OPTIONS TRADING

2 Books in 1: The Complete Guide For Beginners to Investing and Making a Profit with Options by Effective Strategies and Generate Passive Income with Low Risks

Byron McGrady

© Copyright 2021 - All rights reserved.

Table of Contents

BOOK 1: OPTIONS TRADING FOR BEGINNERS

Introduction

I f you have heard about the world of options trading, you might be wondering what investment you can make with options. You can make money out of trading options with anyone, whether you are a complete beginner or an experienced trader.

This is for those who are yet to find out about the market and are unsure how it all works. You will learn the market and how much profit can be made as a beginner.

The name "Options Trading" might make it sound like a complicated process, but that's far from the truth. The options market has been known for years and remains one of the most profitable and exciting investment opportunities available to us today. With technology constantly being developed, it's now easier than ever to trade options without worrying about complicated strategies or trading platforms.

A basic understanding of options will help you decide whether this is the right investment for you or not. As a beginner, it is easy to get lost in the world of finance and move into investing without knowing the basics.

Options are very different from stocks since they're designed as derivatives. That means that options are tied to an underlying asset (stock, index, or commodity) and are traded outside of their relationship with that asset. They're considered more speculative than conservative investments. Stocks were designed as equity investments, which means that they represent ownership in the firms that issue them. Even though you can't cash out your shares before they mature, they provide a reliable way to earn passive income.

This explains how, as an options trader, one can gain passive income. It is possible by using different strategies while trading options and also making profits through this. The strategies explained here are tested as profitable in the market, but one should apply common sense.

Options are a very popular and effective way to make money. However, options trading has become extremely complicated and complex over the years. In this ***Options Trading for Beginners***, we'll show you step by step how to start your investment journey.

Investors use options to speculate whether they believe that a stock's price will go up over time. If the investor anticipates that stock to increase, they will buy an option to gain exposure to that increase. If they do not predict that the price will increase, they may sell their option.

If you're new to the world of options trading, there are a few things that you need to know before you begin trading. You have to learn the basics of options trading at the outset before moving on to a more detailed explanation of each option's characteristics.

You will learn what kind of option you should buy and how to trade it. This gives you an idea about how to trade options to manage your risk while making profits.

Remember this is not a complete guide on options trading. It is intended to give you a general idea of how options trading works. Before you begin trading options, it's important to know a little about what they are and how they work.

CHAPTER 1:

What Are Options?

An option is a financial contract called a derivative contract. It allows the owner of the agreement to have the right to buy or sell the securities based on an agreed-upon price by a specified period.

As the name suggests, there is no obligation in this type of transaction. The trader pays for the right or the option to buy or sell a purchase such as security, stock, index, or ETF (exchange-traded fund) by a certain amount of time. An alternative is a contract.

The option derives its value based on the value of the underlying asset, hence the term derivative contract. This contract states that the buyer agrees to purchase a specified asset within a certain amount of time at a prior agreed-upon price.

Derivative contracts are often used for commodities like gold, oil, and currencies, usually in US dollars. Another type of derivative based on the value of stocks and bonds. They can also find interest rates such as the yield on a specified amount of time, as a ten-year Treasury note.

In a derivative contract, the seller does not have to own the specified asset. They have to have enough money to cover the asset's price to fulfill the contract. The seller also can give the buyer another derivative contract to offset the asset's value.

An option contract usually contains the following specifications:

Agreed-Upon Price

Also known as the strike price. It does not change no matter how much time has passed, and it is so named because the trader strikes when the underlying value makes the desired income.

Specified Time

Also known as the expiration dates. This is the date at which the option (contract) expires. The trader can exercise the option at the strike price at any time up until the expiry date reaches. In some countries, such as Europe, a trader can only exercise the right to the option at the strike price exactly on the expiry date. We will more largely focus on the American way of trading options, which allows for exercising right on.

Rights Acquired With the Purchase of an Option

They can be call (right of purchase) and put (right of sale).

Trading options and trading stocks are different because stocks and options have different characteristics. Stocks stand for shares of ownership in individual companies or opportunities. It allows the stock trader to bet in any direction that they feel the stock price headed.

Stocks are an excellent investment if you think of long-term yields, such as for retirement and have the capital. They are very simplistic in the approach in that the trader buys the stock and wagers on the price they think will rise at a particular time in the future. The hope is that the price will increase in value, thus gaining the trader a substantial yield.

Stocks are an excellent option for those who want to invest without keeping a steady eye on the growth of the investment.

The risk of investing in stocks is that the price of shares can plummet to zero at any moment. It means that the investor can lose their entire investment at the drop of a hat because stocks are very volatile today. They are very reactive to world events such as wars, politics, scandals, epidemics, and natural disasters.

On the other hand, options are an excellent option for traders who would like flexibility with timing and risks. The trader is under no obligation and can see how the trade plays out over the time specified by the option contract. In that period, the price is locked, which is also a great appeal.

Trading options also require a lower investment compared to stocks typically.

Another excellent appeal for options trading is that the specified time is typically shorter than investing in stocks. For regular buying and selling as options have different expiration dates. Expiration dates extent from just a few days to several years.

The drawback that makes some people hesitate in trading options is that it is more complicated than trading stocks. The trader needs to learn new jargon and vocabulary such as strike prices, calls and puts to determine how they can set up effective options. Not only does the trader have to learn new terms, but they also have to develop new skillsets and the right mindset for options trading.

CHAPTER 2:

What Is Options Trading?

Trading options may seem overwhelming in the beginning, but it's easy to learn some key points. Investor portfolios are generally made up of different asset classes. These can be bonds, securities, mutual funds, and ETFs. Options are also asset class and, if used correctly, offer many benefits that trading in securities and ETFs alone cannot offer.

Options are contracts whereby the holder is entitled, but not required, to buy or sell an amount of the underlying asset at a default price before the contract's expiry. Options with brokerage investment accounts may be purchased as most other asset classes.

The options are powerful since they can improve the portfolio of an individual. You do this by adding income, protection, and even leveraging. Usually, a scenario corresponds to the investment goal depending on the situation. A common example would be the use of optional measures as an effective way to hide downside losses from a declining stock market. You may also use the options to generate recurring income. They are usually used for speculative purposes, for example. Bet on title direction.

There are no free stock and bond lunches. The options are no different. Trading options involve certain risks that investors need to be aware of. For this reason, when exchanging options with a broker, a disclaimer typically looks like this:

Options as Derivatives

The options belong to the largest group of securities called derivatives. The price of one derivative depends on or is derived from the price of another. For example, wine is a grape derivative, ketchup is a tomato derivative, and a stock option is a stock derivative. Options are financial instrument derivatives—their interest depends on the price of another currency. Calls, puts, futures, forward, swaps, and mortgage-backed securities are examples of derivatives.

Call and Put Options

Options are derived from a security type. An option is a derivative since its price is inseparable from the price of such goods. You are entitled but not obligated to buy or sell the assets underlying the contract at certain dates or before fixed prices.

The buyer has a right to purchase interest, and the investor can sell an interest. Imagine the future deposit of a call option.

Example of a Call Option

A potential homeowner sees new development. This person may wish to have the right to buy a home in the future but will not want to exercise that right until certain developments have developed in the area.

The prospective homebuyer would benefit from the purchase option or not. Imagine being able to purchase a call option from the developer to buy the house anytime in the next three years, for example, $400,000. Well, you can—it is a non-refundable deposit. Of course, the developer would not grant this option free. The prospective homebuyer needs to deposit to secure this right.

These costs are referred to as premium concerning an option. This is the cost of the contract for the option. The down payment the buyer pays the developer in our home example may amount to $20,000. It is now two years since the developments have gone and zoning has been approved. The homebuyer exercises this option, and the house is purchased for $400,000.

The market value of this home could have doubled to $800,000. However, since the deposit is tied to a fixed price, the buyer pays $400,000. For example, in an alternative scenario, zoning approval is not granted until the fourth year. This is one year after the expiration of this option. Now the homebuyer has to pay the market price because the contract has expired. Either way, the developer keeps the $20,000 originally raised.

Example of a Put Option

Now imagine an insurance policy option. You probably know how to take homeowners' insurance if you own your home. A homeowner purchases a homeowner protection policy against damage. For a period, say a year, you are paying a sum called a premium. In cases where the house is damaged, it has a nominal value and protects the policyholder.

What if your wealth was not a house but a capital stock or indexed investment? An investor will buy options when they need the S&P 500 index protection. An investor may be afraid a bear market is close and unable to lose over 10% of their long S&P 500 position. If the S&P 500 has a trade of $220, it can acquire the put option, for example, to sell the index at $2,250 for the next couple of years.

If the market collapses 20% over the next six months (500 index points), then a combined loss of only 10% will result in a 250-point scale of $2,250 at trading at $2,000. The loss would only be 10% if this option were kept, even if the market dropped to zero. Also, in this case, it is expensive (prime) to purchase the option. If the market does not drop, the maximum loss of option is only the premium paid.

You can do with the options four things:

- Buy calls.

- Sell calls.

- Buy puts.

- Sell puts.

Buying stocks gives you a long position. Buying a call option offers a potential long position in the underlying security. Short sales of stock give you a short position. If you sell an uncovered or uncovered call, you get a potential short position in the underlying action.

Buying a put option offers a potential short position in the underlying security. If you sell a naked or unmarried put, you get a potential long position in the title below. It is essential to keep these four scenarios clear.

People who buy options are called owners, and those who sell options are called option authors. This is the major difference between owners and authors:

Call holders and customers are not allowed to purchase or sell. You have the chance to exercise your rights. This limits the risk of option buyers to justify the premium.

However, Call Writer and Put Writer (seller) must buy or sell if the option expires in cash (more information below). This means that a seller may have to keep a promise to buy or sell. This also means that sellers are exposed to greater and, sometimes, limitless risks. This means that authors can lose far more than the price of premium options.

Why Uses the Options?

Speculation

The future direction of the price is the bet on speculation. A speculator could believe that security prices would increase probably based on fundamental analysis or technical analysis. A speculator can buy the stock or purchase the inventory call option. It is interesting for some traders to specify a call option rather than purchasing the inventory directly because it leverages options. A money-free call will cost just a few bucks or even cents compared with the full price of a 100 bucks allocation.

Validation

The options were developed for hedging purposes. Hedging with options is designed to reduce risk at a reasonable cost. We should find solutions here like a scheme on insurance. As you insure your home or car, you can take the options to protect your investment from the recession.

Imagine wanting to buy tech stocks. Your losses, too, are restricted. You can limit your downside risk and take full advantage of all the advantages by using put options. Call options for short-sellers can be used to limit losses, especially in a shorter compression, when they are wrong.

CHAPTER 3:

Options Trading Basics

The options contract has an expiration date, depending on what type of options you are using. It may be in weeks, months, or even in years, unlike stock with no expiration date. Numbers usually define stocks, but on the other hand, there are no numbers in options.

Options drive their value from something else. That's why they fall into the derivative category, unlike stocks.

Stock owners have their right to the company (dividend or voting). On the other hand, options have no right in the company.

Some people may find it challenging to understand the option method though they have even followed it in their other transactions (car insurance or mortgages).

Few things make the difference between options trading and stock trading:

- In options trading, the value is taken by someone else and had a contract with it. It does not get the values on its own. This is entirely different from stock trading. Option trading belongs to the derivative category.

- In stock, the numbers are definite, but an option, the numbers are not definite.

- The options trading uses the contract, which has the expiration date; the person has no meaning after the expiry date. The date can be in months or years according to the option there are using. Stock trading has no expiration dates.

- In options trading, the owner has no right to the company. They have no affair of any kind related to the company. In stock share, they had the rights to the company.

Options trading may not suit all types of investors, but they are among the most flexible investment choices.

Options in investment are most likely used to reduce the risk of a drop in stock prices, but a little risk is involved in every investment type. Returns are never certain when investors look for options to control risks for ways to limit a potential loss.

Investors may choose to take options because the loss is limited to the price you pay for the token money. And in return, they gain the right to buy or sell stock at their desired price, so trading options benefit the investors.

Option Practicing Method

Stocks are purchased, and the investor sells call options on the same stock which they have purchased. The number of stock shares you have purchased should match the number of call options you have sold.

The investor purchase put options to gain equal shares after buying the stock shares. Married acts as an insurance policy in contrast to immediate losses call options with a particular strike price. At the same time, you will sell similar call options at a higher strike price.

An investor purchases an option with cash from outside while simultaneously works an out of the cash call choice for a similar stock.

The investor purchases a call option and a put choice simultaneously. The two alternatives ought to have a similar strike cost and expiry date.

The investor purchases the call option out of cash and the put choice simultaneously. They have a similar termination date; however, their strike cost is extraordinary. The expense of the information strike ought to be not exactly the expense of the call strike.

Features of the Options

Option contracts include typical terms and conditions for exchange-traded options. The following four elements for any exchange-traded option are specified in each contract option:

Underlying Security

Only a limited number of company shares referred to as the underlying securities, offer options traded on the ASX. The exchange determines these underlying securities based on their own set of guidelines. There is no control over the exchange-traded options issued with their shares by the companies themselves.

Contract Size

On the ASX, all contracts for exchange-traded options have a standard contract size of 100. Before that year, for all exchange-traded options contracts in Australia, the standard contract size was 1,000 shares. It aligns the ASX with the US markets, where the standard contract size is 100 shares per contract offer.

Expiration Date

Every option has a limited life depending on the expiry date of the option. The expiry date is the last day the contract can be exchanged (bought or sold), and all untrained options expire.

American style options can be exercised before the expiry date at any time. The bulk of options traded on the ASX are called in the American style. Nevertheless, there is another design type called choices for European style. It is only possible to practice European style choices on the expiry date and not before.

The expiry date of stock options is Thursday before the month's last Friday. Therefore, the expiry date is quoted as a month instead of a specific date. Options will be cited as having expiry dates set on the March, June, September, and December financial quarters, plus monthly expiry dates for the next three to six months, depending on the options category.

Strike Price

The exercise price or strike price is when the remaining stock price can be acquired or sold if the right is exercised. For all options listed on the ASX options market, it sets the strike prices. For each underlying security, there are several strike prices set for each expiry date option. As the market value of the underlying security increases, new strike orders will be released.

Premium

The premium alternative is the only part that the exchange does not standardize. The premium is the amount at which a buyer and seller buy and sells the contract.

The price of buying and selling shares on the stock exchange is dictated by the supply and demand powers. Buyers put in offers to buy the stock, and sellers put in bids to sell their stock, which decides the market price when they touch. For alternatives, this is not the case.

Option premiums are calculated by a mix of factors, including the underlying security's market value, the option's strike price, and the expiry period.

Option premiums (or prices) are quoted as "cents per share" overstocks. You need to subtract the "cents per share" by the number of shares protected by the option (usually 100) to determine the overall premium for a particular option. Therefore, a $1.50 swap traded offer will cost you $150.00 to purchase ($1.50 per share or 100 shares per contract). With the trading and exchange fees, you would also have your transaction fees on top of that.

CHAPTER 4:

Learning the Lingo

Options traders speak their language. It's not meant to confuse you, and it's just the natural process of creating a shorthand by which one trader can converse with another more easily and thoroughly.

Of course, it does make it difficult to plunge into the waters of options trading if you can't speak the language. It is a lot like trying to decipher road signs in a foreign country. It makes it hard to know the right direction—or even where you're standing right now.

We're going to take a look at the common terms you'll be dealing with as you enter the world of options trading before, we begin taking a deeper look at your strategies.

Don't worry about trying to learn the terms by rote. They will all become clear as you forge onward. This glossary will always be available to you so that you can check on meaning if you need to.

- **Strike price:** A price per share agreed upon before an option is traded. At that price, a stock may be bought or sold under the terms of your option contract. This price is also known as the "exercise price."

- **Bid/ask:** The latest price that a market maker has offered for an option is its "ask" price. In other words, it's what the seller is willing to accept for the trade. The latest amount that a buyer has offered for an option is the "bid" price.

- **Premium:** The premium is a per-share amount paid to the seller to procure an option. The seller will keep that premium whether the buyer exercises their right to buy or sell the stock at the deadline.

- **In-the-money:** Often shortened to ITM, that means that the stock price is above the strike price for a call or below the strike price for a put. In other words, it is now at the right price to be traded.

- **Out-of-the-money:** Often shortened to OTM, that means the current price is below the strike price for a call or above it for a put. Such an option is priced according to "time value."

- **At-the-money:** The strike price is equal to the current stock price.

- **Long:** In this context, "long" is used to imply ownership. Once you purchase a stock or option, you are "long" that item in your account.

- **Short:** If you sell an option or stock that you do not own, you are "short" that security in your account.

- **Exercise:** The option owner takes advantage of the right to buy or sell what they purchased with the option by "exercising" it.

- **Assigned:** When an owner of an option exercises it, the seller is "assigned" and must make good on the trade. In other words, the seller must fulfill their obligation to buy or sell.

- **Intrinsic value/time value:** The intrinsic value of an option refers to how much it is ITM. Most options also include time value, and that refers to how long is left until the option expires. That time has value because, during that time, the stock can still change in price.

- **Time decay:** Linked to time value, that term refers to the fact that, as time ticks on, the amount of time value slowly decreases. At the expiration date of an option contract, the contract has NO time value and is worth only its intrinsic value.

- **Index options/equity options:** Index options are settled by cash, whereas equity options involve trading stock. The main difference between those two options is that an index option usually cannot be exercised before the expiration date, while an equity option usually can.

- **Stop-loss order:** That is an order to sell either an option or a stock when it reaches a particular price. Its purpose is to set a point at which you, as the trader, would like to get out of your position. At that price, your stop order is activated as a market order. In other words, a market order looks for the best available price at that moment to close out your position.

Those are the most common terms you will hear used as you venture into the world of options trading. It's worth mentioning that, as you extend your understanding, you'll encounter more terms. However, the above terms are enough to help you understand your first trades.

CHAPTER 5:

Types of Trading Options

There is a wide range of types and styles of options accessible. This segment gives a picture of each kind just as some essential wording each option investors should be comfortable with.

Call Options

A call option gives the investor the right (not the commitment) to buy the fundamental stock, security, item, or other instruments, at a particular cost within the contract's time. The predefined cost is known as the strike cost. A speculator who is bullish on the stock, which means they anticipate that the stock should go up within a short time or inside the particular period, would buy a call option.

For instance, say Investor A thinks stock XYZ will post high income one month from now, and the stock will go higher. So, they buy a call option on the stock for $20. The option agreement determines that they can buy 100 portions of XYZ at a strike cost of $100 within the following sixty days. If the cost of the stock falls beneath $100, then they won't practice the option. The agreement will terminate uselessly, and they will have lost the $20 price tag. In any case, if the cost of the stock transcends $100, state to $130, then they will practice the option, buy the stock for $100, and afterward, sell it at the higher market cost. They have now made a pleasant benefit.

Put Options

A put option is something contrary to a call option. It gives the owner the right (however, not the commitment) to sell the fundamental stock at a predetermined value (the strike cost) inside the predefined period. An investor who is bearish on the stock, which means they think the stock cost is going down, would buy a put option.

For instance, say Investor B thinks stock XYZ is overrated and will decrease in cost throughout the following sixty days. Then they buy a put option on the stock for $20. The agreement gives them the option to sell the stock for $120 within the following sixty days. If the stock transcends $120 per share, then they would not practice the option. It would lapse useless, and they have lost their underlying speculation. If rather the cost of the stock dips under $120, to state $90, then they would practice their entitlement to sell the offers at $120 and pocket the distinction as a profit.

Make a Profit Using Call and Put Options

There are various ways you can use call and put options. For instance, assume you believe that portions of US banks selling for $200 per share are undervalued and will go higher in the following couple of months. You need more money to buy at least 100 portions of stock, yet you might, in any case, want to bring in money from the ascent in the stock. For this situation, you could buy a call option on the stock, which would cost just a small amount of the stock's cost. So, you buy the call option, and you presently reserve the option to buy 100 portions of the stock at $200 whenever in the following sixty days.

You may be thinking about buying the stock in the next sixty days for $200 per share if I don't have the money; the appropriate response is that you don't need to buy the stock to make a profit. If your impulses are right and the stock cost rises above $200, then your call option will turn out to be increasingly important. At the end of the day, as the stock value rises, the value of your option agreement likewise rises. You will have the option to sell the option agreement itself, rather than the stock, and make a benefit. The higher the value rises, the more your agreement will be worth.

This works a similar route for a put option, but you need the stock cost to fall in this situation. As the cost of the hidden security drops, the value of your put option will rise. The further the value falls, the more important is your option.

As should be obvious, by buying options, you can profit whether or not the stock is going up or down in cost.

Styles of Options

The past segments have reviewed the two essential sorts of options, calls, and puts. This segment will assist you in understanding the different styles of options accessible.

Most options you will buy will be categorized as one of two classifications: American or European. These are once in a while known as vanilla options. The principle distinction between the two is the point at which you can practice the option.

- **American options:** American options can be practiced whenever before the expiry date. Most options on stocks and value are of this sort. These are additionally the kind of agreements exchanged on fates trades.

- **European options:** European options must be practiced on the lapse date characterized in the agreement. These sorts of options are, for the most part, exchanged over the counter (OTC) advertisements.

The two options styles' values are determined marginally distinctively, and their termination dates are also unique. American options lapse the third Saturday of the month, while European options terminate the Friday before the third Saturday of the month.

Similitudes between the two incorporate the result and the strike cost. The result, either for calls or puts, is determined similarly for the two kinds. In like manner, the strike costs ordinarily are the equivalent.

Extraordinary Options

While the over two styles are the primary ones most investors will manage, there is an assortment of increasingly colorful option sorts to know about too:

- **Bermuda options:** Bermuda options are in the middle of American and European options. In this kind of option, you are permitted to practice them on numerous dates during the agreement time frame.

- **Barrier options:** Barrier options are not the same as the different sorts talked about so far in that all together for the option to result in the cost of the basic security must cross a specific level. They can be either be put or call options. There are four sorts of barrier options, which are plot beneath:
  - **Down-and-out:** A Down-and-out barrier option gives the holder the privilege, however, not the commitment to buy (on account of a call) or sell (on account of a put) portions of a hidden resource at a foreordained strike cost since the cost of that advantage didn't go beneath a foreordained barrier during the option lifetime. That is, when the cost of the hidden resource falls underneath the barrier, the option is "took out" and no longer conveys any worth. Hence, the name out for the count.
  - **Down-and-in:** A down-and-in option is something contrary to a done for barrier option. Down-and-in options possibly convey value if the fundamental resource's cost falls beneath the barrier during the option's lifetime. If the barrier is crossed, the holder of the down-and-in option has the option to buy (if it is a call) or sell (if it is a put) portions of the hidden resource at the foreordained strike cost on the termination date.
  - **Up-and-out:** An up-and-out barrier option is like a done for barrier option, the main contrast being the arrangement of the barrier. Instead of being taken out by falling beneath the barrier cost, up-and-out options are taken out if the cost of the hidden resource transcends the foreordained barrier.

- o **Up-and-in:** An up-and-in barrier option is like a down-and-in option; anyway, the barrier is set over the present cost of the hidden resource, and the option might be substantial if the cost of the basic resource arrives at the barrier before lapse.

- **Basket options:** A basket option, otherwise called a rainbow option, is an agreement wherein the worth depends on at least two basic resources. The option to practice the option is reliant on the costs of every fundamental resource.

- **Capped style options:** In this kind of agreement, the most extreme benefit is set up. Capped options contain an arrangement where the option is practiced consequently if the fundamental security arrives at a specific set up cost. These kinds of options offer the author of the option a most extreme sum that can be lost.

- **Compound options:** These are fundamental options to buy an option. Additionally, it is called split-expense options because the holder must compensate two premiums, one forthright and one if the option is worked out.

- **Lookback options:** This style of option supplies the holder of the option to either buy or sell the fundamental security at its top (on account of calls) or most reduced (on account of puts) cost over a predetermined period.

- **Asian options:** Asian options, otherwise called normal options, depend upon the mean (normal) cost of the fundamental security over a particular period.

- **Binary options:** Binary options have a payout that is either a fixed sum or nothing by any stretch of the imagination. There are two sorts: money or-nothing and resource or-nothing. The holder will get a fixed measure of money in the primary kind if the option lapses in-the-money. In the advantage or-nothing assortment, the holder would get the value of the hidden security. Otherwise called digital options, win big or bust options and fixed bring options back. The bit of leeway to this kind of option is that the potential return is a known sureness before the option is bought. Notwithstanding, once bought, they can't be sold before the lapse.

- **Forward start options:** Forward beginning options start with a vague strike value that will be resolved later on.

- **LEAPS:** LEAPS represents Long-Term Equity Anticipation Securities. LEAPS are equivalent to customary options except the more drawn out lapse dates. A LEAP can have a lapse date that is as long as three years away. The favorable position to this kind of option is there is much more opportunity for the basic stock, and along these lines option, to move toward the path you need it to.

- **Index options:** Notwithstanding buying options on singular protections, you can likewise buy options on a stock list. These can be engaging even though they give an introduction to a whole gathering of stocks. List options are adaptable and can fit both moderate and theoretical investors' systems during both a bull and a bear showcase. Most file options are European style options.

CHAPTER 6:

Options Pricing

Anther useful aspect of options trading that you need to be familiar with is pricing options. The option price is also known as the option premium and consists of two distinct components. These are the intrinsic value and extrinsic value. The put-call parity principle governs both.

How to Price Options?

Another factor that you need to be conversant with is how to price an option. You must be able to price options correctly and accurately so that you do not incur unnecessary losses. The first step in pricing options is to understand all the elements that are involved.

The pricing process is a science and not an art. Once you master this science, you will be able to price options quite easily. Numerous external factors determine options prices. However, 90% of the time, volatility, stock price, and time till expiration are influenced by volatility.

Factors to Consider

Stock Price

When pricing options, the first place to begin is the market price of the underlying security. The security could be an index, a stock, or even ETF (electronically traded fund). This price is the predominant factor in determining the price of a stock.

Imagine Apple's stock trading at $500. The company then introduces a new gadget in the market. This new product is even greater than current gadgets like the iPhone. The shares then gain value and tend towards $550. In such an instance, many shareholders will want to secure exclusive rights to buy the shares at $520. As the price of the shares goes up, so do the call prices.

Time

Options are a factor of time. This means that they are wasting assets. In other words, their benefits are limited within a certain stipulated period. It may be three months or six months. As an option approaches its expiration date, there is less time to benefit from it. As such, its value decreases proportionately. You must always factor in time when pricing options.

Bid and Ask Price

Another crucial factor that plays an important part in option pricing is the bid or ask price. Regardless of whether it is a call or put, each option always has a bid and ask price.

When buying options, you will purchase at the asking price or very close to it and sell on the bid or near it. For instance, if you are looking at September 75 calls and notice prices like $9.60 x $9.90, then the asking price you'd be purchasing is $9.90 while the selling price on this option has its lower margins at $9.60. The difference between these two prices is that the asking price and bid price is known as the spread. If the spread is very tight, then it means that the stock is very liquid.

Volatility

Yet another important factor that determines the price of an option is its volatility. Volatility is the most crucial factor in the stock price. Any options based on very long-term stable stocks will be predictably priced compared to options whose stocks have hugely volatile charts. Apart from past performance, implied volatility is also crucial, so all these factors are considered when pricing a stock.

Other Factors Influencing Prices of Options

In both puts and calls, the market maker or investor receives a premium. The premium is the fee of acquiring an option. Here are some of the factors that affect the price of an option:

Probability

The chance that an option will end up in-the-money is the main aspect influencing an option's worth. The closer the probability that the underlying asset will end up in-the-money gets to 100%, the greater the option's worth becomes; the further away the probability that the underlying asset will finish in-the-money gets from 100%, the lower the value of the option. As a trader, you have to sharpen your analytical skills and determine whether an option is worthy of the premium it demands.

Interest Rates

You must note that rates of interest have a slight effect on the value of an option. When the rates of interest increase, the call's worth will go up, and the put option will go down. The adjustments in the premiums are triggered by the costs of owning the underlying assets. When a trader acquires an options contract, the extra cash can attract interest. A high interest translates into bigger earnings. Therefore, traders are willing to pay higher premiums to own call options.

Dividends

When a trader fails to receive their dividend, the stock will go down by that amount. A dividends increment causes a rise in the value of both calls and puts.

Natural Logarithm

The Black-Scholes calculation of premiums utilizes the natural logarithm. The changes in the price of underlying assets are proportional to the price of the underlying.

Normal Distribution

The normal probability distribution is used in the calculation of an options price. In the Black-Scholes model, price movement is understood to be distributed normally. Small movements have a high probability, whereas large movements have low probability.

News

It seems that financial news plays a critical role in driving the whole derivatives markets. Although chances of it happening are rare, influential finance journalists could drive a plan that could trigger oscillations in the price of options contracts. But the real captains of the industry are the brokers and market makers. These people who are in charge of brokerages and market-making corporations have the power to influence the course of the derivatives market. When they appear on the news, traders and investors hang on their every word, and traders could go on a spree of buying or selling, which affects the value of options.

Crowd Psychology

If there's a sector that asks for mental maturity and discipline, it's the derivatives market. You have to have a plan and know when to take action instead of guessing your way around. But people are still people. It's so easy to get distracted by the trends and lose sight of your trading strategy. For instance, if a certain clique of traders reaps sudden profits, everyone runs into their niche in the hope of reaping quick benefits, thus driving the premium of the option up.

Price of the Underlying Asset

While they often will not move at the same speed or for the same amounts, an option will always follow the lead of its underlying asset. As such, you can always expect the price of related calls to increase along with rising asset prices, while puts will always decrease and vice versa.

Time Value

The amount of time that an option has until it expires is directly related to how likely that same option will ultimately end in a profit greater than the intrinsic value before things are said and done.

To determine the amount of time value that the option you are considering offers currently, you will want to find the option's current price and subtract from it the amount of intrinsic value that the same option currently has. It is common for options to hold onto 70% of their total value, or more, during the first half of their life before losing value much more rapidly after that point. You also have to remember that time value can change dramatically based on the volatility of the underlying asset both in the moment and based on its expectations in the future. As a general rule, the lower the time value, the more stable the option will be.

Intrinsic Value

The amount of value that an option will hold onto, even at the end of its lifespan, is known as the intrinsic value. When working with a call option, you can find the intrinsic value by taking the current price of the underlying asset and dividing that by the difference between the strike price and the current price. When it comes to finding the intrinsic value of a put option, the process is mostly the same; to start, you subtract the amount the underlying asset is currently worth from its strike price before dividing that number by the current stock price.

This equation's results will provide you with a clearer idea of the type of advantage that choosing to exercise the option at the moment would provide you with. It can also be the minimum that the option will ever be worth, even at the moment of its expiration.

CHAPTER 7:

Benefits of Options Trading

There are a few of the primary benefits of trading in options and why you may consider purchasing or offering options as a part of your total trading method. We will also learn the significant dangers in buying and providing options, remembering that the risks included in options are substantially different for buyers of options than the risks for sellers of options.

When purchasing options, you invest in an asset with no real worth, which may be worthless within a few months. As you will quickly find, there are numerous benefits of trading options that can be used in a wide variety of methods.

We will now describe a few of the main advantages of options. These are extended attributes that apply to options. As we talk about the types of options in more detail and the methods used for each kind of option, you will see the benefits (and drawbacks) of trading options.

A benefit to a seller will typically equate to a downside to the buyer and vice versa. The factor this operates in the marketplace is, the reason or strategy used by the seller is different from the idea the purchaser has participated in the agreement.

When evaluating the benefits of using options, you likewise need to think about the risks associated with your particular options method.

Danger Management

Options provide financiers with the ability to manage danger within their portfolio. Options can provide a financier with a hedge versus falls in the price of their present stock holdings. It can effectively allow a financier to lock in some profits on their holding without physically selling their shares.

This can be useful when an investor wishes to maintain their shares for a longer-term or does not want to understand a capital gain by offering their investment at the current time.

Purchasing a put option allows you to buy the right to sell your present shares at an advantageous price if you anticipate a fall in the cost of those shares before the expiry date of the option. The investors are allowed to gain on the put options that will offset a loss on the physical shares on the occasion that the stocks do fall in value.

You own 3000 shares in a stock presently trading at $10.50. You want to secure some revenue at this price as you feel that the price will fall in the brief term. To use this strategy, you purchase 30 put option agreements with a strike cost of $10.50. This costs you to buy $0.20 per share in each agreement (with 100 shares in each transaction).

This purchase allows you to offer 3000 shares at $10.50 whenever before the option's expiry date. Your put option value will increase by a similar quantity (less any ended time worth) if the stock rate subsequently falls. Thus, you are safeguarding yourself against a fall in the price of your stock. A fall in the worth of your stock will be balanced by a rise in your options' value.

If the stock cost stays at or above $10.50, then you would either not exercise your options or sell your option close to the expiration date (although it would deserve very little).

If the stock rate does fall to, state, $9.50, then the worth of your put options would increase by $1.00 (less any expired time worth). You could then offer these options for approximately $1.00 and realize earnings of $3000.00. This will balance out the fall in worth of your shareholding of a similar amount. Effectively, you have paid $600.00 for your options to defend you against the fall in the stock position price.

Speculation

The capability to trade online and the listing of options on the ASX make it very simple to purchase and offer options. The options trading makes it possible for traders to buy an option contract with the intent of selling the options before the expiration date for a revenue. The traders may have expectations of an increase in the option (due to a change in the underlying security cost). And no objective of ever exercising the option if your option has intrinsic value. The value of your options will change much in line with the change in worth of the underlying stock. You will also see a fall in quality that is unrelated to any change in worth of the hidden security but is due to a fall in the option's time value as it nears expiry.

How options move with changes in the value of the underlying stock. These movements are for options that have an intrinsic worth in their premium.

As a speculator, you can acquire call options if you expect the underlying security rate to increase. As the security rate's underlying price rises, your options' intrinsic value will increase by a similar amount if you anticipate the underlying security rate to fall. Your method may be to buy put options as the price of the underlying security drops. The intrinsic options' value will increase by a similar amount. To produce a profit, you need the worth of the underlying security to move in your favor before the expiry date, and you would need to offer your option on or before the expiration date.

When purchasing and after offering American style stock options to generate short-term revenue, you need to ensure you sell your options before the expiry date. This requires the cost of the underlying stock to move in your favor before the expiry date.

Leverage

Leverage can produce the same return level from a prospective financial investment; however, utilizing a smaller sized initial expense. If you owned the real shares, purchasing a call option with intrinsic value exposes you to a comparable gain or loss that you would attain. The cost of a fraction of the price options of the underlying stock. This permits you to benefit from changes in the stock's value without paying the capital's full fee.

Leverage does come with a new threat; the gains are amplified through the usage, so too are any losses. Some examples show how force can create a more significant portion of return than can direct financial investment.

Your returned percentage can be magnified as a result of the leverage achieved through the usage of options. It is necessary to note that your losses can be equally magnified in some circumstances. Nevertheless, your loss will always be limited to the premium you spent on the opportunity when purchasing options.

Idea

When speculating using options, you need to represent the fall in time worth of your option and your ideal costs when assessing your trading opportunity.

Diversification

The use of options can offer you the opportunity to benefit from the motion in a stock rate at a portion of the stock price. This permits you to construct a varied portfolio for a lower preliminary expense. This comes at a cost as your options include a value for the time of expiry, which will decrease to no over the option's life.

Income Generation

When selling an option, you get an advance premium from the purchaser of your option. The premium kept, whether or not the option has worked out. This premium can produce an income stream if carefully selected options are sold on a systematic basis. The seller maintains the premium and has no further commitment if the options are not exercised.

There are several methods based on offering options to generate premium income. The goal is to sell options that are not likely to be worked out or purchase back (closeout) your options before the expiration date if there is a danger they will be exercised.

CHAPTER 8:

Disadvantages of Options Trading

O ptions have many advantages, but just like any other investment, they have disadvantages too. The investor must understand both sides of the coin, the good and the bad, before committing their resources to options trading. Following are some of the shortfalls of options trading (The advantages and disadvantages of options, n.d.):

Tax

Except for extremely rare instances, all your gains are taxed as income. This is the same as taxing your income because the tax rates levied upon your gains are just as high. One clever way investors can step around the taxation issue is to utilize their tax-deferred accounts such as the IRA. Sadly, not everyone has ownership of a tax-deferred account. The tax can reduce the amount of money you take home, but considering the high earning potential, options are still profitable.

Commissions

In comparison to stock investing, commissions for options are significantly higher. For most active traders, their annual commissions usually exceed 30% of the total amount you invested. To guard yourself against paying exorbitant commissions, never sign up with a broker without being clear. Whenever you receive a newsletter, quickly check to see the commission details. Options trades will cost you more in commission for every dollar that you put down. The commissions may even be more for spreads that require you to pay commissions for both sides. A trader should be careful about the broker that they choose to work with. For instance, if you're a beginner, you should stick to brokers who cater to beginners.

Time Value Decay

In stock trading, you can purchase long-term stocks that can take decades to mature. But options contracts come with an expiration date. You can't stop the process of expiring. Also, the option's position relative to expiration dates affects the premium that you will pay to acquire the option. The more the options get closer to the expiration date, the more the rate of time value decay increases. Therefore, monitor your open positions so that your options don't expire worthlessly.

Uncertainty of Gains

Investors try to minimize risk by examining the risk profile graphs. This shows them the projected gains or losses at the next expiration of options contracts. In as much as these graphs are helpful, especially when placing the initial position, they still cannot guarantee you a profit. It can be hard to project the gains from an options trade. Sometimes, after the expiration of options contracts, the expected gains are not generated. But there are other times when, at the expiration of options contracts, the earnings exceed the projected gains. In that sense, your gains or losses become somewhat uncertain—terrible for individuals who loathe uncertainty.

Loss of Investment

The extent of your losses depends in large measure on your investment strategy. If you put together a strategy aimed at the highest possible returns, the risk is considerably higher. During the contract's lifetime, the underlying's price can depreciate, and at expiration, you would not exercise your option. You will only lose the premium; a stock trader would lose their shares.

Regulation

One of the things that bother traders and investors is the regulations imposed by governing bodies. The OCC, Securities, and Exchange Commission (SEC), or even The Court, has the power to impose restrictions on exercising various options. Although it rarely happens, it is still enough of a concern that it can make traders think again before putting down their resources into acquiring options contracts. You should always perform your due diligence over the underlying assets you intend to take options contracts for. If the assets are at the center of legal battles, you might want to take a pass.

Lower Liquidity

A lot of individual stock options don't have much volume. If it is not among the most popular stocks or indexes, the option you're trading is likely to be low volume because each stock will have a different strike price and expiration. Remember that liquidity issue only becomes a huge factor if the trades are big money. In the case of a small trader who purchases around ten options contracts, liquidity is never an issue.

Complicated

It's not beginners alone who can get overwhelmed in the world of options trading. Some professional traders seem to think that they understand options trading when they don't. To understand options trading, you have to dedicate a significant amount of time to study all the aspects of this field. As a beginner, the worst mistake you can commit is to sign up with a broker that caters to professional traders. You have to look for a broker that caters to beginners so that you could utilize their educational resources. There's so much to learn before anyone could become proficient in options trading.

Leverage

When it comes to options trading, leverage is a double-edged sword. On the one hand, it can minimize the risk surrounding an underlying, and on the other hand, it can affect the performance of the asset's market value. When an underlying price is affected negatively, it means that your earning potential is constrained. Leverage is most dangerous when you're selling naked options or entering into unlimited-risk strategies. Options trading affords investors many trading tools. The tools can make or break you. It is upon the investor to use these trading tools for their benefit. The biggest step an investor can take for success in options trading is acquiring the requisite knowledge. Guesswork is bound to get you into major losses.

CHAPTER 9:

Tips for Getting Started on Options Trading

Although it seems complex and can include a wide range of strategic approaches, it's relatively easy to start trading options.

You need a broker, and you will need to compare fees and account minimums so that you can choose one that is affordable and meets your investment style.

From there, it's time to develop your strategy for trading options. Like most investment options, trading strategies is dependent on your personal goals and tolerance for risk and can range from simple to complex.

Create a Brokerage Account

If you're interested in trading options, you'll need to open a brokerage to access your transactions—this can be done online or through a standard broker account. Be sure you fully grasp what's involved in creating a brokerage account before you do that.

Compare the options trading commissions between different brokerages. Some firms do not even offer commissions on trading options.

Carry out some research online and read the reviews of brokerage firms that are on your shortlist. Get knowledge from the mistakes of other people so you won't have to repeat them.

 Observe for scam trading platforms and sites. Always thoroughly research the platform before you deposit any money. Avoid any platform with negative reviews or possible fraud reported.

A cash account will only permit the purchase of options to create a position. If you desire to sell an option to set up an account without the underlying asset, you will need a margin account.

If you want to trade online, make sure that your online brokerage accepts secure payment forms, like a secure credit card payment gateway or a third-party payment service such as PayPal, Payoneer, Skrill, Bitcoin, etc.

Get Approval to Trade Options

You will need approval from your brokerage before you start buying and selling options. Brokerage firms handling an account set limits based on experience and money in the account, and every firm has its own criteria to ensure that the customer knows what they are doing. You can't write a covered call without an options account. Brokerage firms want to make sure before trading that customers have a full understanding of the risks.

Covered call writing means selling the right to purchase your stock at a strike price during the option duration. The buyer has the right to do so, not the seller. The stock must be in the brokerage account and cannot be sold or exchanged while the call is pending.

Understanding Technical Analysis

Options are typically short-term investments, so you will be searching for price movements of the optioned security to make a healthy return soon. To accurately forecast these price fluctuations, you would need to grasp the fundamentals of the technical analysis.

Learn about the level of support and resistance. These are points where the stock hardly ever decreases below (support) or increases above (resistance). Support is the level at which significant security purchases have historically occurred. Resistance is the price level, where significant security sales have occurred in the past.

Understand the significance of the volume. If a stock changes towards a specific direction with a lot of volume behind it, it typically means a strong trend and can be a money-making opportunity.

Understand the patterns of the chart. History usually repeats itself, even in the case of stock prices. There are common trends that you can look for in stock price fluctuations that can show where the price is going.

Learn more about moving averages. The same case is when the stock price is above or below the common moving average of the prices. A thirty-day moving average is perceived to be more accurate than a ten-day moving average.

Start With "Paper Trading"

Resist every temptation to risk hard-earned money with a technique you've just learned.

Instead, go for paper trading or practice. Make use of a spreadsheet or a practice trading software to enter "pretend" trades. Then review your returns for at least a few months. If you make a decent return, work your way to real trading slowly.

Paper trading is different from real trading, as there is no mental pressure or commissions involved. It's a good idea to learn mechanics, but it's not a predictor of actual results. Real options trading is a very high risk, which can result in substantial losses for the investor. You can only trade with money that you can afford to lose.

Use the Limit Orders

Avoid having to pay market prices for options, as the execution price can be higher than expected. Instead, state your price with limit orders and maximize your return.

Reassess Your Strategy regularly

Determine if there is anything that can be done to enhance your return. Learn from your mistakes but repeat your effective strategies as well. And maintain a focused strategy; traders concentrate on a few positions, not on diversification. You should have not more than 10% of your investment portfolio in options.

You Can Join a Forum of Traders of Like Minds Online

If you're experimenting with advanced trading options strategies, you'll discover that a vital source of information (and help, after a few tough losses) is an online trading platform. Locate a forum to enable you to learn from the successes and other failures.

Think of Other Strategies for Trading Options

After you have made some successful trades, you can get cleared for more advanced options trading strategies. However, start trading on paper as well. This will make it much simpler for you to carry them out in real trading.

One such strategy is the "straddle," which includes trading on both sides of the market, purchasing a put and a call option with the same strike price and date of maturation so that you restrict your exposure. This strategy is most successful when the market moves up and down rather than in a single direction. There is also a risk that only one side will be exercisable.

A related strategy is the "strip." The strip is like a straddle but is actually a "bearish" strategy with twice the downward price movement's earning power. It is comparable to the straddle in its implementation, but with twice as many options purchased on the downside (put options).

Know More About the Greeks

Once you've perfected simple options trading and choose to move on to more advanced options trading, you will have to learn about the Greeks. These are measuring that traders use to maximize their returns.

CHAPTER 10:

Options Sellers

Selling options is a strategy that is used to generate regular income. Selling options is a little simpler but carries a higher risk.

Review of Selling Covered Calls

If you have 100 or more shares of a particular stock, you can sell covered calls against your shares. This is a usual strategy used by people to earn money off their shares, but you always face the risk that your shares will be called away if the option is exercised. A strategy that can be used is to sell out-of-the-money calls when you don't expect the share price to rise to the call option's strike price over the lifetime of the contract.

For example, Facebook is trading at $190.25 a share. You can sell a $210 call for $0.64, so for all 100 shares, one option contract would net you $64. This is for an expiration date of thirty days. Or you could take a higher level of risk and sell a $195 call for $4.05, which would give you a premium of $405 per option contract. If you had 500 shares, then you'd receive $2,025 in premiums. Not a bad passive income and all you have to do is hope that the share price stays below the strike price.

If the share price closes in on the strike price, then you will be faced with a dilemma—risk having the option exercised if the share price rises above the strike price, or you can buy back the option and cut into your profits. With a few days left to expiration, the option you sold may be worth $2.05, so you could buy back the five options you sold, and you'd reduce your net profit to $1,000.

You could go further out, even selling LEAPS. In that case, the premium paid is much larger. A Facebook LEAP with a $195 call that expires in eighteen months has a premium of $30.58, so selling five contracts for your 500 shares could bring in an income of $15,290. Of course, there is a higher risk that the share price will rise above the strike price over eighteen months than there is over the short term.

The one principle to keep in mind selling covered calls is that you could lose your shares if the option is exercised. You should select a strike price that is of a higher amount than what you had paid for the shares. If you are forced to sell the shares, you are not taking a loss doing so. That can make losing the shares easier to deal with. So if we had purchased our shares at $200 a share, we would not select a $195 strike price because that represents a potential loss, which would be given by the price we paid for the shares minus the strike price and then less the premium aid, in this case, $200 - $195 - $4.05 so we'd end up losing $0.95 on the trade. If you had purchased the shares at a lower price, say $190 a share, then the $195 strike would make sense since if the stock price rose and the shares were called away, we'd still profit by selling the shares.

Protected puts are the put version of a covered call. The risk with a protected put is that the shares will be "put to you," and you will have to buy the shares, so you will be required to have enough capital in your account to cover the purchase.

Of course, the trick to selling options is to pick a strike price where you think the option will expire worthlessly. There is the risk that you are wrong, but if you think the share price will rise for Facebook, to use an example, you could sell a protected $190 put for $4.95, earning $495 per contract. If the share price rises, the options will expire worthlessly, and you would keep the premium and profit from the deal.

Selling Naked Puts

It is a popular strategy for traders that are given level 4 status. If you can get this level from your broker, you can consider this possibly profitable strategy. Of course, the key is choosing the right strike price.

When a put is "naked," that means it isn't backed by anything. However, you are still required by law to fulfill your obligations should the option be exercised, but one way that traders avoid this problem is by buying the options back if there is a chance they would be exercised. The time value may work in your favor, which will make the options cheaper and so you can buy them back and still profit.

Another consideration is to choose a relatively low implied volatility, which reduces the chances that the stock will move much over the lifetime of the option. But that is a trade-off as well, as implied volatility that is a few points higher can have a large increase in the premium received for selling the option.

Consider IBM. The stock price is at $139.20, but you could sell a thirty-day $135 put for $2.44, or $244. You could even sell in-the-money puts. A $145 put would sell for $748. If you sold five contracts, that would be a thirty-day income of $3,640.

Selling in-the-money puts could be risky but beneficial if it was believed that IBM shares were set to rise in price. When the price rises above the strike price, then the options will expire worthlessly.

Selling LEAPS, while it carries higher risk since a long time to expiration gives a higher chance that the option will move in the amount, also allow you to sell at high premiums. A $130 put for IBM expiring in eighteen months would sell for $13.20, so selling five contracts would give you a premium of $6,600. Bid-Ask spreads can be large for LEAPS, and the volume is probably small. For this particular option, we find that the bid-ask spread is about 80 cents, which isn't too bad, meaning selling it might not be that difficult. Daily volume is small at 10, but the open interest is 1,282. Experienced traders often recommend an open interest of 500 or higher since that indicates enough people are buying the contracts.

The risk with naked puts is that you will be forced to buy the shares. Again, if it looks like that might turn out to be the case, you can buy the contracts back. Selling OTM options that expire in the near term can leave you in a better position since the options will probably expire worthlessly, and you will be able to keep the premium without having to buy back the options. If you have to buy the shares, the loss would be the share price minus the market price. But of course, you'd have to get the capital to buy the shares as well.

So, if you sold a put option on IBM with a strike price of $138 expiring in six weeks, it would sell for $3.70. If the share price dropped to $136, you'd have to use cash to buy the shares at $138 and possibly lose $2 a share by selling them—or you could keep them and wait for the price to go back up. Your loss would be offset by the premium, so your break-even point is the amount of the strike price less premium paid.

Selling Naked Calls

You can also sell naked calls. This means that you sell call options without owning the shares of stock. The risk that the option will be exercised means that you would have to buy the shares at a higher market price and then sell them at the lower strike price. So, the key here would be to sell out-of-the-money calls at strike prices that you doubt the stock will reach over the option's lifetime. The same strategies can be used, and if it looks like the share price is rising, you can buy the options back to avoid being assigned.

Looking at IBM, some modest out-of-the-money call options thirty days to expiration have good prices. A $141 call, which is almost $2 out-of-the-money, is $3.55, so selling one contract would give you $355.

Suppose that stock was trading at $195 a share. You could sell a call with a forty-five-day expiration with a strike price of $200 for $4.46, or $446. If we find that the share price has risen to $197 with ten days to expiration, the calls would now be priced at $1.88, or $188. So, you could buy them back and still have a profit of $258 per contract, avoiding the risk that you would be assigned if the share price kept rising. Of course, at $3 out-of-the-money, you might wait. When the price of the share rises to $199 with seven days left, the calls would be $218, so you'd be cutting a little more into your profits. But if it dropped $1 the following day, then the call option would only be worth $1.58.

Remember, when you sell options, you make money on the time premium. Or put another way, time decay is your friend. Out-of-the-money, options lose value rapidly as the expiration date approaches.

The biggest risk with selling naked call options if you can't buy them back is to buy stocks at a high price and then selling them at a loss to honor your obligations. Supposed that a stock is trading at $95 a share, and you sell a call option that has a $100 strike price. If the stock breaks out and, say, rises to $130 a share, someone might exercise the option. Since you sold the call naked, you'd be forced to buy the shares at $130 and sell them at the $100 strike price, losing $30 a share, which would be partially offset by the premium, which might be around $1 per share.

So, selling naked calls can be profitable but carries a lot of risks as well. The key to selling naked calls successfully is picking the right strike price and choosing a stock that you don't believe will have price movements that are large enough to cause the option to be in-the-money.

Broker May Force Sale

Note that most brokerages may automatically exercise options that expire in-the-money. So, you will not want to let an option expire in-the-money unless you are prepared to buy or sell the shares as required.

CHAPTER 11:

Popular Options Strategies

When you understand the fundamentals of trading options, you can get things going. You should have a business plan if it relates to options trading strategies. Just what will help you decide in your trading plan what kind of strategy to introduce. You will choose to create a strategy that will lead you to achieve your goals, depending on your trading plan.

Trading options stand the chance of failing. Recognizing what you do, however, is, by far, an essential factor. It will always be a threat to trade and invest; you need to have a good outlook on what you are doing. Establishing a successful trading strategy and then implementing a series of strategies to allow you to achieve it is the secret to a consistent and significant edge in trading options.

Traders often get started with trading options with little or no knowledge of the option strategies available. There are several solutions to alternatives that both minimize risk and optimize return. With just a little work, investors can learn to take advantage of the flexibility and flexibility that stock options can offer.

Here we will list some trading options strategies that every trader needs to know to manipulate the market:

Covered Call

A covered call translates as a financial operation where the owner selling call options holds an equal number of the corresponding security. To do this, a trader keeping a long position through an asset sells call options to create a revenue stream on the same investment. The investor's long position in the commodity is "cover," as it means that if the buyer wishes to utilize the call option, the seller will transfer the shares. It is regarded as a "buy-write" trade if the investor purchases the stock at one time and writes call options on that stock.

- A covered call would be a common options technique used in the pattern of options premiums to make profits.

- A trader maintaining a long position through investment then writes call options on the same investment to conduct a covered call.

- Many who wish to retain the underlying asset for a long time are often using covered calls but do not anticipate a substantial price rise in the short future.

- For a trader who thinks the associated price will not change much through the near-term, this approach is perfect.

Covered calls are often a balanced strategy, implying that the investor expects a small rise or decline in the corresponding stock price for the written call contract duration. This approach is often used when a trader has an impartial short-term perception of the commodity and, for this purpose, keeps the asset longer and also has a short position through the option to earn revenue from the premium at the same time.

A covered call acts as short-term leverage on a prolonged position and enables investors to gain revenue for selling the option through the premium obtained. The investor, though, revokes stock profits if the price rises above the option's purchase price. If the trader wants to exercise the option, they are also obliged to offer 100 shares at the market price (for every contract written).

Married Put

An investor buys a share, such as company shares, in a married put approach, and concurrently buys options for an equal amount of stocks. The put option owner is entitled to offer the stocks at the strike rate, and the value of each agreement is 100 shares.

When maintaining a portfolio, an investor can utilize such a strategy to preserve their market risk. This solution operates comparably to an insurance plan; if the stock price drops sharply, it sets a price floor.

A married put is a term referring to an options trading approach in which an investor buys an at-the-money (ATM) put option on the very same share, maintaining a long position in such a product, to hedge against a decline in the stock's price.

A married put is also called a long synthetic call since it has the same pattern of benefit. The method is similar to purchasing a standard call option (without any of the underlying assets) since the same dynamic applies to both: restricted loss and infinite benefit potential.

Bull Call Spread

An investor concurrently buys calls at a particular strike price in a bull call spread technique while still offering the very same number of calls at a higher price. There will be the same expiry date and underlying security for both call options. Whenever a trader is optimistic about the financial commodity, this form of spread strategy is mostly used and projects a modest increase in the asset values. Using this method, the investor can reduce its trade advantage while also diminishing premiums spent (compared to buying a naked call option outright).

Bear Put Spread

Another type of vertical spread is the bear-put spread approach. Concurrently, in this technique, the investor buys put options at a particular strike price and sells the same volume of puts at a lower price. For the same financial commodity, all options are acquired to have the same expiry date. This technique can be used when the investor has a bearish feeling regarding the financial commodity and anticipates its price to decrease. The strategy generates both restricted losses and constrained gains.

Protective Collar

By buying an out-of-the-money (OTM) put option and concurrently selling an out-of-the-money (OTM) call option, a protective collar approach is carried out. The corresponding asset, as well as the date of expiry, must be similar. Sometimes after a long position throughout a stock has seen considerable returns, this technique is also used by traders. As the long put makes it easier to lock in the future sale price, investors also have risk security. The trade-off, though, is that they will be forced to sell securities at a premium cost, leaving aside the prospect of more gain.

Straddles

A straddle is a neutral option technique involving the mutual acquisition of both a call option and a put option with much the same market price and the same expiry date for the underlying stock when the value of the security increases or drops from the market price by a sum more significant than the premium charge's cumulative value. An investor will benefit from such a long straddle as much as the value of the underlying product shifts very abruptly; the profit potential is practically limitless.

A straddle may offer two important clues to an investor about what the market for options feels about some inventory. The first is the uncertainty predicted from the protection by the sector. The second is the stock's estimated trading scope by the date of maturity.

A strategy of extended straddle options happens when an investor buys a call simultaneously and puts an option along with the same asset class with the same purchase price and expiry date. A trader can also use this technique if they assume that the underlying stock's value will move dramatically out of a particular range, but they are not sure which path the transfer will take. This method allows the trader, ideally, to have the potential for limitless profits.

Strangles

A strangle is a technique of options wherein the investor owns a place with varying strike rates, with almost the same expiry date and financial instrument, in both a put and a call option. If you assume the underlying asset will undergo a significant price action in the immediate future but are not sure of the course, a stranglehold is an excellent approach. It is, nevertheless, lucrative primarily if the investment swings in price dramatically.

A strangle is closely related to a straddle, except at varying strike rates, uses alternatives, whereas a straddle utilizes a call and places it at a similar strike price.

The trader purchases an OTM put and an OTM call option concurrently in a long strangle. The call option's market rate seems to be greater than the existing selling price of the associated asset, whereas the put has a lesser market price than the asset's selling price. As when the call option has potentially infinite potential if the asset value increases in value, this strategy has huge benefit prospects. In contrast, the put option will generate income if the asset value falls. The transaction risk is restricted to the premium charged for the options.

Long Call Butterfly Spread

The traditional approaches required the integration of two specific positions or agreements. An investor can mix both a bear spread strategy and a bull spread strategy within a long butterfly spread utilizing call options. There are three different strike rates they can all use. All options are from similar underlying stock and maturity dates.

For instance, by buying one in-the-money (ITM) call option at a lower rate while still offering two at-the-money (ATM) call options as well as purchasing one out-of-the-money (OTM) call option, a long butterfly spread can be established. Relatively similar wing dimensions would be available for a consistent butterfly spread. This instance is termed a "call fly" and a cumulative debit result from it. When they assume that the stocks will not change much until expiry, a trader will move into a long butterfly call spread.

Iron Condor

The investor concurrently owns a bear call spread and a bull put spread within the iron condor approach. By offering one out-of-the-money (OTM) put and purchasing one out-of-the-money (OTM) put off a lesser strike-a-bull put spread and writing one out-of-the-money (OTM) call and purchasing one out-of-the-money (OTM) call of a greater strike-a bear call spread, the iron condor is established. Both options would be on the same asset class and have the same expiry date. The call and put sides usually have the very same spread diameter. This investment thesis provides a net profit framework and is structured to fully leverage a low-volatility stock. Many investors use this technique for its expected high likelihood of receiving a small amount of fee.

Iron Butterfly

An investor will write an at-the-money (ATM) put in the iron butterfly strategy and purchase an out-of-the-money (OTM) put. They would also transfer an at-the-money (ATM) call at the very same time and purchase an out-of-the-money (OTM) call. Both options would be on the same asset class and have the same expiry date. Although this method is close to a butterfly spread, it makes use of both puts and calls.

This approach effectively incorporates the sale of an at-the-money (ATM) straddle and the purchase of defensive "wings." The development can also be interpreted as two spreads. In both spreads, it is customary to get the same dimension. The long, infinite downside is covered by the out-of-the-money (OTM) call. The long out-of-the-money (OTM) put protects against the disadvantages. Based on the price levels of the options utilized, benefits, and losses, both are limited to a particular range. Investors like this method for the revenue it produces and the greater possibility of a small benefit from a non-volatile portfolio.

CHAPTER 12:

Practical Example

We will talk about essential trading habits and give you examples of excellent option trading strategies. Remember this information can be used to decide to take part in any trading.

The medium and long-term investment is ideal for those who want to build capital or diversify and enhance savings over time naturally and at reduced costs. Given their versatility, ETFs can be used in different medium and long-term investment strategies. They can support or replace traditional instruments, thus allowing them to achieve the set objective. Currently, the range of ETFs is so diverse that any FCI can be replicated (at a much higher cost)

A strategy to invest its capital in the medium to long term is to resort to investment funds, whose popularity has grown progressively over the last twenty years. One of the funds' main characteristics is allowing the underwriter to enter the market with modest capital and obtain professional management that will allow them to obtain positive results over time, with moderate risk. Investment funds should favor more active management, even if this does not always happen.

In addition to weighing on their final return, they are the highest management costs to which the same funds are subject. Their impact is felt particularly in times of slowdown or stagnation of the market. In light of this situation, the investor could find it convenient to substitute the investment in funds with that of ETFs that aim to follow the evolution of its benchmark index carefully while offering the maximum possible transparency.

In advance, it cannot be said whether it is better to invest in funds or ETF; to make this choice, you have to decide if you want the manager to move away from the benchmark (and from which benchmark): this possibility is called "active risk." Active risk is not necessarily bad because some managers are better than others. Still, in reality, they are few, and, not always, you can find them. If you decide to move away from the underlying risk, you must be convinced that:

- Good managers exist.

- That they can do better than their benchmark.

- Above all, be able to find them.

If you think you can complete each of the three phases, it is appropriate to rely on active funds. Otherwise, ETFs are preferred because they cost less and carry precisely where you decided to go without additional surprises.

The techniques for choosing the ETF that best suits your investment strategies are different; an interesting methodology is applied to sector rotation. The market is made up of different equity sectors, corresponding to the different economic sectors and their continuous alternation from the origin to the expansion and contraction phases. Thus, the moments in which all the economic sectors grow or decrease simultaneously are quite rare. The concept of sector rotation is useful to identify, on the one hand, the stage of maturity of the current primary trend and, on the other, to select those sectors that have a growing relative strength. For example, sectors sensitive to changes in interest rates tend to anticipate both the minimums and the maximums.

The sectors sensitive to the demand for capital goods or raw materials generally tend to follow the market's overall trend with delay. Through ETFs, it is possible to immediately position on a specific stock without necessarily being forced to buy the different securities belonging to that particular basket. It will be possible to obtain immediate exposure to this sector, benefiting from its value growth, besides the advantages linked to the diversification.

It is also possible to invest using relative strength, investing, perhaps, on a stock exchange index while benefiting from its growth in value and the advantages linked to diversification.

For example, if one thinks that the US market should grow in relative terms at a given moment to a greater extent than the French one, it will be appropriate to make the first one and underweight the second one. This decision can be reached by analyzing the relative comparative strength between the two markets, which compares two dimensions (composed of market, sector, securities, or other indices) to show how these values are performing comparably. Respect for each other. The trend changes expressed by relative strength generally tend to anticipate the actual ones of the financial activity to which it refers. Therefore, it is possible to use the relative strength to direct purchases towards ETFs that show a growing relative force.

ETFs' high flexibility also allows the construction of guaranteed capital investment; in times of financial turbulence, investors often turn to products that provide capital protection: those provided by financial intermediaries often have high charges for customers. It is possible to build a guaranteed capital product by yourself, which respects your personal investment needs. The central point of the logic of guaranteed capital is interest rates and the duration of the investment. At the base of all, there are central concepts of finance: the higher the interest rates, the greater the return on the money as the duration increases, you earn more because money "works" longer.

In many years, the money we will obtain can be brought to today, as for bills that follow the discount law (the technical term of bringing the future money to today). You can quickly answer the question: "to have 100$ in seven years, knowing that the rates are at 5%, how much money do I have to invest?" This statement indicates how much money is needed to invest today to get the desired amount at maturity. The bonds that allow only the fruits to maturity, without paying interest during their life, are called zero-coupon bonds (zcb) and are quite common on the market. If for example, I want to have $100 at maturity and interest rates are at 5% I will have to invest in zero-coupon bonds $95.24 (if the deadline is between one year) $78.35 (if the deadline is in five years) $61.39 (if the deadline is ten years) €48.1 (if the deadline is between fifty years) and $23.21 (if the deadline is thirty years)

In effect, by building investment with guaranteed capital, one only has to decide how to invest the remaining part of the initial $100 that have not been allocated in the zero coupons. An ideal solution could be to invest in options because they can amplify any yield thanks to the leverage effect. If you have a less aggressive investment profile, ETFs are excellent tools to build guaranteed capital investment. If, for example, we assume a ten-year investment with rates of 2.5% for that maturity, the portion to be invested in zcb is equal to 78.12%. In comparison, the remaining 21.88% will be invested in the ETF.

This investment strategy achieves a minimum (not real) "money" return target with few operations, as the zcb provides for the repayment only on the nominal amount of the loan (not discounted to the inflation rate). Therefore, it is a valid methodology for those who intend to make investments with clear objectives and have little time to devote to monitoring the values as only an operation until expiry may be necessary. Unlike a guaranteed capital product offered by any financial intermediary, an investment of this kind built independently with ETFs can be dismantled entirely or in pieces (selling only the zcb or existing assets, ETF) to meet any need.

Naturally, only at maturity will there be a certainty of the pre-established return and, throughout the loan, a temporary adverse trend in financial variables, (rates rise by lowering the zcb and at the same time decreasing the value of the ETF) could result in the liquidation of losing positions. The same consequence would be selling a structured bond, with the advantage that "doing it at home," the commissions are much lower. You can separate the two components and, if necessary, liquidate only one, according to specific needs.

The Profitability of Equity (Roe)

This is the ratio between the net result and a given company's net assets. Mainly from equity investments is an essential parameter as profitability higher than the cost of capital is an index of an enterprise's ability to create value. Therefore, it should guarantee a higher capacity for the securities' growth in the phases of the rise of the market and resistance in the reflexive phases. From this point of view, the Roe is always held in strong consideration by those who choose to invest in shares today.

Price/Earnings Ratio

A low ratio of this parameter makes a share price particularly attractive, but at the same time, it could mean that expectations regarding future profits are not particularly positive. As in the Roe case, this is a factor to be taken into due consideration when choosing the best actions to invest in.

Price-Book Value Ratio

It is the share price and the net asset value resulting from the last balance sheet, especially if this ratio is lower than the unit, which means that the company is being paid less than the value of the net budget liabilities. However, this does not necessarily mean that it is a good deal since it may not produce profits.

Dividend Yield

This is the percentage ratio between the last distributed dividend and the share price. In particular, it measures the company's remuneration to shareholders in the last year in the form of liquidity. This parameter is often taken into account to identify the securities to invest in since a company that can distribute dividends is generally a good company.

In this case, as with all the other selection parameters, it is necessary for a broader and more complete analysis since a high level of this indicator could also mean that the company has made few investments or has little prospect of growth. For this reason, looking at the dividend yield as a primary factor in determining the securities to invest in the options market is reductive. The dividend yield only makes sense if accompanied by considerations of the listed company's business plans and industrial plans.

CHAPTER 13:

Charts to Assist With the Explaining

G raphs that are used to analyze technical analysis are commonly referred to as charts. The technical analysis charts used in the financial markets tend to identify two major components in trading. They narrow down to depicting the trends and patterns that are being experienced in foreign exchange markets. Other chart functions are used in the process of an individual trying to understand the financial markets. It can be hard to interpret the graphs for an individual who is a beginner in the financial markets.

There several forms of graphs that are used in the current world to analyze financial markets technically. However, three common graphs are heavily relied on by traders in this sector of trading. These charts include candlesticks, line charts, and graphs. There is a common similarity that is shared across the three graphs. They are all created by the use of the same price data. However, the difference crops in when it comes to the displaying of data. All three graphs have a different way in which they display the data.

The difference between major types of graphs makes a trader have varied forms of technical analysis. However, the graphs have various advantages that they present to a trader investing their time and resources in financial markets. They help a trader to make informed decisions about the market. The advantages and uses of technical analysis graphs can be effectively used in the trade of options. These analyzing graphs include:

Line Charts

This form of type of graphs is common in financial markets. It is common for people who are known for trading stock. However, this analysis graph's fame and advantage have led it to be used in the trade of options. This sector of financial trading has also proved to be effective in the roles it is tasked with. People who are beginners in options trading and other forms of financial trading are always encouraged to use this graph because one can easily understand it. It is easy for someone to interpret this graph because it focuses on the market holistically. This helps to eliminate the shifts in data that proves to be a heavy task for various people. Emotions are always put aside because this form of analysis uses factual figures presented to it.

What this graph simply does is illustrating the display are the closing prices. There is nothing else that is portrayed in the line charts. Each of the portrayed closing prices tends to be linked to the closing price seen in the last trading session. This makes a continuous line that flows easily. This type of graph has places that easily depict it. They are popular in several web articles, newspapers, and television programs. It is because several people can easily digest them. The graph provides an individual with less amount of information to handle. This is completely different from those bar charts or candlesticks. One can describe the graph as having a simplistic view of the market with just a simple glance.

Something is intriguing when it comes to this graph's advantage of helping an individual manage their emotions. The process of trading is done by humans characterized by having feelings attached to what they do. These emotions are drawn away by the usage of neutral colors. Several choppy movements have easily eliminated the usage of several colors.

Bar Graphs (OHLC)

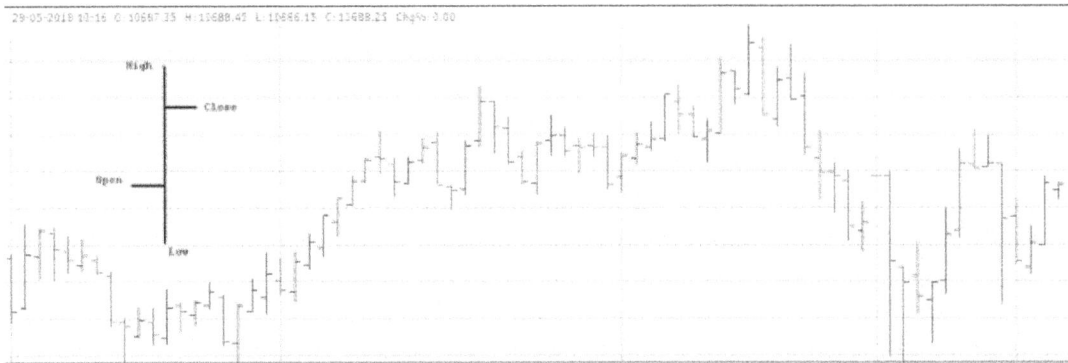

Individuals who commonly trade options that involve commodities as the underlying assets are commonly known to use this graph. It is very popular because of its effectiveness in the financial markets, and its success is vastly experienced in trading stock options and foreign exchange markets. An individual at the intermediate level of options trading will be advantaged to using this graph while studying the market. There is a unique way by which this graph analyses the trends in the market. The data collected on the prices of financial instruments help to sport the trend in the market. They help in the identification of the entry and support or resistance points in the trade of options. The advantage with this graph is it's detailed hence giving added information to a trader.

This bar graph can display closing, opening, high, and low prices for specific periods designated in the bar. The high and low prices in the graph create the vertical line of the graph. There are always two dashes that are present in the graph. The one on the left always signifies the signals of closings price while the one on the right signifies the opening prices' signals. There is a similarity that is presented between this kind of graph and candlestick. Both graphs are easily viewed on the sides though the bar graph tends to have a clearer view.

Candlesticks Charts

Some individuals are used for trading in the financial markets to use this graph to analyze the options markets. They can be equated to the bar graphs since they are commonly preferred by intermediate traders in the trade of options. Candlestick can look easier in a trader's eye compared to bar graphs because of their full nature.

A candlestick graph does a function of displaying the opening, closing (OHLC), low, and high prices for the period that is designated for each candle. The candle body of each stick represents the opening and closing prices. On the other side, the candle wicks tend to signify the high and low prices for each specific period. Several colors are used in this graph, which is green and red. The green color represents the prices closing high than when they were opened. On the other hand, the red color signifies the prices closed low than when they were opened.

CHAPTER 14:

Common Options Trading Mistakes

N

o one can claim to be the perfect trader. We all make mistakes, even the best of us. When we note our mistakes and admit to them, we get a chance to become better. Some mistakes are often repeated over and over again, yet they can be avoided. There are, however, some general mistakes that you need to avoid if you are to trade options successfully:

Trading Without a Definite Exit Plan

You need to learn how to control your emotions as a trader. This is true whether you are trading in stocks or options. You always need to have a plan, work with the plan, and stick to it no matter your feelings. An exit plan is necessary whether you are losing or winning. In short, have an upside exit point and a downside exit point.

Trying to Make Up for Losses Incurred

Most traders will lose money at one point or another. This is a common occurrence. However, many beginners or rookie traders often get into a panic after losing money. Inexperienced traders often panic after losing a couple of trades and will try and pump in more money in a panic. You should not do this as it will only cost you more money. Instead, take a deep breath, relax, and even take a break.

Sometimes, traders tend to double up, a way of investing more money in trades in their attempt to recoup their losses. While this can be a tempting affair, you should learn to avoid and stick to your investment plan. Your plan is very important and will guide all your online trading ventures.

Not Performing Sufficient Research on a Position

You have to conduct due diligence and do your homework. If you do not use the tools provided, study charts, compare performance, and lots of other things that you should, then your trades may not be successful. You will only lose money and not even have a chance to understand why. Ensure that you put in the work necessary and work hard so that you can trade successfully. An informed trader is most often a successful trader and vice versa.

Trading With a Fixed Mind

Many traders often trade with a fixed mind, thinking they are always right. Sometimes, even when evidence is available to the contrary, traders still stick to their positions. Instead of insisting on being right, the focus should be on being profitable, and this means being flexible and having an open mind.

Waiting a Long Time to Buy Back Short Strategies

As a trader, you need always to be ready to purchase short strategies and do so early enough. Sometimes, when a trade happens profitably, and according to your wishes, you may tend to relax. You may form an opinion that this run will continue forever. Such trades or runs can easily change direction.

Should a short option that you have goes out-of-the-money, then you should buy it back. If you can manage to rescue over 80% of your earlier gains, you should buy back the option.

Purchasing Out-of-the-Money Options

Some of the cheapest options in the options market are the out-of-money options. Many beginners often rush to buy these because of their low cost, and this might seem like, therefore, to them. However, there is a reason these options are so cheap. Most of them have very little chance of ending up in-the-money, so that they may be worth nothing eventually.

If you are to purchase these options, you have to be accurate in terms of time and direction. You will still lose out even if the direction is accurate if you sit on them too long. The expiration date is often the most crucial determinant about whether the options will finish in-the-money.

To fix this, try and go for straight long puts and calls. Get these in-the-money options as soon as possible. While they are likely to be more expensive, they possess a better chance of success and will likely earn you a profit.

Letting Short Options Go Unmonitored

One of the most outstanding features of short options is that they carry limited rewards and unlimited risks. While this might be a turnoff to some investors, it should not deter you. Short options can be a very lucrative way of getting an income. However, as a trader, you have to remain in-charge and involved.

You should monitor both the upside and downside of this option and see how it is performing. Many traders, however, try to get as much out of their options as possible. This might see them end up in a loss. The best approach with short options is never to let them go in-the-money. That is unless they are covered calls or when you are applying puts to find stocks. Also, ensure to set your points where you will exit. It could be determined by a maximum loss amount or your technical analysis of the trades.

Trading Low-Volume Options

One of the important factors of options trading is dealing with liquid options. Liquidity here stands for the speed at which you can enter or exit a given position at a desirable price. If the liquidity is low, then the chance of exiting at your preferred time or price is limited.

Remember that just because options are listed on the market does not imply that they are good for trading. Most listed options will not be traded. Smaller companies do not have liquid options. Try and avoid being so far out-of-the-money or even in-the-money.

Not Being Informed as You Trade

It is very crucial that when you start trading, you have all the necessary information, so you make the correct and informed decisions. However, not being informed is a problem experienced not just by rookie traders but even experienced ones. Remember the part about doing your homework? This is very important.

You should always keep abreast of matters about macro and micro-economics. Also, make sure to have the economic calendar to know when a major economic news item is to be announced. Such information is definitely important and will help guide you even as you make your trades' financial decisions.

At a micro-level, you want to look at a company's information. For instance, do they have any major impending announcements? Major announcements can have a great impact on the stock exchange. Stocks may rise drastically or drop significantly. It is okay to trade, but you should have sufficient knowledge to understand how they affect your overall trading strategy.

Trading Options Without Properly Understanding Them

Plenty of beginners often lack a deeper understanding of options. For instance, a trader purchases a call stock option when the share experiences a price increase, but the option loses money. This usually happens due to the volatility of the stocks. It also goes to show the lack of a deeper understanding of stock options.

You don't need to understand every minute detail before you embark on your trades. You need to have at least some basic information about the company whose stocks you are about to deal in. You also need to understand how different stock trading strategies can benefit you and how each strategy reacts to time, direction, and volatility.

Understand a Strategy Before Implementing It

Most advanced traders venture into advanced options trading by implementing intermediate strategies that involve a combination of strategies. There is nothing wrong with this, and it is a good approach. First trades should not be complicated and should not be within an iron condor. The only issue here is that, as a trader, you may get stuck into these strategies and forget that there are many other great strategies out there. If you do not diversify your strategies, then you may lose out.

In options trading, traders can move in any direction and leverage the market. For instance, options can allow you to trade profitably whether the market is volatile or not, is moving upwards, is on a downward trend, or is not moving at all. A good trader can exploit all these different market situations to ensure that they can benefit from them and maximize their profits.

However, not all strategies will work for everyone or in all situations. However, by venturing out with knowledge and understanding, it will be possible to eventually identify the kinds of strategies that work for you in every different situation. Strategies can be tried in small sizes after a proper understanding of how they function.

CHAPTER 15:

Fundamental Analysis

To make the best trades, you have to gather as much data as possible regardless of what market you are working in. There are two ways to get the most out of any of the data you gather, the first is via technical analysis, and the second is via fundamental analysis.

Fundamental analysis looks at specific factors based on the underlying asset for the market that you are working in.

Fundamental analysis is typically considered easier to master than concepts less expressly related to understanding market movement exclusively.

Fundamental Analysis Rules

The best time to use fundamental analysis is when you are looking to gain a broad idea of the state of the market as it stands and how that relates to the state of things shortly when it comes time to trading successfully.

Establish a Baseline

To begin analyzing the fundamentals, the first thing that you will need to do is to create a baseline regarding the company's overall performance. To generate the most useful results possible, the first thing you will need to do is gather data both regarding the company in question and the related industry as a whole. When gathering macro data, it is important to keep in mind that no market will operate in a vacuum, which means the reasons behind specific market movement can be much more far-reaching than they first appear. Fundamental analysis works because of the stock market's propensity for patterns. If you trace a specific market moved back to the source, you will have a better idea of what to keep an eye on in the future.

Furthermore, all industries go through several different phases where their penny stocks will be worth more or less overall based on general popularity. If the industry is producing many popular penny stocks, then overall volatility will be down while at the same time liquidity will be at an overall high.

Consider Worldwide Issues

Once you hold the current phase you are dealing with, the next thing you will want to consider is anything that is going on in the wider world that will after the type of businesses you tend to favor in your penny stocks. Not being prepared for major paradigm shifts, especially in penny stocks where new companies come and go so quickly, means that you can easily miss out on massive profits and should be avoided at all costs.

To ensure you are not blindsided by news you could have seen coming, it is important to look beyond the obvious issues that are consuming the 24-hour news cycle and dig deeper into the comings and goings of the nation's going to most directly affect your particular subsection of penny stocks. One important worldwide phenomenon that you will want to pay specific attention to is anything in the realm of technology. Major paradigm shifts like the smartphone's adoption of electric cars' current move can create serious paradigm shifts.

Put It All Together

This is to compare what has been and what might to what the current state of the market is. Not only will this give you a realistic idea of what other investors are going to do if certain events occur the way they have in the past, but you will also be able to use these details to identify underlying assets that are currently on the cusp of generating the type of movement that you need if you want to utilize them via binary options trades.

The best time to get on board with a new underlying asset is when it is nearing the end of the post-bust period or the end of a post-boom period. Depending on if you are going to set a call or a put.

You will have the greatest access to the freedom of the market, and thus, have access to the greatest overall allowable risk you will find in any market. Remember, the amount of risk that you can successfully handle without an increase in the likelihood of failure will start decreasing as soon as the boom or bust phase begins in earnest, so it is important to get in as quickly as possible if you hope to maximize your profits truly.

Understand the Relative Strength of Any Given Trade

When an underlying asset is experiencing a boom phase, the strength of its related fundamentals will determine how other investors are going to act when it comes to binary options trading. Remember, when it comes to fundamental analysis, what an underlying asset looks like at the moment isn't nearly as important as what it is likely to look like in the future, and the best way to determine those details is by keeping an eye on the past.

Quantitative Fundamental Analysis

The sheer volume of data and a large number of varying numbers found in the average company's financial statements can easily be intimidating and bewildering for conscientious investors who are digging into them for the first time. You will quickly find that they are a goldmine of information when determining how likely a company is to continue producing reliable dividends in the future.

At their most basic, a company's financial statements disclose the information relating to its financial performance over a set period. Unlike qualitative concepts, financial statements provide cold, hard facts about a rarely open company for interpretation.

Important Statements

Balance Sheet

A balance sheet shows a detailed record of all of a company's equity, liabilities, and assets for a given period. A balance sheet shows a balance to a company's financial structure by dividing its equity by the combination of shareholders and liabilities to determine its current assets.

In this case, assets represent the resources that the company is actively in control of at a specific point in time. It can include things like buildings, machinery, inventory, cash, and more. It will also show the total value of any financing that has been used to generate those assets. Financing can come from either equity or liabilities. Liabilities include debt that must be paid back eventually, while equity, in this case, measures the total amount of money that its owners have put into the business. This can include profits from last years, which are known collectively as retained earnings.

Income Statement

It takes a closer look at the company's performance exclusively for a given timeframe. There is no boundary to the length of time an income statement considers, which means you could see them generated month to month or even day to day; however, the most common type used by public companies are either annual or quarterly. Income statements provide information on profit, expenses, and revenues that resulted from the business that took place over a specific period.

Cash Flow Statement

The cash flow statement frequently shows all of the cash outflow and inflow for the company over a given period. The cash flow statement often focuses on operating cash flow, which is the cash generated by day to day business operations. It will also include any cash that is available from investing, which is often used to invest in assets, along with any cash that might have been generated by long-term asset sales or the sale of a secondary business that the company previously owned. Cash due to financing is another name for money paid off or received based on issuing or borrowing funds.

The cash flow statements are quite important as it is often more difficult for businesses to manipulate them than many other financial documents. While accountants can manipulate earnings with ease, it is much more difficult to fake having access to cash in the bank where none exists. This is why many savvy investors consider the cash flow statement the most reliable way to measure a specific company's performance.

Finding the Details

While tracking down all the disparate financial statements on the company's you are considering purchasing stock in can be cumbersome, the Securities and Exchange Commission (SEC) requires all publicly traded companies to submit regular filings outlining all of their financial activities, including a variety of different financial statements. This also includes managerial discussions, reports from auditors, deep dives into the operations and prospects of upcoming years, and more.

These types of details can all be found in the 10-K filing that each company is required to file every year, along with the 10-Q filing that they must send out once per quarter. Both types of documents can be found online, both at the corporate website for the company and on the SEC website. As the version that hits the corporate site doesn't need to be complete, it is best to visit SEC.gov and get to know the Electronic Data Gathering, Analysis, and Retrieval (EDGAR) system automates the process of indexing, validating, collecting, forward, and accepting submissions. As this system was designed in the mid-90s, however, it is important to dedicate some time to learning the process as it is more cumbersome than 20 years of user interface advancements have to lead you to expect.

Qualitative Fundamental Analysis

Qualitative factors are generally less tangible and include name recognition, the patents it holds, and its board members' quality. Qualitative factors to consider include:

Business Model

The first thing that you will want to do when you catch wind of a company that might be worth following up on is to check out its business model, which is more or less a generalization of how it makes its money. You can typically find these sorts of details on the company website or in its 10-K filing.

Competitive Advantage

You have to consider the various competitive advantages that the company you have your eye on might have over its competition. Companies that will be successful in the long-term are always going to have an advantage over their competition in one of two ways. They can either have better operational effectiveness or improved strategic positioning. Operational effectiveness is the name given to doing the same things as the competition but more efficiently and effectively. Strategic positioning occurs when a company gains an edge by doing things that nobody else is doing.

Changes to the Company

To properly narrow down your search, you will typically find the most reliable results when it comes to companies that have recently seen major changes to their corporate structure as it is these types of changes that are likely to ultimately precede events that are more likely to see the company jump to the next level. The specifics of what happened in this instance are nearly as important as statistically speaking; 95% of companies that experience this type of growth started with a significant change to the status quo.

CHAPTER 16:

Before You Enter a Trade

You have to know a few things before you enter the market to understand how to filter out and consistently pick good trades.

Portfolio Balance

Before you do anything, you need to look at your portfolio balance first. When you're planning a new trade, it's always important to ask yourself why you need that trade and how it will affect your portfolio. Do you even really need it? For instance, if your portfolio already has plenty of bearish trades, it would generally be better for you to avoid adding more.

You need to reduce your risk in every situation, so the key here is to balance out your trades. That's how one develops a great portfolio, risk diversification. When you have many bearish trades in hand, look for bullish trades to offset the risk and vice versa. Once you internalize this, it becomes far easier to focus on your portfolio needs and filter out the rest from the first moment you start looking for a new trade.

Liquidity

Liquidity is straight-up one of the essential qualities of a good, tradable option. You don't want to remain with an illiquid option, no matter how lucrative it looks. Here's a simple rule to follow when looking for a new trade: for it to be a good trade, the underlying stock should be trading at least 100,000 shares daily. If the numbers are less than that, the trade isn't worth your time.

In a market as big and efficient as the one we have, the calculations only become more accurate over time. Similarly, when considering the underlying options, there should be a minimum of 1,000 open interest contracts for the strikes you are trading for it to be a good trade. It ensures quick entry into and exit from the market. Remember, liquidity is important.

Implied Volatility Percentile

When a trade satisfies the two criteria, it's time to move on to the next step—the IV percentile. You need to check how high or low the implied volatility of an option is, which is measured by using percentile scores. Let me explain with an example:

Say, if AAPL has IV of 35% but IV percentile of 70%, it means that while the current volatility is low, in the last year, it was higher than what it currently is (35%) for more than 70% of the time. So, the implied volatility for AAPL is relatively high, and you should be looking to employ premium-selling strategies.

Picking a Strategy

Picking a great strategy is as much a matter of eliminating as it is a matter of selecting, perhaps even more so. You can easily eliminate many strategies once you have a good idea of the IV and the IV percentile of the underlying stock and how it affects the options. For example, it's easy to eliminate strategies like debit spreads and long single options when you know the IV is high and the pricing rich. Then it's time to consider our risk tolerance and account size to pick the best strategy out of the ones left (iron condors, credit spreads, strangles, etc.).

Strikes and Month

Your trading style and goals also play a big part in how you decide to pick trades. Some people are more risk-averse than others, and that's okay. You should always select the right strategy based on the risk level you're comfortable with. If you're selling credit spreads, let's say, and you have the option to sell them at either a strike price that has a 90% chance of success of a strike price that has a 65% chance of success, you need to decide which option you want to go with based on the level of aggression you're comfortable with. It needs to fit your trading style and your goals.

You also need to do is give yourself sufficient time. This makes sure the trade can work out. This means that you should place low IV strategies at sixty–ninety days out and high IV strategies at thirty–sixty days out. You should read up on Theta value (one of the Greeks) and how it affects volatility.

Position Size

It is one of those areas where even some of the more experienced traders fail. You must understand this concept so you can make great trades often. Before placing a trade, you should always carefully assess your position size. As your trading position gets bigger, so does the risk, but this isn't linear, as many studies have shown. The risk increases exponentially, and one bad trade could easily lead to a blown account in this case. I strongly advise you to start with small positions as a beginner and continue to do so even when you're an intermediate. Your risk scale should be a sliding scale of 1–5% of your total balance on which all your trades need to be placed.

The cash or margin you use to cover a trade is what we call risk. For example, when selling a $1 wide credit put spread for 50 cents, you would need to cover it up with a $50 margin. You use this $50 margin to base your trade-off for each trade you make. If your account is worth $20,000 and you wish to allocate 3% of your account (it fits the 1–5% sliding scale criteria), you can take $600 of risk (3% of $20,000). You divide this by $50, and you get 12, which is the number of spreads you should sell at most. If this number is a fraction, always round down and never up.

Future Moves

You must've heard the popular saying that a chess grandmaster can foresee as many as 20 moves ahead. A good options trader also plans and foresees future moves. You're going to lose to the market more often than not if you're not thinking a few moves ahead. Always have another plan in case things go nasty and you need to shield yourself from losses. And while shielding yourself from a losing trade is important, it's also important to plan how to turn a loss into a winning one.

Sometimes, you won't be able to make a winning trade. That's just how the market works; some trades go wrong no matter how well you plan. But you need to keep asking yourself important questions constantly. When you do this, your mind stays sharp and ready to jump into action to formulate a new plan or make an adjustment as and when the need arises.

CHAPTER 17:

Choosing a Broker

For selecting brokers, you have many options available. There are full-services, discounts, online, etc. Understanding the differences between them and selecting the ones best suited for your purposes is crucial if you wish to succeed. Another area that many beginners ignore and then receive a rude lesson in is the regulations surrounding options trading.

There aren't too many rules to comply with, but they have significant consequences for your capital and risk strategies.

Generally, there are two major varieties of brokers: discount and full-service. A lot of full-service brokers have discount arms these days so that you will see some overlap. Full-service refers to an organization where brokerage is just a part of a larger financial supermarket.

The broker might offer you other investment solutions, estate planning strategies, and so on. They'll also have an in-house research wing, which will send you reports to help you trade better. Besides this, they'll also have phone support if you have questions or wish to place an order.

Make a good relationship with them, a full-service broker will become a good organization to network. Every broker loves a profitable customer since it helps with marketing. A full-service broker will have good relationships in the industry, and if you have specific needs, they can help you with the right people.

The price of all this service is you paying higher commissions than average. It is up to you to see whether this is a good price for you to pay. You need not sign up with a full-service broker to trade successfully. Order matching is done electronically, so it's not as if a person on the floor can get you a better price these days. Therefore, a full-service house will not give you better execution.

Discount brokers, on the other hand, are all about focus. They help you trade, and that is it. At least not intentionally, they will not advise from a business perspective, and phone ordering is nonexistent. That doesn't mean they reduce customer service.

Margin

Margin refers to the number of assets you currently hold in your account. Your assets are cash and positions. As the market value of your positions fluctuates, so does the amount of margin you have. Margin is an important concept to grasp since it is at the core of your risk management discipline.

You must make a choice when you open an account with your broker. You can open either a cash or margin account. To trade options, open a margin account. Briefly, a cash account does not include leverage within it, so all you can trade are stocks. There are no account minimums for a cash account, and even if they are, they're minuscule.

A margin account is subject to weird rules. First, the minimum balances for a margin account are higher. Most brokers will impose a $10,000 minimum, and some will even increase this amount based on your trading style. The account minimum achieves nothing by itself, but it acts as a broker's commission.

The thinking is that with this much money on the line, the person trading will be more serious about it and won't blow it away. If only it worked like that. Anyway, the minimum balance is a hard and fast rule. Another rule you should know is the Pattern Day Trader (PDT) designation.

PDT is a rule that comes directly from the SEC. We classify anyone who executes four or more orders within five days as a PDT ("Pattern Day Trader," 2019). Once this tag is slapped onto you, your broker will ask you to post at least $25,000 in the margin as a minimum balance. Again, this minimum balance does nothing, but the SEC figures that if you screw up, this gives you enough of a buffer.

Margin Call

One other aspect of margin you must understand is the margin call. This is a dreaded message for most traders, including institutional ones. The purpose of all risk management is to keep you as far away as possible from this ever happening to you. A margin call is issued when you have inadequate funds in your account to cover its requirements.

Remember that your margin is the combination of the cash you hold plus the value of your positions. If you have $1,000 in cash, but your position is currently in a loss of -$900, you'll receive a margin call to post more cash to cover the potential loss you're headed for. You'll receive it well in advance. If you don't post more margins, your broker has the right to close out your positions and recover whatever cash they can to stop their risk limits from being triggered.

The threshold beyond which your broker will issue a margin call is called the maintenance margin. Usually, you need to maintain 25% of your initial position value (that is: when you enter a position) as cash in your account. Most brokers have a handy indicator that tells you how close you are to the limit.

The leading cause of margin calls is leverage. You can borrow money with a margin account and use that to boost your returns. Let's look at an example: If you trade with $10,000 of your own money and borrow $20,000 from your broker to enter a position, you control $30,000 worth of the position. Let's say this position makes a gain of $10,000 to bring its total value to $40,000.

You've just made a 100% return on this investment (since you invested only $10,000), although the total return on the position is 33% (10,000/30,000). What happens if you lose $10,000 on the position, though? Well, you just lost 100% despite the position losing only 33%. Leverage is a double-edged sword.

It is far too simplistic to call leverage bad or good. It is what it is. If you're a beginner, you should not be borrowing money to trade under any circumstances. When you're experienced, you can do so as much as you want. Please note the difference between the leverage where you borrow money and the leverage options provide.

A single contract gives you control over a larger pie of stock with options, but the option premium still needs to be paid. It is, therefore, cheaper to trade options than the common stock. If you were to borrow money to pay for the option premium, then you're indulging in foolish behavior, and you need to step away.

There's a difference between leverage being inherent within the instrument's structure and using leverage to increase the amount of something you can buy—the latter when you're a beginner.

Execution

A favorite pastime of unsuccessful traders is to complain about execution. Their losses are always the broker's fault, and if it weren't for the greedy brokers, they'd be rolling in the dough, diving in and out of it like Scrooge McDuck. Complaining about your execution will get you nothing. A big reason for these complaints is that most beginner traders don't realize that the price they see on the screen is not the same as what is being traded on the exchange.

We live in an era of high-frequency trading, and the markets' smallest measurement of time has gone from second to microseconds. Trades are constantly pouring in, and the matching engine is always finding suitable sellers for buyers. Given the pace of the market, it is important to understand that it is impossible to figure out an instrument's exact price.

Therefore, within your risk management plan, you must make allowance for high volatility times when the fluctuations will be bigger. For now, I want you to understand that just because the price you received differed from what was on screen doesn't mean the broker is incompetent.

Price Quotes

Many traders are stumped when they first look at their trading screens and see that there are two prices for everything. After all, every financial channel always displays one price for security, but you'll be quoted two different prices within the price box when trading. This is a small but crucial detail for you to understand.

The lower price you receive is called the bid, and this is the price you will pay if you sell the instrument. The higher price is asked, and this is what you will pay to buy the instrument. The single price you see on your TV screen is the "Last Traded Price" or LTP. Don't think the LTP is the actual price since the market moves constantly.

Even the spread (the difference between ask and the bid) doesn't accurately reflect the genuine state of things thanks to constant movement. Just remember to look at the spread to understand what you'll be paying. The spread increases and contracts constantly, but if you see that it is getting too big, this is a sign that too much volatility exists, and you're better off staying out.

CHAPTER 18:

Options Trading Platforms

A trading platform is the most important feature of a broker, which you will use to trade.

Many of us do not usually take this issue into account, and we only look at commissions. Still, as necessary as the broker service itself is the trading platform it offers us.

Why? Because the failure or success of our investment depends mainly on the power and reliability of the tool.

A trading platform and broker are not the same.

The broker is the midway that acts directly between us and the stock market. On the other hand, the trading platform is the work tool (software) through which we will operate and launch orders.

Thus, the broker will offer us a service while the platform will allow us to execute our strategy. Therefore, if the investment platform is not right, we can have serious problems when trading.

When hiring an online broker, we are going to come across two possibilities:

- Brokers who have developed their trading platform.

- Brokers using a multi-broker platform (also available to other providers).

Although there are powerful tools developed in-house by some brokers, keep in mind that a multi-broker platform can open many doors for you when it comes to trading and trading with other brokers.

- **Find the best trading platform:** There are some criteria you must take into account to choose a trading software:

- **Offer the instruments with which you want to invest:** Not all systems offer trading with any instrument.

- **The platform should be friendly and easy to use:** The best platform suggests the most comfortable and most intuitive usability for the user. With possibilities on the market, it makes no sense to continue using a complicated idea that is comprehensive.

- **Access to the tool code:** Some platforms such as MetaTrader 4 allow you to modify the programming code to create your indicators or scripts, among others.

Different Platforms

These are some of the top options trading platforms in the market today.

Firstrade

It is an online investment company that offers one of the best options trading platforms on the market. It became one of the first companies to launch into online trading when it launched in 1997 under First Flushing Securities.

The company changed its name to Firstrade a year later and has since been a pillar of online investing.

Competitive costs per order: Firstrade does not have the lowest fixed cost per order of the best options brokers on our list, but at a base rate of $6.95 and $0.75 per contract, it remains competitive.

Extended opening hours: One advantage of trading options with Firstrade is its ability to trade extended hours. This feature allows you to jump into exchanges likely to be affected by recent developments in the hours before and after exchanges on the standard market.

If you read something in the morning news that made you want to place a pre-market operation, you can do it between 8:05 and 9:25 a.m. with Firstrade.

Are you interested in participating in the aftermarket? You can do this too with Firstrade. It will allow you to place orders from 4:05 p.m. to 5:25 p.m.

TradeKing

It is an online broker found in 2005 and part of the TradeKing Group, Inc. It is merged with its sister company Zecco Trading.

Notable features of TradeKing: In recognition of excellence and excellence in customer service, TradeKing has received numerous awards over the years. Some of them include:

- Ranked 2019 Best in Class for Commissions and Fees by Stockbrokers.com

- Rated four stars by Barron Online corridor survey between 2006–2016

- Stockbrokers.com 2019 #1 innovation broker for its TradeKing Live platform

- Ranked # 1 in the merchant community for 2013–2014 according to the survey conducted by StockBrokers.com

Main base rates and competitive commissions: The base rate for TradeKing is $4.95. It only competes with OptionsHouse by offering the lowest base rate for the cost-conscious options trader.

And while TradeKing's $0.65 contract fees are not the lowest in the industry, they remain incredibly competitive with lesser-known companies.

However, compared to large companies, TradeKing rates offer a distinct advantage. These general cost-saving advantages make TradeKing the solution of choice for the best options broker.

All-in-one options trading platform: TradeKing software gives you everything you need on a fully functional trading platform. It hosts a page in its education center that specializes in options trading. This page presents options trading tools, option strategies, and on-demand videos to deepen your knowledge of options. Bank and make the most of TradeKing technology.

TradeStation

TradeStation is an online options trading platform offered by TradeStation Group, Inc. and TradeStation Securities, Inc.

The TradeStation group is located in Plantation, Florida. It is a subsidiary of Monex Group, Inc., located in Japan. It is considered the best broker because of its flexibility.

It has been known across as one of the best buy and sell options. Some of the awards and distinctions that the software has received include:

- Highest rating by Barron in the category Best for large merchants 2016

- Stockbrokers.com rewarded for the best platform technology 2012–2016

- Best in class from Stockbrokers.com for Mobile Trading 2016

- The top five online brokers in Business Daily 2016

Flexible and staggered price structure: You may think that option trading platforms of the type offered by TradeStation are reserved for high volume professional traders. While professional operators can use the TradeStation platform, TradeStation has enabled its software to benefit even those who do not trade as often.

You can do this thanks to its tiered price structure. Depending on your operations' frequency and volume, you can take advantage of a contract or a business plan.

By contract, it is better for rare merchants or those who do not work with large volumes. You pay a lump sum of $1.00 per contract with no base rate applicable. However, a minimum of a contract is required.

Those of you who can trade as "whales" are bets. They save money with the operating price plan.

Under this plan, you pay underlying fees for each transaction, as well as contract fees. These rates vary in volume. The higher the amount, the lower the rate.

For example, if you execute more than 200 transactions per month, your base is $4.99 plus $0.20 per contract. Fewer operations result in higher costs. The following key details the full price structure of TradeStation:

- Base of $4.99 plus $0.20/contract for 200 transactions/month.

- Base of $5.99 plus $0.30/contract for 100–199 transactions/month.

- Base of $6.99 plus $0.40/contract for 30–99 operations/month.

- Base of $7.99 plus $0.50/contract for 10–29 operations/month.

- Base of $9.99 plus $0.70/contract for 1–9 operations/month.

Trading at the base rate of $9.99 ($10.69 total) with TradeStation is not as profitable as some of its competitors, as shown in the table above. Even in this case, the price of TradeStation remains very competitive.

However, when you exceed this base rate, the comparison table clearly shows that TradeStation is the most profitable option than the most critical company names. This is true regardless of the volume.

OptionStation Pro

TradeStation set out to create the best platform for trading options, and there is no doubt that it has become one of the leaders in the online options trading industry. It is a powerful and feature-rich platform that allows you to take control of your options trading. Some of the benefits you get with OptionStation Pro include:

- Ability to quickly discover and classify potential business opportunities.

- Use a pre-established strategy to reduce the time between the discovery and execution of the transaction.

- Create, analyze, and track almost all option positions.

- Place one-click orders directly from an options chain.

- Fully customizable interface, which includes position management, dispersion types, graphic screens, etc.

TradeStation Mobile

It has been ranked among the best options brokers by the variety of access points offered to its customers.

You can still view appointments, view charts and tables, view data continuously in real-time, and execute operations. Not only that, but you can easily track locations and closely monitor your watch lists, among other features.

Other Notable Platforms

- Plus500

- eToro

- Capital.com

- IG

- XTB

- OANDA

- OptionsHouse

CHAPTER 19:

Passive Income

Making passive nature of income by using options trading might sound like a real dream. But, can it be turned into reality? To answer this very question, we first need to learn about the various aspects of active income and passive income to understand the major differences between the two. Right after that, we will be exploring some ways in which passive income can be generated by using various techniques of trading.

Passive money is the money generated regularly, which requires very little effort right on the recipient's side to maintain the same. Gains on interests, stocks, lottery winnings, commodities, and capital are often the earning types in mind. But this fits the most popular definition of passive income; there are still some countries that impose a definition of technical nature for passive income for the very purpose of taxation.

Active Trading vs. Passive Trading

Various people often ask about stock trading as being a source of passive income or not. The active nature of traders will be investing a great amount of effort and time in turning a profit. Well, their activity of the trade will be taken as the primary form of focus.

In the case of passive income, the earnings are derived from a limited partnership, rental property, or by using other enterprises, in short, anything in which any individual is not involved actively. Passive income is generally taxable. So, suppose you are looking out for generating passive income by using options. In that case, you must hand over the capital to a broker whom you trust, any automated system, or by investing your capital through copy trading.

Passive Income Pros and Cons

Right before we start with the various techniques of earning passive income by using options, it is very important to first learn about the benefits of passive income and its drawbacks. An obvious benefit related to passive income is the limited amount of time you will have to commit. But this also indicates the extreme pressure on the decisions of investments that you are going to make. Passive trading might sometimes end up in a very slow profit stream when you compare it with active trading. There are also certain dangers that you are most likely to oversee while monitoring your income. Ultimately, this might result in losing a great amount of potential profit.

Techniques for Generating Passive Income

There are some ways in which passive income can be made:

Automation

To make the whole game of passive income a lot easier, some people often opt for automation. When used properly, the automated systems can make you capable of generating substantial nature of profits. This is because there is only a specific trade number that one can make in a day. A unique algorithm can easily enter and exit the positions as soon as the pre-determined criteria have been met.

They will also permit you to trade in several markets at one time. Right after you have successfully programmed your criteria, passive income can also be generated while sleeping. Some of you might doubt the capabilities and efficiency of this system. But, around 75% of the trades made on New York and NASDAQ's stock exchange originate from all these algorithms and define their efficacies.

Software

Right before you start having passive income by using automated trading, you must lookout for the perfect software. Try doing your research, and never forget to check the assessments first before you start investing. Once done with your research, and you have chosen your software, you must develop a great strategy. You can start by creating a small checklist for your parameters of trading. You can easily consider these:

- When to enter positions and when to exit them.

- Size of the position.

- Trading timeframe.

- Stop losses and targets.

Backtesting

Before starting any automated system for generating passive income from options, you will need to backtest the strategy first. This will permit you to test the entire system right before you risk in your capital. You need to run the software you chose right against any historical price data to gauge how efficiently it performs. You can easily identify the issues, if there are any, and fix them before investing.

Copy Trading

Another great way of developing passive income is by the method of copy trading. In place of giving in all your energy and time for developing the strategy and monitoring all the tasks, you can easily benefit by following the experienced traders' success. You need to select a trader, and a program will then be mimicking the trader's buying and selling by using your capital. But it might happen that the traders will take a minimal percentage of the profit that you make. But it also comes along with certain drawbacks:

- Risking your capital: You need to be always prepared because of the market volatility. You might also lose the entire capital you have invested in. If you are risk-averse and if you cannot see yourself with huge losses, it is better not to opt for this option.

- Choosing a trader: Picking a trader might turn out to be a challenge. Any aggressive nature of options trader can clear you out within several days. Always consider the instrument of approach and choice that they use. You are also required to check the updated history of the trade of the trader. All you are looking out for is a consistent and steady form of results.

- Not keeping up with the trades proportionally: Certain sites might not permit you to trade proportionally. But, for good, the traders, most of the time, invest only in particular quantities. So, you need to ensure that you only focus on copying the trader.

Using Put-Selling Strategy

It is often regarded as the most efficient way of developing passive income. The best strategy that can be used is by buying stocks when they are overvalued instead of being undervalued. As you sell puts that are overvalued, you can rake in huge premiums from the buyers. You can also determine the option value based on the implied volatility of the same. Implied volatility can help in measuring the amount of greed and fear that is priced into any option. When the implied volatility is considerably high, the prices of the options will tend to be overvalued. This can easily attract many investors.

The stocks that are your own will be trading much above the strike price for the duration of the option's lifespan. This indicates that you will be collecting the option's premium, and you are not required to purchase any of the underlying stocks. While this is taken as an ideal scenario, there are other scenarios for you to understand.

When the underlying stocks fall under the right level in the middle of the strike price and strike price that is less than the option's premium is the second scenario. The investor will be winning as the adjusted cost basis is better than the one currently present in the market, right after considering the received premium of the option.

The third scenario is when the stock price goes below a point below the strike price, subtracting the option's premium. This is often taken as the worst-case scenario for any trader of cash-secured put.

How You Can Make Money by Selling Puts?

Selling puts will be allowing you to set the stock strike price according to you at which you want to buy it. Selling puts is much more attractive than selling covered calls as you are not required to post your capital, which is beneficial for purchasing the shares. You need to follow certain steps right before selling the puts:

- Finding out a stock that you would like to buy.

- Deciding the entry price that you want to buy the shares.

- Evaluating the implied volatility.

- Setting the risk parameters.

CHAPTER 20:

Technical Indicators

What are technical indicators? These are useful indicators that provide information about trends and even possible turning points in stocks and securities prices. Technical indicators are among the tools used by traders and even analysts to predict the best times to purchase or sell stocks and options. The technical indicators also indicate the cycles.

A technical analyst will calculate the essential particulars of a stock. Many of the technical indicators are calculated using data such as:

- Closing price.

- Highs.

- Lows.

- Trading volumes.

- Opening prices.

- Among others.

Stock prices from the past couple of trades provide most of the raw data required to work out technical indicators. Data mostly used is often from the last thirty days. The data is then utilized to develop a chart or trend that indicates what has been happening and what will happen to a particular stock. This is because past performance is a great indicator of future trends.

Options traders widely use technical indicators to predict the future movement of the price movement of stocks. They also indicate trends within the market. When it comes to technical indicators, there are two main types. These are:

1. Lagging Indicators

Lagging indicators are indicators that closely monitor and follow a stock's price pattern. This is why they are called lagging. These indicators are solely based on the last data. They are hence excellent at indicating any trend developing in the market or if a stock has entered a trading range. Lagging indicators can, for instance, point to a stock with a major downward trend and will most probably continue falling.

Future Trends and Pullbacks

Keep in mind that lagging indicators are not recommended when it comes to predicting future pullbacks or rallies. These indicators can indicate the trends that have developed until the latest point. However, they cannot point to future trends or events, even just for the following couple of days. Some common lagging indicators popularly used by options traders include ADX indicators, the Moving Average, and the MACD.

Therefore, lagging indicators are excellent at pointing at the developing trends but are poor at predicting or forecasting future stock price movement.

2. Leading Indicators

The other very useful technical indicators are the leading indicators. These technical indicators are beneficial at predicting future events. They often provide relevant information regarding possible crashes and future price gains. Some of the leading indicators include momentum indicators. These are capable of predicting or gauging the momentum of the price movements of a stock.

Momentum indicators are more like tossing a football in the air. No matter how high the ball rises, we know that it will eventually fall back to the ground. We may not know when it will stop going up, but we are sure that it will do so at one point. This is the genesis of momentum indicators.

Leading indicators such as the momentum indicators are excellent at revealing if a stock price has gone too far down or too high up. They also let us know whether there is a reduction in the momentum of the price movement. When the price moves too high, it simply means there has been an over-purchase of the stock. In such cases, then, the stock has been overbought.

Should the price move too low, then this says an oversupply of the stock, and buyers are possibly dropping it. If the stock has been overbought or oversold, it will not remain in this state for long. We can, therefore, make a deduction that a pullback is likely to happen. Most momentum indicators and the RSI are good examples of leading indicators.

Lagging and Leading Indicators

Most traders appreciate both lagging and leading indicators because they are both invaluable. You are informed of any possible price pullbacks and slowdowns as a trader. Ideally, you should never rely on just one of these indicators but both. This way, your predictions, and trades will always be accurate and reliable.

Most indicators sometimes produce false signals occasionally. Since this is a risk that you want to avoid, we recommend using at least two or three different indicators. Identify 3 specific indicators that you like, and if they all give you positive information about a stock, you can feel confident enough to invest in it. There are essentially hundreds of different indicators in use across the world. Most seasoned traders will have developed their technical indicators to predict the markets accurately. You should learn how to use about 5 different technical indicators. This way, you will have a wide variety of options to choose from.

Top Technical Indicators

We have noted above that there are hundreds of different technical indicators currently in use. However, some are absolutely crucial for options traders. If you can learn how to use about 5 of them, you will have a strong foundation for your technical analysis. Here is a look at some of the more important ones:

Average Directional Index Indicator, ADX

The ADX or average directional index is a popular indicator that is mostly used for confirmation purposes. It essentially works to confirm the information or signals that are produced by other indicators. This technical indicator works by measuring the strength of any given trend. For example, you can use the ADX to measure if an upward trend or maybe even a downward trend is slowing down or gaining momentum.

This average directional index, ADX, combines the positive directional indicator, +DI, and the negative directional indicator, -DI. The -DI or negative directional indicator tracks the downward trend, while the +DI or positive directional tracks the upward trend in the stock market. When these two indicators are combined together, we get the Average Directional Index. This combination of two strong indicators produces one powerful and unified trend strength indicator.

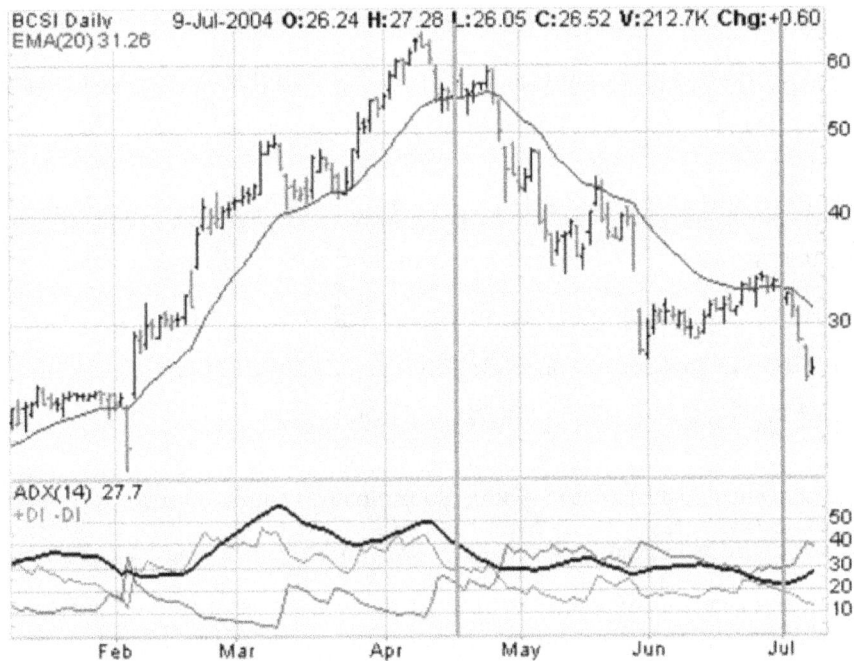

The +DI is showcased as a green line in the chart above, while the –DI is shown as a red line. The ADX indicator itself is shown as a fat black line. We note that there was a strong stock trend from late February until mid-April, as indicated by the ADX. The stock was trending upwards.

It is possible to notice that the ADX indicator never went below the 20 marks. This is a clear indicator of when the stock ever traded flat. An accurate assessment is mostly visible from the stock price. In general, we notice that this is an accurate assessment as it is visible from the strike price. There was a remarkable uptrend for the first three months and the last three months indicate a downward trend.

Oscillating Indicator

The ADX technical indicator also happens to be oscillating. Its oscillations range from zero to a hundred, with zero representing flat trades while a hundred represents a plunging or rising stock. Please note that the ADX indicator showcases the strength of a trend only without pointing its direction.

Also, the ADX values often range between 20 and 40. Rarely will you see ADX values above 60. The reason is that high values above 60 point to a trend that usually appears when there is a long recession or a long bull run. Any values that are below 20 often point to a stock entering the trading range.

According to our chart above, we notice that signals produced by the Average Directional Index, or ADX, indicator, any move that is way below 40 points and above will indicate the trend's slowdown. The options strategies always rely on large volumes of shares, so a trend that is slowing down is undesirable. Therefore, as a trader, if you notice any ADX indicator is a simple pointer, the trend is slowing down, and that now would be the best time to buy out.

Similarly, any index indicator that moves above 20 indicates that the sideways trading strategies are over because a new trend is currently developing. It is an indication that the current upward trend is almost drawing to an end. As such, it is time to make a positive movement that can be either bullish or bearish. Also, sometimes the ADX indicator can move way above 20. This is always a clear indication that the current upward trend has started to fade.

Again, in our chart above, the ADX technical indicator produced a signal right in the middle of April. You should learn how to look for stuff and be observant. Signals on this example can be obtained by observing and noting where there is. When the +DI, green, and wring signal process above +61422 –5840364. When the two indicators, the +DI, and the –DI cross paths with each other, we will identify our signal here. When they meet together, they should form a bullish signal. You should, therefore, always base your investment opportunity on recommendations from the map. Experts advise that you make use of only one or additionally two types of indicators. This way, you will be sure of what to do and when to do it.

Bollinger Band Strategies

Another technical strategy that is commonly used to showcase the voracity of stocks is the Bollinger strategy. There will always be an opportunity to learn from the boss. A Bollinger Band strategy or theory is mostly meant to showcase how volatile the stocks are.

This is a simple technical indicator as it is composed of a simple moving average and both its upper and lower bands. These upper and lower bands are only about 2 standard deviations away.

We can confidently say that standard deviation is more like statistical tools. This is because the majority of movement occurs around these positions. When you use the Bollinger Band theory, you will discover that it only works as a guide or gauge and should, therefore, be used in conjunction with other indicators. If you learn how to apply these indicators, then you stand a great chance for success.

The Bollinger Band theory operates optimally in conjunction with the twenty-day SMA or simple moving averages. We also need the standard deviations of the twenty-day SMA to create the Bollinger Bands. Some of the strategies that emanate from this indicator include long-term and short-term Bollinger Bands. The shorter-term bands which are less than twenty days are highly sensitive to price movement while the longer-term bands that exceed twenty days are less sensitive and more conservative.

CHAPTER 21:

Daily Routine for a Trader

Missteps occur in options trading. They regularly happen because an excessive amount of data is coming in without a moment's delay. You feel over-burden, froze, and forceful, or they frequently happen during calm/bring times when your watchman is down. Furthermore, there are constantly irregular mix-ups, for example, hitting an inappropriate catch—purchase rather than sell—or putting out an inappropriate position size. Such blunders can even occur with robotized methodologies.

Before each trading day, take a couple of minutes to experience a multi-day trading routine to help limit mistakes for the day. Here are the means to experience. Contingent upon the market you exchange, you may wish to include a couple of extra advances. This entire procedure takes a few minutes, however, spares you a great deal of dissatisfaction and cash.

Conditions in the Market

Make a brisk appraisal of trading conditions up until now. Is the pre-advertise demonstrating a great deal of instability, or is it steady? Is there a pattern or explicit propensities you take note of?

Such an evaluation tells you how to continue and whether you ought to exchange your framework by any stretch of the imagination. This is particularly significant if utilizing an emotional framework—a framework that fluctuates marginally dependent on economic situations. For instance, in unpredictable conditions, you may have a bigger expected benefit focus than on a multi-day when there is no unpredictability.

Keep Notes

On your graph, put content notes expressing when high effect news discharges are. Whenever fascinated in exchange, you may disregard one of these occasions, which could cost you beyond all doubt. Record it on your diagram. If the occasion happens later in the day, look over and put the content note close to the declaration's estimated time. That way, you will see it when the opportunity arrives.

Launch Platform Is Vital

Dispatch your stage. Ensure statements are gushing (not slacking or sporadic), and the program is running easily. Most intermediaries give dependable information encourages, yet issues can emerge. If the information feed is irregular or appears to be erroneous, don't exchange until the issue is fixed. On the off chance that it looks right, continue.

Automated Strategies Should Be Confirmed

Regardless of whether your day exchange physically, you may have some robotized orders. For instance, in Ninja Trader and Meta Trader, you can convey stop misfortune requests and focuses on the minute you enter a position. Ensure these stop misfortune requests and targets are set properly. If trading with a "robot," ensure all settings are exact before beginning it.

Have an End Time

If you see a time you pattern to give back benefits all the time, compose a note to yourself to quit trading around then. Numerous informal investors will, in general, lose cash in the time encompassing (and including) the New York lunch hour if trading U.S. markets. If you see this inclination, don't battle it. Quit trading during portions of the day you commonly lose cash. Help yourself to remember this when you start trading every day.

Have a Starting Position Size

If you exchange with a default position size, ensure it is set fittingly. Adding a digit to a position size could spell catastrophe. Dropping a digit implies exchanging a small amount of what you could have, and you pass up a chance.

Once you change your position size dependent on your entry point and stop misfortune areas, note your record balance before trading. A legitimate position measuring limits risk to a small level of record capital, for example, 2%. If you have a $40,000 account, you can risk up to $400 on an exchange. Remember this greatest risk for the duration of the day (or compose a content note on your screen) to remind yourself this is the most you can risk on one exchange.

The Economic Calendar Must Be Considered

High effect monetary occasions can cause value spikes/holes, making critical slippage (the distinction between the value you expect and the value you get) on stop misfortune orders. It's ideal to abstain from being in exchanges for a couple of minutes encompassing high effect planned news occasion. Check your monetary schedule before trading and note the high effect news-times. For U.S. stocks and prospects, you can utilize Bloomberg. For Forex, look at the Daily FX financial schedule.

On the off chance that you exchange individual stocks all the time, check if the organization does not have income or different declarations due out that day. The Yahoo! Finance profit schedule functions admirably. Know about these occasions, to abstain from trading directly before the declaration.

Important Thoughts

Help yourself to remember your risky propensities and how you will deal with those circumstances should they emerge. Go over your Key Trading Thoughts.

Be Mindful as You Start Trading

You are set to exchange. This procedure should help dispense with certain errors identified with position size, trading an inappropriate record/contract, trading during news, or just not setting up your brain to exchange.

As you begin searching for potential exchange arrangements, remember your Key Trading Thoughts. This will help keep you out of awful exchanges (ones not in your trading plan) and keep your caution and prepared to jump on great chances.

Use the Right Trading Account

In Meta Trader and Ninja Trader (for instance), you can sign various records utilizing a similar stage. Ensure you are trading the right record. When you practice day trading in a mimicked record, yet additionally have live records. You would prefer not to have an incredible day, to acknowledge you traded in recreation rather than with genuine capital. In the event, that day trading prospects, ensure you are trading the rightmost noteworthy volume contract. Know about termination dates on the agreements you exchange.

Make a Trading Routine

Your day trading routine may shift marginally from this, contingent upon your trading style and the market you exchange. Make a daily schedule, however. It just takes about a moment or two to experience and can spare you from a great deal of dissatisfaction.

CHAPTER 22:

Day Trading

An important part of day trading is understanding the different options available to you, which will best suit your available time, finances, and interests. Although all-day trading activities seek to profit by purchasing stocks and selling them at a higher price within the same day; there are several different types of day trading:

Options

The two types of options are puts and calls. A stock option is a contract between two people. As the buyer of the option, you will purchase the right to buy shares from a different party at a set price within a set time frame. A call means you have the right to buy at the agreed price, while a put means you can sell.

If you are trading on the stock market, this can be very beneficial; you can purchase the option at a low price and wait for the price to rise. Once the price has risen, you can then complete the purchase by buying the shares and selling them immediately to someone else, making a profit along the way.

Day traders will often deal with the options, buying the right to buy shares from someone, and selling the option to someone else. In principle, this is the same as dealing in options on the stock market, but the risk is lower as you do not expend any funds until you find a buyer. The option to buy is yours, but this does not mean you have to.

Futures

One of the most approved options for many day traders and an excellent place for a beginner to start. On the stock market, a futures contract has been created between two parties; one agrees to sell a certain amount of stock to the other in the future, but the price is fixed at the time of the contract. These can be purchased and sold on the market as different speculators decide whether they can profit on the futures contract's maturity value.

Day trading in futures means that you are focusing on the future contracts and looking to buy and sell any which will turn you a profit within a day. Future trading is a good guide regarding the market and going in general; this makes it easier to trade in as they produce a more reliable picture of prices than many other trading types.

Currencies

When you are abroad and needed to change your money into another currency, you will already understand that currency rates vary daily. This volatility allows people to trade on two currencies of their choice and make a profit.

In simple terms, you seek to purchase a set amount of a certain currency, for example, 200 US$. This may cost you 150 GBP. If you then wish to change your funds back, the exchange rate may have moved. This results from market demand; the more popular a currency is, or the more the country's resources are needed, the better the exchange rate will be. If the US market improves, you may need to pay 175 GBP to get the same 200 US$. If you have already purchased the currency, you will change it back and make yourself a 25 GBP profit, less any transaction charges.

Day trading in currencies works on the same principles; you will be able to trade online with any currency worldwide and potentially make good profits. Of course, every trade involves you being a buyer and a seller; this does increase the risk.

Stocks

Shares are the first thing most people think of when considering the stock market. Purchasing shares and holding them for the long term to make money from increased value and dividends is a very successful tactic by many investors.

It is also possible to day trade in the same way; however, your window of opportunity is much smaller! Shares you purchase should be at the bottom of their fall or already on the way up. This should allow you to purchase some and then sell them again later the same day for a profit.

To successfully trade in stocks, you will need to keep a close eye on the stock market and which companies are performing well. The best ones to invest in are those who normally do well but have had a blip thanks to an unforeseen but fixable event. These shares will usually dip and then re-climb throughout the day.

Arbitrage

You need to be informed that there are many different markets, and you can trade in any of these. You can trade in more than one market simultaneously and make money doing so. This type of trading involves locating a product selling for less in one market than another. Once you have located the product, you purchase as many as possible in one market and sell them instantly in the other market. The risk is minimal as you hold the stock for only a few moments. The price difference needs to be enough to provide a small profit after allowing for the trade costs.

There are usually very small windows of opportunity available to make funds trading this way. The process of arbitrage helps to consolidate the prices across the different markets; it is an excellent way of keeping trading fair. It provides the opportunity to create a decent profit simultaneously, depending on how much you can afford to invest in the process.

Momentum Trading

Big companies can be hugely affected by news in either the wider economy or by events inside their business, but the information is publicly available. It is important to wait until you see the market movement.

Once you are certain that the share price is climbing or dropping, you will purchase your shares. Only buy as the share price climbs; the momentum builds. Generally, events like this will hit a share price and then naturally rebalance later in the day. So, it is essential to monitor the trend and sell when it starts to go back down.

Always buy in a rising (bullish) market and sell in a decreasing market (bearish). It is best to set yourself a target price. This should be at a level that will allow you to make a reasonable profit after allowing for buying and selling the transaction costs.

Swing Trading

It is natural for the price of any commodity to change during the day. Swing trading attempts to profit from these movements of prices. You need to identify the products or stocks which are moving throughout each day. At some point, they will go from higher to lower and then back again. Operating as a swing trader means buying at the low end of the swing and waiting for it to go back to the top end of the swing, all within a day's space. Remember that you do not need to buy and sell at the top and bottom of the swing; as long as the difference between the two prices will give you a profit and cover costs. Even a product with very small swings can be a good investment; small, consistent profits can quickly mount up.

No matter which option you choose to trade in, it is important always to have a professional approach and treat your day trading as a business. Many people have attempted day trading and lost substantial funds as they have not prepared or had the right approach. Any trading on the stock market requires research, patience, and understanding of how the stock market works. The more you know about your chosen market sector, the better you will predict the up and down movements and purchase the right day trading option for the occasion. It is possible to day trade in all the different options listed above; it is even possible to day trade as part of a larger investment strategy. The key is to be prepared!

No matter which type or types of trading you commit to, you should always sell and consolidate your position at the end of the day. The prices listed on the market can change dramatically overnight, and you will have little ability to recover your capital. You will only be able to watch your funds disappearing and hope they recover, to some extent, in the morning.

CHAPTER 23:

How Much Do Day Traders Make?

Day trading can sound exciting, and it certainly is. And if you have more significant amounts of capital to invest, and you're very good at it, then day trading can help you make large amounts of money over short periods. But if you are just getting started, how much can you earn day trading? Let's try looking at some realistic scenarios before having visions of millions of dollars.

The first thing to consider when trying to gauge the potential for success in any endeavor is the Pareto principle. This principle tells us that 20% of the people get 80% of the spoils. It doesn't matter what you're talking about, and you could be talking about farmers. In that case, 20% of the farmers will be responsible for 80% of the output. In the stock market, 20% of the investors will take 80% of the returns, which most certainly applies to day trading. Most days, traders will have to keep their day job, and many may end up losing their initial capital investment.

This isn't too out and out discouraging anyone from taking up day trading. Many factors will decide success or failure. For example, many people start off with high excitement levels when taking on something new, like day trading, but they quickly fizzle out. In short, they fail to put in the work required to excel. There would be a million reasons for it. Some people might wilt at the first sign of a challenge. Others may become bored with it. Some people are downright lazy—day trading takes work, and they were hoping for a get rich quick scheme.

Just like only a small percentage of basketball players are ever going to be NBA stars, only a tiny percentage of day traders are going to rise to become the cream of the crop and make millions of dollars. That said, you can take action to seriously tip the odds in your favor. After all, many people practice basketball with an all-out effort and become top-level players. Even if they aren't Kobe Bryant or Lebron James, they still may be very successful. The same principle applies to day trading. You may be a budding star or not—but if you dive in 100% to study the markets and finance and trading, you will significantly increase your odds. Even if you don't become a star, if you are a smart trader who hedges risk well, then you may be able to make a solidly upper-middle-class income from it even if you don't become a top-level trader.

One rule is that disciplined traders, at least in the long run, are going to make more money than people who are flying by the seat of their pants kinds of people. The more capital you start with, the more money that you're going to make. But let's have a look at the minimum. Suppose that you start off with the recommended minimum amount of capital, which is $30,000.

Using leverage at 4:1 means you can potentially control $120,000 worth of stock. Remember that there is a 1% rule on risk per trade, and starting with $30,000, that means you'll be trading $300 at a time. Assuming you're a disciplined trader, you will have a good stop-loss strategy. Standard values are a win rate of 50% (that is, half your trades are profitable), and your winners are around 1.5 times bigger than your losers. These figures sound like no big deal, but it may take you a couple of years to get to this level. Now let's use these assumptions together with a guess that you make, on average, 5 trades per day or about 100 per month. With a 50% success rate, you'll have 50 profitable trades per month. A reasonable stop loss is $0.10, so with a 1.5 times ratio of the winner to the loser, you're making $0.15 per share in profits. You can control 3,000 shares per trade. So that gives you a monthly profit of $22,500. Your losses come from the stop loss figure of $0.10 a share, so you're going to lose $15,000 per month.

Your gross income will then be the difference, or $7,500 a month. However, remember that you'll need to pay lots of commissions. Brokers don't let you trade stock for free. In the end, your actual profit will probably be about $5,000 a month.

Now, this isn't bad to get started. So, you're able to work from home, doing something fun and exciting that is even a little bit risky, and make an OK middle-class income from it. But it's probably not the kind of income you were hoping to see.

That isn't to say that you can't grow your business over time and make huge amounts of money. You absolutely can do that. However, we're trying to show here that day trading isn't a get rich quick scheme. It's not dissimilar from any other kind of business that takes time, work, and energy to grow.

Of course, you might be better than average. If you are really good, maybe 65% of your trades turn out profitable, and you're banking $8,000–$9,000 per month depending on the size of commissions you have to pay. That's not an unrealistic possibility; however, remember that not everyone is as talented as anyone else. Some people are going to do worse than the 50% success rate that we initially started with, and in those cases, they will make less money, maybe a couple thousand a month or less. Still, more won't make anything, and some are going to end up with losses.

CHAPTER 24:

Designing a Trading Plan

Y ou need to have a long-term plan of success that will serve as your reference guide, as well as a business plan.

Trading Plans

You'll hear a lot of trading gurus tell you to make a plan. Well, what exactly is a trading plan, and why do you need one? A trading plan by itself is not going to matter too much. However, when done right, it can help you focus and nail down your vision when it comes to trading.

Perhaps a more appropriate term for this is to call it a trading business plan instead of just a trading plan. Much like how you need to record all key information (both financial and in terms of vision) in your business plan, your trading plan needs to do the same for your trading business. At a minimum, it needs to have the following information:

Instruments to Trade

What instruments will you be trading? List them all out here. You can also list out the individual stocks you will be trading. When starting, it's best to pick a single instrument and trade just that. The methods described here work for any instrument in any time frame.

This doesn't mean you go out and try to trade everything under the sun. You build a base with one, then two instruments, and then expand outward. Much like individuals, stocks have natures of their own in terms of liquidity and volatility. Some stocks have certain tendencies, depending on the time of the day.

You need to observe and learn all this to trade successfully and doing so one by one is the way to go about it.

Markets and Timing

Which markets will you be trading? When will you trade them? Most of you reading this will have full-time jobs or something else going on. So, you need to note down your session time and stick to it.

Which is the best session for beginners or busy people to trade? Well, there's no such thing as "best" to begin with. In terms of liquidity, the open is probably the best. The other side to this is that the volatility can be pretty extreme. Things pick up toward the end of the day as well, so it's not as if the open is the only worthwhile time to trade.

The afternoon session is usually seen as something of a graveyard, with many traders stepping out for lunch. Don't just assume this is so. Observe the market and check its tendencies. While the more active stocks tend to slow down quite a bit, some instruments provide easy pickings.

Risk Limits

What is your daily risk limit? Weekly, monthly, etc.? It is also a good idea to execute a gain-protection plan. What this means is that if you have a bunch of winners during the session (say two or more) or if you make a certain percentage of your account during the session (say anything about 0.5%), then you could decide to stop trading during that session if your gains dip below 0.25% or if you lose two more trades.

The idea is that you've made money during the session, and you would like to hang on to it. This is to protect a string of winners or a huge gain. Once you've had a great day, it's perfectly fine to set a lower loss limit to protect some of it so that no matter what happens, you'll end the day up.

Events

The markets have many external events that affect them, such as earnings announcements, dividends, splits, interest rate announcements, press conferences, and on and on. Generally speaking, you need to pay attention to the following events:

- Earnings.

- Special events of the individual stock or political events like elections.

- Interest rate announcements.

- Nonfarm payrolls (NFP).

That's it. These events are always scheduled in advance, and as a beginner, stop trading an hour before the announcement and resume an hour after it has passed. The reason is that volatility jumps like crazy, and your stops will get triggered.

If you have any positions open that are close to profit, take a lower profit just before the announcement, as long as it doesn't affect your risk numbers too much. Similarly, if you have a trade that is in a loss and is near its stop-loss, you have to close the trade out just before the event.

If your trade is in the middle of the road or is even break even, ride the event out and hope for the best. Some stocks are better than others in this regard. Stay away from flashy companies run by Twitter-wielding CEOs who tend to send their products into space instead of building profits. You know who I'm talking about.

Aside from being annoying, you can bet there will be several algorithms and bots tracking every character such people type into Twitter, and all it takes for a flash tumble to occur in the stock is a typo or a rash tweet. Stick to boring names no one has heard of, and you'll be much better off, no matter how much you love or hate the company.

Review System

Every successful trader spends a lot of time reviewing their trades and actions over the week. Mention the time you will spend reviewing.

Practice

When will you practice your skills? What skills will you practice? Each strategy has some skills you need to execute, not to mention mental skills. Set aside time to practice each of these individually to perfect it.

Journals

As important as your trading plan is, the document that is of primary importance for your trading success is your trading journal. This will list all the trades you took over the past week and serve as a record for you to review. In addition to written records, you should also save screenshots of your trades on entry and exit.

Remember to also save screenshots of the market condition on the higher time frame on trade entry. You will often notice how you might have misjudged the higher time frame action. Below are the things your trading journal needs to record at a minimum:

- Date.

- Instrument (the ticker or name of the stock).

- Entry price.

- Stop-loss level.

- Stop distance.

- Position size.

- Reasons for entry (describe in as much detail why this entry was in line with your strategy and what you saw).

- Reasons or exit.

- Exit date.

- P/L.

- Mental state on entry.

- Mental state on exit.

You can either have this recorded on a spreadsheet or in a notebook; it doesn't matter where as long as you can review it easily. Save your screenshots in a numbered manner and appropriate folders. In addition to this, you can also record your screen and yourself during the session and review your demeanor and market action at the time of entry to verify whether you saw things correctly.

Remember, the more information you record at the time, and the more potential things there are for you to improve and learn.

Aside from the trading journal, you should also keep a mental journal. This is simply a record of what your mental state was during the session and if anything was bothering you at the time. It's up to you as to how much information you want to put in here, but you must aim to record whether you followed your preparation routines properly on that particular day.

Your prep routine can include physical exercise, meditation, visualization, affirmations, skill practice, and so on. It's up to you to decide what you want to include. Your aim should be to include things that are as repeatable as possible. Don't include too many things because you like its idea but will be stretched for time when it comes to implementing it.

The last journal you need to have is an assessment journal. You can incorporate this within your trade journal itself or as a separate document. When you're starting out, if it is logistically possible, I'd recommend reviewing your session after a thirty-minute break once it ends. This way, the action is still fresh in your mind, and you're more relaxed.

Go through all your trades and review the screenshots. Review the video recording as well to confirm and check if what you saw was true. Record what you did incorrectly and, even more importantly, record what you did right. The review is not just about finding things to improve; it's also about celebrating things you did right.

Doing a review after each trading session will increase your rate of improvement instead of doing it weekly. Remember, even a session where you place no trades should be reviewed for mental state and whether you were tuned in or zoned out. Did you miss any opportunities? Leave no stone unturned.

Training

Trading is a unique endeavor in that we spend more time in the market (that is, game day) than in practice. Every other high-performance activity requires a minimum of double the amount of time spent in practice than in games. So how do you achieve this when it comes to trading?

Well, first off, you're not going to be able to achieve anything like double the amount of practice time as trading time. However, by simply assigning time every day to practice and improve your skills and strategy, you'll be putting yourself way ahead of the curve.

Make at least 15 minutes every day to train your skills in simulation. Break down your strategy into its elements and practice each skill separately. You can also commit to practicing your skills in session if it happens to be slow or if there aren't any opportunities available.

Simulation software has a market replay feature, so you can simulate a market at a much faster pace and hone your skills instead of letting dead market time go to waste. Finally, schedule a month of each year or a couple of weeks off every quarter to review your existing skillset and to improve yourself as a trader.

Remember, do not trade every single day that the market is open. This is the easiest way to go insane. Take some time off and schedule breaks to keep yourself fresh.

Progression

Your progression should always be from simulation to demo and only then to live. You need to place at least 200 trades on the demo and make money from the demo before going live. It simply isn't worth it otherwise. Your practice should be done on simulation software to ensure you're keeping your skills fresh.

Once you've completed 200 trades on the demo and have made money on the instrument, you then add the next instrument on simulation and backtest your strategy on it. Once this passes, you demo trade it for 200 trades. Once you make money on this, you begin trading it live.

You first do it on simulation to see if it works any changes you choose to make to your system. If so, trade it on demo and compare it with your live results. If it is more successful, then push it live.

CHAPTER 25:

Money Management

Money management is how you handle your finances, your savings, your expenditure, and investments. It is making sure you can survive a financial crisis. It means planning a budget for your long-term goals and making investments to achieve your goals successfully. When you manage your money, you will be able to make wise purchases. Otherwise, you will always complain about having less money no matter how much your income is. It is known as investment management.

Money management is more about risk. When you have better money management skills, you will reduce the risk. You must understand all the areas of money management to avoid any risks—plan with a negative bias. Always asks yourself "what-if" scenarios, act, and technique. When budgeting for money management, make sure you are spending less than what you save. Excellent money management will help you monitor your spending before going beyond your budget. By doing this, you will secure your savings.

You will be able to invest if you make the right decisions. Avoiding taking on more risks will help you reach your financial goals. The strategies you use in your investments play a significant role in your success. When you decide to invest, the first important thing to focus on is the risk involved, and you can avoid it. Here are some of the basics, advantages, and disadvantages of money management.

The Basics of Money Management

Money management is a broad term that involves solutions and services in the entire investment industry. You can now have a wide range of resources in today's market and also phone applications to help you manage all your finances. Investors can also seek services from a financial advisor for professional money management. Financial advisors work with private banking and even brokerage services to offer money management plans involving retirement and estate planning services.

The Advantages of Money Management

Better Tracking of Your Money

When you have a reasonable budgeting plan, you can track how you use your money and monitor every expense. It is a significant benefit to you, as you can spend less and end up saving more money. Monitor your costs for some months and then change your budgeting by removing the less required payment and allocate that money to your savings plan, a retirement plan, or a vacation fund. Excellent money management will help you stay on track; you will be able to pay your bills on time, will be able to stay within your limit, and avoid bank account overdraws. Poor money management can put you in bad debt quicker than a blink of an eye. You can prevent those nasty fees charges when you go over your limit. By having an excellent budgeting plan, you will avoid overspending.

A Good Retirement Plan

Better money management and savings programs will help you in the long term. You will be able to secure your future and have an excellent retirement plan. With better money management skills will give you a better retirement plan. No matter how much you save, even when you save and invest a small amount of money, it will provide you with a more significant amount for your retirement later in life.

Peace of Mind

Proper money management brings you peace of mind. Having bills on the counter and having no idea how you will pay the bills or not having the money to purchase something you needed. All these issues can be difficult to face each day. Managing your money wisely and experience all the benefits of sound money management, you will enjoy peace of mind, and you can provide for yourself and your family, too.

The Disadvantages of Money management

Rapid Changes

With the rapid changes in the financial world, it can change your management plans every time. It is sometimes challenging to adjust your planning to incorporate fast-changing situations. Unless your project can help to adopt the new techniques, it will be limited.

Time-Consuming

Managing your money can sometimes be a time-consuming exercise. It requires you to make the estimates as accurate as possible. However, you can use software and mobile applications to assist you with planning, and this may reduce the time you will take if you were not using the technologies. And if you have less knowledge about money management, it will take you more time to achieve this.

Inaccuracy

When planning, you make a lot of assumptions in terms of estimation of your expenses. Any shift like an economic downturn or the change in the currency rate or interest rates can change your planning estimates.

Why Is Money Management Important?

Money turns to wealth when it is well-managed. It is an instrument used to pursue wealth. For wealthy people, having and spending money does not bring them happiness, which gives them joy, a steady income, achieving their goals, and leaving a legacy to their loved ones. Money management focuses on your habits, and your decision making can have affected the outcome of your long-term strategies. In pursuit of wealth, there are many powerful elements such as debts, risks, and taxes that can take away all the hard work you have put in to achieve your goals. It is a life skill that everyone must learn. You don't have to be financially savvy to start managing your money. There is plenty of information available to help you better understand your finances. The following are the importance of money management:

- **You are establishing clear goals.** Have a transparent approach to your decision in money management to build your wealth. Making the best decision will bring you closer to your goals. Also, set some clear and realistic goals you want to achieve and set a time horizon to perform them. Setting up clear goals will help you track where you are, and this will help you see your progress towards your goals. Some people give up earlier due to not being able to see their progress. You can see your progress and stay encouraged if you break your goals into short term milestones. Finally, have clear and quantifiable goals to help you to make clear decisions. Abandon any choices that will not get you closer to your destination.

- **You are controlling your cash flow.** Spend less than what you earn will help you accumulate wealth. You can't be financially successful if you are not tracking and monitoring your expenditure. Drawing up a spending plan and religiously following the program might seem trivial, but it's central to the world's wealthiest people's success. If you own a business, your goal will be to increase your monthly profits, which you will invest in for more growth. You will learn how to prioritize your spending when you have a solid money management plan and make the right decisions, which will bring you closer to your goals.

- **Budgeting.** Creating a household income budget is an essential part of personal money management. Budgeting will help you better understand your cash flow, thus giving you a clear understanding of your current financial situation.

- **Debt management.** There is proper financial education to help you understand consumer debt and how it works. Financial advisers and credit counselors advise how you can review your debts, your loan terms, and how you can pay off the debt quickly and stress-free.

- **You are managing your risks.** Your risk exposure increases as you continue accumulating your wealth. You might think that wealth can make life easier, but it does not. The ignored reality is that it can make life more complicated. You are getting a bigger house, expensive cars, and lavish lifestyles. These bring financial exposure and the potential to lose if all is great.

Have a risk management assessment in your money management plan with protection strategies to prepare you for the unexpected. Some of the unintended exposure include:

o   Income loss due to illness or accident

o   Death of the breadwinner in the family

o   Asset exposure to liability claims

Money management will provide you with a 360-degree view of your financial status and having financial discipline will help you overcome these obstacles. With a solid money management principle, you will have better control of your financial goals.

- **You are taxing efficiently.** Paying taxes is a responsibility; however, there is no obligation to spending more than necessary. Most people are not aware of how much taxes they are paying and unnecessary taxes and how it affects their wealth accumulation abilities. Money management does not focus on what you make but what you get after paying your taxes. Consider the tax characteristics of your investment and your overall portfolio. The first thing to consider is the account location, the money allocation on different accounts based on respective tax treatment. Secondly, the asset location, wherein you allocate different types of investments among the different types of funds on the tax treatment, giving your least tax-efficient assets to a tax-deferred account such as 401(k). The taxable accounts can hold in a tax-efficient investment such as low turnover funds. It will give you more income distribution options in the more tax-efficient retirement, thus enabling you to accumulate more wealth faster.

CHAPTER 26:

Better Options Trading

A trading scheme of options is a mechanism for creating and selling signals using a validated stock analysis tool.

The program can be based on some alternative approach and includes both basic and technical evaluations. Options trading systems may concentrate on changes in the underlying stock price, interest, decay time, unusual purchasing/selling behavior, or a mix.

Essentially, it is a checklist of conditions that must be met before entering the trade. When all conditions are fulfilled, a signal is produced to buy or sell. The criteria for each type of options trading strategy are different.

Whether it's long calls, covered calls, bear spreads, or naked index options, each has its type of trading system. An optional salt trading program can help you get out false signals and create trust in entries and exits.

How Relevant Is a Trading Network for Options?

The demand for options is very complex. Trading without a framework is like building a house without a plan. Movements of price, time, and stock will all impact your earnings. You must be mindful of each of these variables. Emotion can easily be swayed as the market shifts.

With a program, the response to these natural and usual emotions can be controlled. How much did you sit and watch a trade losing money when your order was filled?

Have you seen a stock price spike when you think of buying it? It is important to have a clear strategy in place to make rational and reasonable trade decisions. You can boost your trade executions by designing and following a good program, as emotionless and automatic as a machine.

Advantages of Trading Scheme Options

- **Leverage:** Selling options have the stock market leverage. You can manage hundreds or thousands of shares with options at a fraction of the stock price itself.

  A change in stock values from 5–10% may be equivalent to an increase of 100% or more. Seek to focus on percentage gains against dollar losses in your exchange. It needs a radical shift in traditional thinking, but it is necessary to effectively manage the trading system.

- **Objectivity:** A successful trading scheme of options is focused on observable parameters that allow signals to be bought and sold. It takes the subjectivity of your business so that you can focus on predetermined variables that trigger explosive trade.

- **Flexibility:** Most options traders can tell you that options give your trading flexibility. The demand for options makes it remarkably easy to take benefit of short-term positions.

  You may build strategies for overnight gains with clearly specified risk with earnings events and weekly options. There are ways to benefit from the trend to the range of any market situation.

- **Security:** The options trading program will serve as a hedge against certain investments, depending on an acceptable strategy in prevailing market conditions. This is a way of using defensive puts.

- **Risk:** The trading structure of good options reduces the risk in two essential ways. Cost is the first method. The option prices are very small relative to the same quantity of inventory. The second way issues end. A successful system will easily reduce losses and keep them low. The more tools in your toolbox, the more able you are to adjust business conditions. Unless the markets were to act in the same way every day, trading would become a play for children. To start designing your options trading, you have to build a trading strategy or strategy to lead you in the right direction.

Start with the basic framework and tweak it to identify and enhance your trading criteria. It takes time and experience to develop a productive options trading program that can return 100% or more in consistently profitable businesses. If you are pleased with your machine parameters, you can look at your own program's automatic trading.

Steps to Options Trading System

- **Pick a strategy:** You can select any strategy to start developing a program. The best way to get going is to buy calls and puts. You will add new approaches to your trade to boost your method by researching and understanding more about how prices move.

  Adding long-term equity protected calls and protections is a sensible next step so that you can debit your account by generating a monthly or weekly cash flow.

- **Trade:** It is time to trade once you have established the fundamentals of your strategy. Start small contracts, one or two contracts, and keep detailed transaction records. Be sure to include the underlying inventory price at the time you purchased or sold your right.

  Notes will allow you to evaluate how and where you can change. When you add new trading requirements to your system, your statistics should be strengthened. If not, it is time to re-evaluate your given criteria.

- **Measure-assess the successes and shortcomings:** The duration of the research depends on the amount you traded. If you trade actively, it is important to have a weekly or monthly summary. Compare your winnings to your losses. Zero on the main factors that make up a good trade and seek to change your parameters to boost your results.

  Analyze your mistakes as frustrating as they can be. Tune the requirements to avoid the same errors again. Analyzing your errors is as critical, if not more, to research your productive businesses.

- **Change:** If there is a losing streak or spot in your options trading scheme, change it. Adjust it. It's no shame to be wrong. This is part of the trading industry. The irony is that you are blind to and repeat your mistakes.

You will keep the device in line with changing business patterns and conditions by identifying the blind spots and making modifications. It sounds so basic, but perseverance and discipline are important.

- **Know:** A method of trading is not static. Keep your mind engaged by learning always. The more you research the stock market and the trading system of options, the more you learn and the better.

CHAPTER 27:

How to Become a Top Trader?

You are the one responsible for turning your venture into foreign exchange into a successful endeavor. That is one of the great things about the stock. You do not have a boss screaming down your neck, telling you to do something you do not agree with. You can come up with your trading plan based on your own research and your knowledge. That being said, success can come more quickly for some than for others, and a lot of the time, this has to do with approaching this endeavor with the right strategy. We will provide you with three strategies designed to help you make this stock as profitable as possible (with as little loss as possible):

Strategy 1. Buy Low and Sell High

If you began stock trading today with $25,000 in your pocket and access to a trading platform, all ready and raring to go, how would you know what is low and what is high? It's your first day. Naturally, for you to understand what would represent a good low investment and conversely what is high, you need to know the exchange rate history of that currency. Maybe the exchange rate for the Japanese yen seems low, but actually, compared to last year or a few months ago, it's a little high. Now it would not be a good time to buy.

Maybe the pound seems low right now, but yesterday the British government announced that the first round of the Brexit negotiations with the EU failed and therefore the pound may have room to go lower than it is was when you logged onto your trading platform. You can wait and see what the pound is today or tomorrow and buy then.

The point here is that buying low and selling high requires understanding the patterns associated with that stock and what might cause it to go up or down. And that's merely the buying side of things. Once you have bought low, you need to figure out when you are going to sell. This is where a good trading plan will come into play. A good plan will prevent you from selling too soon, or even not selling soon enough.

Strategy 2. Focus on Not Losing Money Rather Than on Making Money

This may not be an easy strategy to understand initially, in part because not losing money and making money seem like two sides of the same coin. They are, but they are not identical. One of the personality types that is associated with difficulty in finding success in trading is the impulsive type. This type of person wants to make money and they want to make it quick. They have a vague strategy about how they plan on doing that, but the most important thing to them is that they have a high account balance to make as many trades as they need to turn a profit. This is the wrong approach. Currencies are not the same as stocks. A stock's value may change very little even over a week, so the strategy that involves a lot of trades to make money is usually not the best strategy. You need a clear idea of when you are going to but, yes, because you want to make money, but mostly because you don't want to lose.

Every market that involves exchanges, like the stock market, has some implicit risk, and stock trading is risky, too, because you may be tempted to give up the advantage you have to try and make money quickly.

Strategy 3. Develop a Sense of Sentiment Analysis

Alright, the third strategy was going to be about Fibonacci retracement, which is a type of technical analysis of the market, but as this is the basics of stock trading, we are going to go into a different strategy that is not any easier than a Fibonacci retracement, just different. Sentiment analysis is a term that is used in many different specialties, not just finance, and it is not easy to describe.

It is essentially a type of analysis that is not based on a chart showing exchange rates over time (technical analysis) or understanding a factor that might today be affecting the value of the stock (fundamental analysis). Sentiment analysis attempts to gauge the tone of the market, the direction the market is heading in, by parsing all of the available information.

A key to understanding sentiment analysis is likening it to public opinion. The economy may be booming, people have more money in their pocket, so this hypothetical country's stock should increase in value, but maybe it doesn't. Maybe there is something that is causing the market to be bearish, which might cause the stock to drop.

As you perhaps can tell, as this analysis is not based on any concrete information, it can be thought of as intuitive and no one has intuition on the first day. Let's be honest about that. Intuition comes from experience. But the purpose of this strategy is to introduce to you the idea that not the foreign exchange market, like any market is not going to behave like a machine because it's not a machine.

Markets are places where human beings come together and humans are unpredictable, often in a frustrating way. Perhaps one day, stock trading may be handled by machines (that wouldn't be fun), but that day is far off and so you will have to develop your own sense of where the market seems to be going and use this as a strategy to achieve success in this endeavor.

Regardless of the investment that you make, be sure always to do your research. Doing research is a must. It is what will increase your chances of making the right investment decision.

The more that you understand something, the more likely that you will be able to predict how it will move in the market. This is why doing research is essential. It will allow you to know if something is worth investing in or not. Remember that you are dealing with a continuously moving market, so it is only right that you keep yourself updated with the latest developments and changes. The way to do this is by doing research.

Whether you will start forex trading or trade in general, it is always good to have a plan. Make sure to set a clear direction for yourself. This is also an excellent way to avoid being controlled by your emotions or becoming greedy. You should have a short-term plan and a long-term plan. You should also be ready for any form of contingency.

Make your plans practical and reasonable. Remember that you ought to stick to whatever project you come up with, so be sure to keep your ideas real. Before you come up with an idea, you must first have quality information. Again, this is why doing research is very important.

What if you fail to execute your plan? This is not uncommon. If this happens to you, relax and think about what made you fail to stick to your plan? Was it favorable to you or not? Take some time to analyze the situation and learn as much as you can from it. Indeed, having a plan is different from executing it. It is more challenging to implement a plan as it demands that you take positive actions.

Learn From Your Competitors

Pay attention to your competitors and learn from them. Studying your competitors is also an excellent way to identify your strengths and weaknesses. You can learn a great deal from your competitors, especially ideas on how you can better improve your business.

Your competitors can also help you promote your trading goals and draw more techniques. This way, you get a better idea of how to trade. You do not have to fight against your competitors; you can work together.

It is prevalent for people online to support one another. It is a good practice that you connect with other traders, especially those who are in the same niche. Do not think of them as your direct competitors, and you might be surprised just how friendly they can be.

Now, a common mistake is to consider yourself always better than others. This is wrong as you are only deluding yourself, making you fail to see the bigger picture. Instead of still seeing yourself better than your competitors, learn from them, and see how you can use this knowledge to improve your trading endeavors.

Cash-Out

Some people who trade forex or invest in cryptocurrency commit the mistake of not making a withdrawal. The reason why they do not cash out is so that they can grow their funds. Since you can only earn a percentage of what you are trading/investing, having more funds in your account means making a higher profit return. Although this may seem reasonable, it is not a recommended approach. It is strongly advised that you should request a withdrawal. You should understand that the only way to enjoy your profits truly is by turning them into cash; otherwise, it is only as if you were using a demo account. Also, by making a withdrawal, you lower your risks, since the funds you withdraw will no longer be exposed to risks.

You do not have to remove all your profits right away. If you want, you can withdraw 30% of your total profits, allowing the remaining 70% to add up to the funds in your account. The important thing is to make a withdrawal still now and then.

Take a Break and Have Fun

Making money online can be exciting and fun but it can also be a tiring journey. Therefore, give yourself a chance to take a break from time to time. When you take a break, do not spend that time thinking about your online business. Instead, you should spend it to relax your body and clear your mind. You will be more able to function more effectively if you do this. This is an excellent time to go on a vacation with your family or friends or at least enjoy a movie night at home. Do something fun that will put your mind off of business for a while. Do not worry; after this short break, and you are expected to work even more.

Making money online is a long journey, so enjoy it. Making money online can be lots of fun. Do not just connect with people to build a good following, but also try to make friends with your connections. You do not have to take things too seriously. Keep it fun and exciting.

CHAPTER 28:

Rolling Positions

Sometimes options traders wish to adjust positions they hold in the market. When this happens, it means the trader's market outlook has changed. It is possible to roll a short or long option position.

The term rolling refers to changing the outlook on the underlying security of an option. This change is often driven by a change in the outlook of the markets and positions held on certain trades. In such situations, a trader is often worried that certain positions will be assigned.

Rolling is like making a different turn other than the one initially planned. Think, for instance, you leave home heading to the grocery store only to end up at the movies. This is very similar to what rolling is about.

Rolling aims to either deter or cancel the assignment. Managing positions through rolling is an advanced technique that should only be applied by seasoned traders and experienced investors. Therefore, as an intermediate trader, you need to thoroughly understand this process before applying it.

Anytime that a trader rolls a position, they will be purchasing options very close to a current position in the marketing then sell this position to start another one. This process will cause small, minute, but significant tweaks to the trader's options' strike prices. This will shift the expiration times further out, so positions do not expire as initially planned. Even then, this process is not a guarantee that the strategy will work. In extreme cases, rolling will only compound losses, so only experienced traders should apply this technique.

How to Roll a Covered Call?

When you hold covered calls, you can choose to sell them to reduce the cost of holding them in long positions. When rolling calls forward, you will improve the break-even position and make it easier to succeed in the long run. However, you need to know if a position should be rolled on and when to do so. For instance, should rolling of a position occur twenty days to expiration or possibly at expiration?

Also, just about any trader can write a covered call. The most crucial thing is to manage such a position appropriately. Certain factors should be considered when rolling a position, especially near expiration Fridays.

First, you need to confirm whether the underlying stock is suitable for this kind of management. Then you will need to confirm the option chains for statistics involving the current and following month.

Now use the Ellman Calculator and enter the statistics to determine whether the dates are viable for rolling management. The first-month goal for initial returns stands at 2%–4%. With this information, you will finally need to conduct a thorough evaluation chart, technical information, and the prevailing market conditions. This way, you will comfortably be able to adjust your trades to benefit more.

If the stock price increases and you have no intention of selling the stock, you will need better management skills and high assignment risks simply because the covered call you have is now in-the-money. As such, you choose to purchase all your covered calls to cancel out any obligation to sell the stock. At this stage, it is advisable to then sell a call option that has little chance of being assigned at a better strike price.

The common strategy when a stock forecast or objective changes is to adopt a rolling process. Seasoned traders usually adapt rolling covered calls. Even then, as a trader, you should understand that there is no specific formula for the implementation of a rolling plan. For instance, as a trader, you may be wondering the current covered call should be shut down and replaced with yet another call that is in line with the new changes.

How to Roll the Short Strangle?

Rolling is the process of adjusting options strategies that a trader sets up. There are varied reasons why traders adjust their trades. These include erroneous initial predictions, changing market positions, and news that will affect a stock's performance.

Now on a strangle strategy, you always have a negative delta on the put and a positive delta on the call option. Therefore, we can deduce that we have a neutral delta in this instance. A neutral delta is okay at the onset. However, if the position remains that way, then you lose money. As a trader, you desire to make money; therefore, you want this movement to be huge when there is movement in the stock price. As such, you may use gamma, which will ensure the price goes up. However, should the stock price remain constant without any movement, then you will lose money.

The short strangle is sometimes considered by traders as a very risky strategy. However, as an experienced trader who knows what they are doing, this is not necessarily the case. Here is a look at some circumstances where risk is reduced by rolling action.

First, the premium is considered rather rich. As it is, a short straddle requires a trader to sell a put option and a call option based on an underlying option with similar expiration dates and strike prices. The best ones offer a very rich premium under near-the-money or at-the-money conditions.

Also, short straddles must have expiration dates that are within one month or less. It is time decay that causes the value of options to decline. Therefore, short straddles should be limited to only short-term options. Time decay often happens extremely fast within the first month.

Traders should focus their eyes on the current price and the strike price then note the relationship. It is advisable to close positions once it becomes practically possible. This should happen, especially when positions begin to move in-the-money. It is always a great idea to close at a profit because time decay will affect the trade value.

How to Roll a Short Call Spread?

When you roll a spread, the action is like rolling a single option. A trader who rolls a short call spread is most probably exit a position in a timely fashion with the strike prices moving down or up. The difference between rolling the short call spread and an individual option is that you will be engaged in a four-way trade with the short call spread. You will essentially be trading four different options instead of the usual two. This means opening two new positions while closing two existing ones.

If you implement a rolling process on a stock option position, be careful not to compound your losses because this is quite possible. Therefore, if you are confident about your initial predictions, you should try and stick to your game plan. Alternatively, you could choose to exit the strategy rather than roll and incur even larger losses.

This roll management process applies to most two-legged trades and not just the short spreads. Rolling also applies to other formations, including back spreads and straddles.

CHAPTER 29:

Trading Varying Time Frames

Weekly Options Trading

Weekly options are listings that provide an opportunity for short-term trading as well as plenty of hedging possibilities. As the name states, they have an expiration time of exactly one week; in general, they are listed on Thursday and expire the following Friday. While they have been around for decades, they have primarily been the domain of investors who work with cash indices. This exclusivity level changed in 2011 when the Chicago Board of Options expanded the number of ways they could be traded, especially to make them more easily acceptable to traders like you. Since then, the number of stocks that can be traded weekly has grown from 28 to nearly 1,000.

In addition to having a short time frame, weekly options differ from traditional options in that they are only available three weeks out of the month. They are also never listed in the monthly expiration style. The week that monthly options expire, they are technically the same as weekly options.

Advantages of Weekly Options

The biggest benefit of buying into weekly options is that you are free to purchase exactly what you need for the exact trade you are looking to make without worrying about coming up with extra capital or dealing with more options than you currently need. This means if you are looking to start a swing trade, or even an intraday trade, weekly options will have you covered. For those looking to sell, weekly options provide the ability to do so more frequently, rather than wait a month between sales.

Weekly options trades are also useful in that they lead to reduced costs for trades that have longer spreads, such as diagonal spreads or calendar spreads, as they can sell weekly options against them. They are also useful to higher volume trades as they are useful for hedging larger positions and portfolios against potential risky events. When the weekly options bind the market, the market can still be utilized through the iron butterfly or iron condor.

Disadvantages of Weekly Options

The biggest disadvantage when it comes to weekly options is the fact that you will not ever have very much time for a trade to turn around if you make the wrong choice in the first place. If you are selling options, then you will also need to know that their gamma will also be much more sensitive than it would be with more traditional options. This means that if you are planning to short options, then a relatively small move overall can still lead to an out-of-the-money option entering in-the-money very quickly.

Weekly options are also known to require a good deal more micromanaging of risk. Without taking the time to size your trades and guarantee your profits properly, you will find that your available trade balance disappears quickly. Furthermore, all of your trades' implied volatility is going to much higher than it would have been otherwise due to the time frame you are dealing with. Near term, options are always going to be more open to large price swings as well.

Buying Weekly

Because you are always going to have much less time when it comes to turning a profit with a weekly option, your timing for when to move on a specific decision needs to be much more precise than it would otherwise have to be. If you choose poorly at either strike selection, time frame, or price direction, you can easily find yourself paying for a generally worthless option. You will also need to consider your level of acceptable risk as the option will be cheaper per unit, but you will need to purchase more in a week than you otherwise would.

It is also important to avoid making naked calls or puts when trading weekly as these typically work out to be lower probability trades as a whole. If you have a bias regarding the direction you want your trades to move in, then using a debit spread or structured trade is generally preferred.

Selling Weekly

Selling reliably for the long-term can generate steady profits if done properly. It only works this way if you are defining your profits upfront, which means it is important always to know what your options are worth to prevent you from selling yourself short. Selling trades weekly will make it easier to collect the full premium if they guess correctly while still leaving you exposed to unmitigated losses if you choose poorly, which requires an extra margin.

The ideal types of the underlying stock to use for these types of trades will be lower priced as they each ultimately consume a smaller amount of your total buying power. This also means it is easier to move forward on trades with lots of implied volatility as it is more likely to revert to the mean in the allotted time. As a rule, selling a put in the short-term is always better than selling a call as it tends to generate an overall higher return in the shorter period.

Spreads

Spreads are a great way of making a profit in the weekly market. The overall level of implied volatility will be much higher in the weekly market than in the monthly variation, so the spread can help you when you find yourself dealing with an unexpected directional change quickly enough that you can actually do something about it. Selling an option against a long option will naturally decrease the role volatility plays in the transaction. The best point to use the debit spread will be near the current price, providing you with a 1 to 1 risk and reward ratio.

Intraday Trades

While options are frequently left out of day trading strategies, this trend is slowly changing. Traders are slowly but surely realizing that they can apply many standard day trading techniques to successfully sell and buy options.

Intraday Trading Challenges

When attempting to day trade options, you will likely run into some unique challenges that you should be able to best with the proper consideration.

Price movement will decrease value more significantly due to the time value naturally associated with options that are only in-the-money so close to their period of expiration. Remember, while their inherent value is likely to increase along with the underlying stock price, which will be dramatically countered by the time value loss.

The bid-ask spreads are typically going to be wider than they would otherwise be due to the reduced liquidity that you will typically find with the options market. This will frequently vary by as much as 0.5 of a point, which can cut into profits if things move at an inopportune time.

Some types of options are naturally a better fit when it comes to day trading than others. Perhaps the most effective is the near month in-the-money option, which is appropriate for those traders who are a fan of trading stocks with a high level of liquidity. The premium on this type of option is based more closely on its overall value as it is already in-the-money and getting close to its expiration date. If this occurs, the time value drain is decreased dramatically. This type of option is generally traded most effectively in periods of high volume, resulting in a decrease in the gap between the asking price and bidding price.

Protective Put

The protective put is a type of option that is useful when you purchase put orders along with shares of the related underlying stock. This is a reliable strategy when the underlying stock is likely to experience a high degree of volatility. It is especially effective when used to purchase the same option throughout the day to capitalize on short bursts of positive movement. It is also useful for providing insurance when purchasing shares of a risky underlying stock as you will always be limited in your potential losses to the price of the options you purchased.

Protective puts are also useful in a strategy known as bottom fishing. It is common for many underlying stocks to regularly break through existing support levels and continue moving down into an entirely new lower trading range. When this occurs, it is in your best interest to seek out the bottom point of the downturn so that you can catch it before it starts moving back up. It is possible for a stock to give off false signs of having hit bottom and buying in at that point will only lead to serious losses. This is where the protective put comes in, however, and limits the possibility for risk substantially.

While models can be used to calculate the likelihood of the bottom of a given trend, they too can be fooled by the exhausted behavior, which can indicate a false bottom. As such, when you feel that a given stock has bottomed out, then you can buy in with a protective put and then be protected regardless of the outcome.

Directional Options Trading

The most effective directional strategies for intraday options trading are those with the overall highest degree of making it possible to make quick moves time and again. These moves are typically going to occur at specific retracement levels or around breakouts.

Trades that are based around the Fibonacci retracement on the charts for time frames less than ten minutes. Fibonacci retracements can be used to determine reasonable reward/risk levels either by selling a credit spread to the level in question or buying options that are already in-the-money that are likely to experience a bounce at these levels. It is generally going to be in your best interest to look for Fibonacci levels that are likely to overlap at multiple time frames and correspond to the most recent trend experienced by the underlying stock. If you are so inclined, you can also utilize candlestick price patterns as a means of confirming a buy at specific Fibonacci levels.

Alternately, you may find success with oversold or overbought indicators when it comes to range-bound or trendless stocks. You can then sell credit spreads or buy into options already in-the-money and near the current level of resistance and support with tight stops. It is important to keep in mind that a given stock might not move quickly enough to make these levels worthwhile, so it is important to do your research ahead of time to have a reasonable expectation about the future movement.

Indicators used to signal lower than average volatility, such as Bollinger bands, are especially useful for place trades that you anticipate big moves from. Breakout indicators time, especially for the shorter charts, are also especially useful.

High Volatility Options Intraday Strategy

Trading volatility by selling options with high volatility, such as credit spreads currently out-of-the-money, will allow you to profit when anticipating a volatility drop. This is a commonly used professional strategy to employ when it comes to earning season or other scenarios where the underlying stock has developed a big price gap. The front-month short-term options will then have an extra-large amount of volatility that makes it easier to generate a positive reward and risk ratio when selling.

CHAPTER 30:

Swing Trading With Options

The most straightforward way to trade options is to make a bet on the stock market's direction and buy a call or put options accordingly. Most beginning options traders will have to start with this method because more advanced strategies are closed off to beginning options traders. However, that isn't all bad because you should feel for the options market before attempting more complicated trades.

What Is Swing Trading?

Swing trading is a simple trading philosophy, where the idea is to trade "swings" in market prices. There is nothing special about swing trading in a commonsense kind of way because it's a buy-low and sell-high trading method with stocks. You can also profit from a stock when the price is declining by "shorting" the stock.

So, what distinguishes swing trading from other types of trading and investing? The main important distinction is that swing trading is different from day trading. A day trader will enter their stock position and exit the position on the same trading day. Day traders never hold a position overnight.

Swing traders hold a position at least for a day, which means they will hold their position at a minimum overnight. Then they will wait for an anticipated "swing" in the stock price to exit the position. This time frame can be days to weeks, or out to a few months, maximum.

A swing trader also differs from an investor, since at the most, the swing trader will be getting out of a position in a few months. Investors often put their money in companies they strongly believe in. Alternatively, they are looking to build a "nest egg" over one to three decades or even more.

Swing traders don't particularly care about the companies they buy stock in. They are simply looking to make a short-term profit. So, although swing traders may not be hoping to make an instant profit like a day trader, they will not be hoping for profits from the long-term prospects of a company. A swing trader is only interested in changing stock prices. Even the reasons behind the changes in the stock prices may not be important. So, whether it's Apple or some unknown company, if it is in a big swing in stock prices, the swing trader will be interested.

Swing Trading Options

Since options are time-limited, they are a natural fit for the concept of swing trading. Although many of the advanced strategies attempt to take out the direction of share price movement from the equation, if you are buying single call or put options to make a profit, then you're behaving at least in a qualitative sense like a swing trader.

Since put options gain in value when stock prices are declining, buying put options is like shorting the stock. It's quite a bit more accessible, however. You must have a margin account to borrow shares from the broker to short stock. Shorting stock's basic idea is to borrow shares from the broker when the stock price is at a relatively high point and sell them. After this, the trader will wait for the share price to drop. When the share price is low enough to make a profit, the trader will buy the shares back and return them to the broker.

Of course, shorting stock using options is far easier. The reason is you never have to buy the stock to make a profit from the declining price. You profit from the prices of put options, which will increase as the stock price goes down.

Going Long on a Stock

If you believe that the price of a stock will rise, you want to buy call options. So, call options to represent the most straightforward or commonsense way to trade options. You are betting on that stock when you buy a call option. Another way to say this is that you are bullish on the stock.

A good way to go about trading options is to pick a few companies and limit yourself to trading them. The reason is that you are going to have to be paying attention to the markets, company news, and general financial news for any option that you invest in. You will not be able to stay on top of things and find yourself getting caught up in losing trades if you spread yourself too thin. The best approach is to keep your trading limited in scope to know what is going on. That doesn't mean you only trade a single call option; you might trade many of them on the same stock.

There are two ways to go about swing trading options. The first way is to look for ranging stocks that are trapped in between support and resistance. Then you can trade call and put options that move with the swings. So, the idea of this type of trading is very simple. First, you need to study a stock of interest and determine the price levels of support and resistance. Then, when the price drops to the support level, you buy call options. Now hold them until the price goes back up near resistance. It can be a good idea to exit your trades before the price gets to resistance so that you don't end up losing some of your potential profits if the price reverses before you get rid of the options.

Trend trading call options can also be very lucrative. In this case, you are looking for significant news and developments related to the stock or even the economy at large. For example, when a company announces that it had big profits, this can be an opportunity to earn money with call options, as the price will go up by large amounts as people start snapping up the stock. When trading in this fashion, you're going to need to know how to spot trend reversals. The idea is the same when you identify a trend in the making, buy call options, and then ride the trend until you are satisfied with the level of profit and sell the options.

Again, it can't be emphasized too much. You always need to take time to decay into account when trading options. So, remember that with each passing day, your options are going to lose value automatically. Check theta to find out how much value they are going to lose. Other factors overwhelm time decay in the short term.

A big opportunity with call options is trading on index funds. SPY, which we mentioned earlier, is one of the top choices for trading call options. In the case of SPY, you will be paying attention to overall economic news to look for opportunities. Any information related to the economy at large can cause large moves with this index fund. This includes changes in interest rates (or even leaving them the same when that is what the market would prefer), announcements of GDP growth rates, changes in trade policy, or the release of jobs numbers. One of the best things about SPY options is that they are extremely liquid, making it very easy to get in and out of your trades. You can also trade many other index funds, tracking virtually anything financial.

Shorting Stock Using Put Options

Put options may be one of the most powerful tools available to the individual trader. To earn profits from shorting stock, you have to be a big player in the market. That means you have to get a margin account and have enough financial resources that you can borrow large numbers of shares from the broker. Remember that to earn profits from shorting stock, and you'll have to be shorting 100 shares or more of stock to make money.

With put options, you can leverage the stock through the option. By investing in put options, you get control of the stock and earn profits from the stock's price movements without actually having to buy shares. A single put option might cost $30, $100, or $400, but you will control 100 shares.

Some traders hope to profit by selling the shares when they buy put options. Still, most traders want to get into a put option early when a downward trend in stock price is expected and then sell the put option for a profit when stock prices have declined. The same basic things to look for apply, except you'll be doing it in reverse. So, you can trade put options for profits when stocks are ranging. In this case, you start the trade by purchasing put options when stock prices are relatively high, at the resistance level. Then you hold your put options until prices drop down again to support and sell them for a profit.

Likewise, for an options trader, downward trends in stock prices are just as nice as upward trends. When a downward trend is developing, you invest in Put options and then sell them when the stock price has dropped enough such that you are taking an acceptable profit. As with call options, traders using put options will need to learn about signals that indicate trend reversals to have some quantitative tools to help them make solid trades.

Remember there are no guarantees on the options market. When trading options, we are looking for probabilities. This means that you can expect to have some losing trades, and the goal is to be profitable overall without worrying about specific trades.

Swing traders use tools that help them estimate changes in the direction of stock market prices. Some of these tools are more qualitative and involve spotting particular chart patterns that usually indicate a trend reversal is coming. You can think of these tools more in the sense of being rules of thumb or even the art of trading.

CHAPTER 31:

Understanding Trading Orders

As a trader, you will need a broker through whom you will place, buy, or sell orders for any asset. You can decide whether you will buy or sell any stock and then place an order accordingly on your online trading platform.

Usually, exchanges use a bid and ask process for fulfilling orders placed by traders. This means that there must be a buyer and seller to complete a single order, and they both should agree on the price. For example, if a trader wants to buy a stock at X price, a seller must be willing to sell that stock at the same price. No transaction can occur unless a buyer and a seller agree at the same price.

In stock markets, the price moment is directed by a struggle between the bid and ask prices. These prices keep constantly changing. As trading orders get filled, the price levels also keep changing, reflected in the technical charts.

While day trading, one must keep in mind this bid and ask process because this will determine at what price the order will be executed. When markets are moving slowly, the price change is also slow, and one can wait to get the trading orders filled at the desired price. However, when markets are highly volatile and see big up or down moves within split seconds, the order may get filled at a higher than expected rate. This can cause losses to day traders as the price changes quickly and can reverse by the time their orders are filled.

Different markets have different methods of matching buyers' and sellers' prices. These methods are called trading mechanisms. The two types of trading mechanisms are order-driven and quote drove. In markets that use quote driven trading, a constant stream of prices (quotes) is available to traders. These prices are decided by market makers; therefore, these types of trading systems are better suited for over the counter (OTC) markets or dealers.

Exchanges mostly adopt the order-driven trading mechanism. Here, orders are executed when buy orders match with a sell order. In this type of trading mechanism, dealmakers are not involved.

Mechanism of Trading Orders

In electronic day trading, orders are placed on online trading platforms. These orders are the trader's instructions to the broker or the brokerage firm to buy or sell some security. When you are trading stocks, you place orders to buy or sell a stock fulfilled by the brokerage firm with whom you have a trading account. The ease of electronic trading has given traders the freedom to initiate various types of order, where they can use different restrictions in order conditions. By these restrictions, traders can control the price and time of order execution. Such instructions help increase traders' profits or restrict the losses.

In systems where the trading mechanism is order-driven, traders can also control any specific order's timeline. For example, a trader can place an order which will remain open until its execution. Traders can also place orders that last till the end of the session, or one day, or a specific time.

Understanding how trading orders are placed and how they can impact one's day trading is important because it can affect one profit or loss in day trading. For example, a novice day trader may not be aware of the slippage between the bid and ask prices. It occurs in every trade, and every trader faces it, whether buying, selling, entering a position, or exiting from a position. This is also called the spread between a bid and ask price. So, when you place an order to buy a stock at $4, the slippage may increase its cost to $4.05 when your order is filled. Likewise, when you exist in any position, you place an order to sell at $3, but the slippage causes it to get filled at $2.98, thus chipping away at some of your profits.

Professional traders advise beginners to stay away from highly volatile market situations because of slippage increases during those choppy moments. For example, on a central bank policy declaration day, stock prices become highly volatile and move with big numbers within seconds. The ordered price and executed price may be different in such a situation, causing financial harm to the day trader. Such big moves may look tempting to day traders from the outside, making them greedy, thinking they can make big profits with such huge price moves. But the reality is, the slippage between the bid and ask price is equally high, and it can change considerably by the time the trading order gets filled or immediately after the order is executed, creating a loss-making situation for the trader.

Different Types of Trading Orders

Most individual traders use a broker's or dealers' trading platforms to place their trading orders. These platforms provide the facility of placing various types of orders, which are helpful in trade planning. Placing an order on the trading platforms is instructing the brokerage firm to buy or sell a financial asset on behalf of the trader. Based on the execution type, here are some common order types:

Market Orders

These orders do not have any specific price. A market order is an instruction to the broker to complete the trade at the available price. Because there is no fixed price, these orders almost always get executed unless there is some liquidity problem. Traders use market orders when they want their trades executed quickly, and they are not bothered about the execution price.

These orders are good if there is not much slippage between the bid and ask price. But a big slippage can cause loss to the traders, especially those who day trade options.

Limit Orders

Traders place limit orders when they want to buy or sell stocks (or other assets) at a specific price. For example, if Apple shares are trading at $220, and traders expect the price to dip low, they can limit order to buy the shares at $219 or lower. It can be used for both buying and selling. Traders use these orders when trading with technical levels and are sure of price touching those levels. For example, if a trader has bought Apple shares at $220 and thinks it can touch $222, they can place a limit order to sell their shares at that higher price. When the share price reaches that level, their sell order will get executed.

Stop Orders

These are also known as stop-loss orders and make a part of traders' money management techniques. A stop-loss order can stop the trade from going below a specific price, thus restricting losses for the trader. These orders are used for both buy and sell trades. The price specified in a stop-loss order is called stop price; once that price is reached, the order is executed as a market order.

Day Order

This order is valid only in the same trading session where it is placed. If the specified price is not achieved by the end of the session, the order is automatically canceled. This saves day traders from carrying forward their orders to the following day.

Preparations for Placing an Order

When preparing day trading plans and strategies, many day traders forget to pay attention to placing orders for trades. The simple act of placing a trading order can have a big impact on the success of your day trading business.

Successful day traders always prioritize order processing techniques and plan their trades around the stock price they will focus on during the trading. The trading plan itself means planning at what price you will enter a trade, and when you will exit. Online trading platforms provide many methods of placing your orders around your planned trade prices. You can prepare charts of your trade, mark entry and exit points, place orders for both trades together and separately.

A good trading plan always includes trade entry, exit, profit booking, and loss stopping points. The margin trading facility provided by various brokerage firms also includes placing a stop-loss order together with the primary buy or sell order. This ensures that your trade will never suffer a loss beyond a specific price level. Here is an example to illustrate this:

Suppose a trader has bought stock "A" at $10. They are expecting the price to go up, so they will make some profit. However, anything can happen in stock markets, and in case of price reverses, they want to restrict their losses to $3 only. So, they will place a stop-loss order at $7, which is $3 below their buying price. If the price keeps moving up, the stop-loss order will be kept inactive. In case the stock price falls, nothing will happen till it reaches $7, at which time the stop-loss order will be triggered and automatically sell the stock they have bought.

A stop-loss order ensures that even if the trader is not available to check prices, their position will be safe till a certain price.

Similarly, traders can also use limit orders to exit their positions after earning a profit. Taking the above example, if a trader has bought a stock at $10, they believe that the price will move up to $15; they can place a limit order to sell at $15. When the price reaches its target ($15), it will be automatically executed, and the position will be squared off with a profit of $5.

These examples show that day traders can use different order types for money management and manage the risk and reward ratio. By technical analysis of any stock chart, day traders can find at what price the stock will make a big move and be ready to place their orders near that price level.

Some Other Order Types

Apart from the basic orders, some other order types are not common but can be used for money management or specific trading strategies.

For example, someday, traders are more active during the market closing hours, as they create trading strategies for the next session. To take advantage of the price movement during the closing hours, they can place "Limit-On-Close" (LOC) orders. As the name shows, it is a limit order and is specified for getting executed when markets close. As you know, a limit order controls at what price any security will be bought or sold. LOC has an extra parameter of "on close," which adds another condition to this order that it should only get executed if the closing price matches the order's price limit. For this order, both the limit price and the market's closing price are important.

CHAPTER 32:

Market Environment

While the strategies by themselves will limit your risk and give you rewards according to their risk profiles, the most significant risk is applying the wrong strategy to the wrong market conditions.

No strategy can eliminate the risk of you making a mistake, unfortunately. Like the straddle or strangle, even a neutral strategy will not work if you misread a range for a trend.

Technical and fundamental analysis will help you determine what market conditions are appropriate. Every trader has different perspectives towards technical analysis regarding determining which stocks to operate in. This is because fundamental analysis favors longer timelines, of over 5 years, for investment purposes. While the earnings announcements are important, a fundamentally low valuation doesn't play out over a few months.

Learn some basics about the market environment: namely, what is a trend and what is a range.

Trends and Ranges

A market is a chaotic place, with several traders vying for dominance over one another. There are countless strategies and time frames in play, and at any point, it is close to impossible to determine who will emerge with the upper hand. In such an environment, how is it then possible to make any money? After all, if everything is unpredictable, how can you get your picks?

Well, this is where thinking in terms of probabilities comes into play. While you cannot get every single bet right, if you get enough right and make enough money on those to offset your losses, you will make money in the long run.

It's not about getting one or two right. It's about executing the strategy with the best odds of winning repeatedly and ensuring that your math works out with regards to the relationship between your win rate and average win.

So, it comes down to finding patterns that repeat themselves over time in the markets. What causes these patterns? Well, the other traders, of course. To put it more accurately, the orders that the other traders place in the market create patterns that repeat themselves over time.

The first step to understanding these patterns is to understand what trends and ranges are. Identifying them and learning to spot them when they transition into one another will give you a massive leg up with your options trading and directional trading.

Trends

In theory, spotting a trend is simple enough. Look left to right, and if the price is headed up or down, it's a trend. Most of the time, you have countertrend forces operating in the market. It is possible to have long counter-trend reactions within a larger trend, and sometimes, depending on the time frame you're in, and these counter-trend reactions take up most of your screen space.

Trend vs. Range

The key to deciphering trends is to watch for two things: countertrend participation quality and turning points. Let's tackle countertrend participation first.

Countertrend Participation

When a new trend begins, the market experiences an extremely imbalanced order flow tilted towards one side. There's isn't much countertrend participation against this seeming tidal wave of with trend orders. Price marches on without any opposition and experiences only a few hiccups.

This is where countertrend traders start testing the trend and see how far back into their trend. While it is unrealistic to expect a full reversal at this point, the correction or pushback quality tells us a lot about the strength distribution between the with and countertrend forces.

Eventually, the countertrend players manage to push so far back against the trend of stalemate results in the market. After all, you need an imbalance for the market to tip one way or another, and balanced order flow will only result in a sideways market.

While all this is going on behind the scenes, the price chart is what records the push and pull between these two forces. Using the price chart, we can anticipate when a trend is coming to an end and how long it could potentially take before it does. This second factor, which helps us estimate the time it could take, is invaluable from an options perspective, especially if you're using a horizontal spread strategy.

Here's what you look out for to gauge countertrend participation:

- Quality of countertrend candles: Are they strong/weak/have wicks/small-bodied, etc.?
- Several countertrend candles within the movement: Is this changing over time?
- Length of pushbacks: Are the pushbacks increasing in number? Are they lasting for longer?

In all cases, the greater the number of them, the greater the countertrend participation in the market. The closer a trend is to end, the greater the countertrend participation. Thus, the minute you begin to see price move into a large, sideways move with an equal number of buyers and sellers in it, you can be sure that some form of redistribution is going on.

The trend might continue or reverse. Either way, it doesn't matter. What matters is that you know the trend is weak and that now is probably not the time to be banking on-trend strategies.

Starting from the left, we can see that there is close to no countertrend bars, bearish in this case, and the bulls make easy progress. Note the angle with which the bulls proceed upwards.

Then comes the first major correction and the countertrend players push back against the last third of the bull move. Notice how strong the bearish bars are and note their character compared to the bullish bars.

The bulls recover and push the price higher at the original angle and without any bearish presence, which seems odd. This is soon explained as the bears slam price back down, and for a while, it looks as if they've managed to form a V top reversal in the trend, which is an extremely rare occurrence.

The price action that follows is a more accurate reflection of the market's power, with both bulls and bears sharing chunks of the order flow, with overall order flow in the bull's favor but only just. The price here is certainly in an uptrend but looking at the extent of the bearish pushbacks, perhaps we should be on our guard for a bearish reversal. After all, order flow is looking sideways at this point.

So how would we approach an options strategy with the state's chart at the extreme, right? Well, for one, any strategy that requires an option beyond the near month is out of the question, given the probability of it turning. Secondly, looking at the order flow, it does seem to be following a channel.

While the channel isn't very clean if you were aggressive enough, you could consider deploying a collar with the strike prices above and below this channel to take advantage of the price movement. You could also employ some moderately bullish strategies as price approaches the bottom of this channel and figuring out the extent of the bull move is easier thanks to you referencing the channel's top.

As the price moves in this channel, it's all well and good. Eventually, though, we know that the trend must flip. How do we know when this happens?

Turning Points

As bulls and bears struggle over who gets to control the order flow, price swings up and down. You will notice that every time price comes back into the 6427–6349 zone, the bulls seem to step in masse and repulse the bears.

This tells us that the bulls are willing to defend this level in large numbers and strength. Given the number of times the bears have tested this level, we can safely assume that bullish strength is a bit weak above this level. However, it is as if the bulls have retreated at this level and are treating this as a last resort for the trend to be maintained.

If this level were to be breached by the bears, it is a good bet that many bulls will be taken out. In martial terms, the largest army of bulls has been marshaled at this level. If this force is defeated, it is unlikely that there will be too much resistance to the bears below this level.

This zone, in short, is a turning point. If price breaches this zone decisively, we can safely assume that the bears have moved in and controlled most of the order flow.

Turning Point Breached

The two horizontal lines mark the decisive turning point zone, and the price touches this level twice more and is repulsed by the bulls. Notice how the last bounce before the level breaks produces an extremely weak bullish bounce, and price caves through this. Notice the strength with which bears breakthrough.

The FTSE was in a longer uptrend on the weekly chart, so the bulls aren't completely done yet. However, as far as the daily timeframe is concerned, notice how price retests that same level but this time around, it acts as resistance instead of support.

For now, we can conclude that if the price remains below the turning point, we are bearishly biased. You can see this by looking at the angle with which bulls push back and the lack of strong bearish participation on the push upwards.

This doesn't mean we go ahead and pencil in a bull move and start implementing strategies that take advantage of the upcoming bullish move. Remember, nothing is for certain in the markets. Don't change your bias or strategy until the turning point decisively breaks.

Some key things to note here are that a turning point is always a major S/R level. It is usually a swing point where many with trend forces gather to support the trend. Don't hang on to older turning points as this will not always be the case.

CHAPTER 33:

Q&A to Help You Get the Most Out of Trading

1. Why Is It Better to Trade in Options Than Other Forms of Investing?

Many benefits come with options trading compared to some of the other investment choices that you can make. To start, you don't have to purchase the underlying asset. With the options contract, you are purchasing the right, but not the obligation, to either purchase or sell the asset at a later time. You get the benefit of making a profit once you decide to exercise this right. But if the trade goes oppositely, you don't have to exercise your right to use the underlying asset, and your losses are often limited to the fee or the deposit that you placed on the trade in the beginning.

2. What Are Some of the Ways That I Can Limit My Losses?

We spent some time talking about some of the different ways to limit the number of losses you have. There are several risks with any investment, and you could end up losing money along the way. Even those who have worked in the options market for some time may experience losses on occasion. These are the things that you can do to help limit these losses a bit, including:

- Make a plan and stick to it.

- Know your stop-loss points.

- Invest in something you know.

- Never risk capital than you can afford to lose.

- Learn how to keep the emotions out of the trade.

3. What Are the Differences Between Puts and Calls?

This will refer to the right that you have when it comes to working with your options trading. When we talk about a call option, it means that you have the right to buy the underlying asset. But when we are talking about the put option, we are talking about having the right to sell that underlying asset. Ensure that you know each of these and that your plan is set up to work with the right one before you start.

4. What Assets Can I Trade-In?

Options trading can technically be done on any asset that you want. Remember that with options, you will purchase the right, but not the obligation, to purchase the underlying asset. But the underlying asset can be almost anything that you want. With that said, most of the time, the underlying asset will be some stock option. Ensure that you research the different types of assets that can be done in options and determine which one is the best for you.

5. What Are Some of the Characteristics of a Kind Options Trader?

As an options trader, you need to be careful with your investment and be sure that you are taking all the necessary precautions before entering the market. A good investment trader, in options and in other forms of investing, will have some of the following:

- **Capital to invest.** You won't even be able to talk to the broker until you can bring some money to the table. It is preferable if you have some extra money set to the side that isn't earmarked for some other purpose in your life.

- **Some time.** You must have at least a little bit of time to ensure that you will be able to look at the charts and watch your trade to make sure you are successful.

- **Research abilities.** The investments that you take are going to need some research behind them. If you can do your research, hear about the news surrounding your trades, and look through many charts, you will do better with options trading.

- **Controlling emotions.** If you aren't able to control your own emotions, then you are going to fail. For those who let their emotions take over all the time, finding another investment opportunity is a much better option to help you do well. If you are levelheaded and can pay attention to your investment without losing your cool, options are a great choice.

6. Can I Trade-In Options Even if the Market Is Going Down?

Unlike some of the other investment opportunities that you may run into, you can trade-in options even if the market is in a downward trend at the time. You can trade-in options even if the market is stagnant, volatile, and whether it is going up or down. There are various strategies that you can choose no matter how the market is doing at the time. This is one of the biggest reasons that people choose to go with options as their investment vehicle. They can make some good profits from their work, no matter what the market is doing around them.

7. Is it Safe to Invest in Options?

Compared to some of the other choices you have for investing, especially with day trading and swing trading, options trading is much safer. Many investors choose to go with options trading to help protect themselves from any downturns that could harm their other investments. With that said, there is still an element of risk that can come with investing in options, and you should still make sure that there is some plan in place before you decide to enter into the market. Other risks come with using this form of investing, and you have to be careful and stick with your plan if you want to see success.

Conclusion

Options trading is a form of financial speculation that allows investors to buy or sell stock options without owning the underlying stock. This tends to result in much higher returns than investing in stocks directly.

One of options trading's biggest benefits is that it does not require a great deal of initial capital. Even a small sum can be used to buy stock options. However, the cost can quickly add up if large quantities are traded. The monthly premium will need to be paid using the profits generated when the option is exercised.

The basic principle of options trading is that an asset's price can rise or fall in a given time frame. It is a strategy of hedging your position in the market by purchasing a call or put option, which provides you with the right to sell or buy an asset at a specified price, respectively. You also have the right to buy or sell an option at a set price within a set time frame. There are only two types of options at *Options Trading for Beginners*, calls, and puts.

Options trading is thought to be the more sophisticated form of investing because it allows you to trade for price moves rather than simply for the stock itself. It requires more knowledge and understanding of the market.

To use options trading, you must predict how a stock or index will move in the future and what the potential price range is for that move. The more information you learn, the better you'll be able to predict these movements and buy a call or put options accordingly.

You should know the risks involved in options trading. You can reduce some of the risks by trading limit orders, but many traders prefer to trade with both put and call options. This is known as "buying straddles" or "selling strangles." Even though these strategies often work well for experienced traders, they can backfire if you are not prepared for losing money while trading. If you choose to trade options, you should do so only after getting professional advice and guidance from a licensed financial advisor or broker.

Trading options is one way to profit when a stock goes up or down, but it isn't the only option available. You can take positions without using any of your capital by simply buying puts or calls on a stock you want to own. You can sell puts when you think there will be a downward price movement, and you can sell calls when you believe the price will go up.

Although it might sound complicated, options trading is very straightforward and can be learned quickly with a little guidance from professional traders. Make sure to study this guide, and you'll soon be making profits from options trading each month.

With options, there are several different trading platforms and strategies you can choose from. You must choose the type of trading which suits your personality the most.

If you're a beginner or live in an area with high stock market volatility, then I'd recommend that you stick to only index options and invest in only stocks for a while. This way, you can test out your options trading capability without the added risk of losing your money.

It is highly recommended that you read this guide and make some notes to learn more about options trading. This will help you understand it better and avoid common mistakes.

BOOK 2: OPTIONS TRADING CRASH COURSE

Introduction

The world of finance can be a complicated place, but it doesn't have to be. Options Trading is a great way to get involved in the world of finance without the heavy learning curve. If you want to get involved in the world of Options Trading, but don't know where to begin.

This guide will introduce you to Options Trading basics, and how it fits into the world of financial markets. We'll show you what options are, how they work, and how you can use them to your advantage.

It is one of the most profitable and exciting ways to earn money. Although options trading can be complicated, it is not difficult to understand. In this article, we'll cover the basics, strategies, and information you need to know about options trading.

Options trading is similar to investing in stocks and bonds, except instead of buying shares of a company or buying paper for cash; you are buying an option on it.

Options trading is a type of derivative trade. It is the practice of buying and selling options contracts to control the price of stocks, commodities, indices, foreign currency, and other financial assets. Options are financial securities that give the holder the right to buy or sell a particular asset at a specific price and date.

Options have been traded since the dawn of civilization. Invented in 1801 by a French financier named Pierre de Fermat, options were initially used as a form of investment instrument to speculate on future stock market movements.

It can be used to gain exposure to particular asset classes without having to purchase the underlying investments. They also provide traders with an opportunity to control their risk when trading a high-risk investment asset. It is important to note that options were traded before they were invented. The first documented use of options occurred over 2,000 years ago during Roman times.

Options trading made its way into the United States in 1790 when pioneers brought it from England with them when they migrated across the Atlantic Ocean. The term option was coined in 1790 by Alexander Hamilton, who wrote that "a merchant can be made to owe his entire fortune to an option."

Options trading is an innovative way to invest in the market. Traders can profit from both rising and falling prices of stocks.

Trading options can be extremely profitable for experienced traders who know how to manage risk and choose to open and close their positions. Options trading also offers investors an opportunity to own shares in what otherwise may be extremely volatile stock markets such as Brazil's Ibo Vespa or China's Shanghai Composite Index. Those who trade options regularly can be financially rewarding to see the value of their investment double overnight when a company goes public or is bought out by another company.

Options trading continues to gain popularity. It is becoming easier for first-time investors to enter this lucrative market through online brokerages, and discount brokerages like Options Trading Crash Course Online Brokerage (Options Trading Crash Course).

CHAPTER 1:

Financial Freedom

While there are many things that you may dream of accomplishing in your life, you will find that almost everyone is interested in gaining financial freedom. Being free financially means that you can maintain the lifestyle that you want without a regular paycheck. It is like having a retirement where you can live comfortably and maybe go out, and have some fun without worrying about stretching yourself too thin.

There are a lot of ways that come with gaining financial freedom. It is not a single point in time, but rather four stages that will lead you to this. The four stages of financial freedom that you should follow include:

No Freedom

Everyone is going to start the journey in the same place. You will rely on your monthly paycheck during this stage. You will see that a job and the reliable income stream that it provides are required so that you can pay the bills. If something happened to your income and you no longer received that paycheck, your savings would be depleted quickly, and you may end up defaulting on your monthly expenses. It is the starting point to be financially free, and you will work from here.

Temporary Freedom

You will still need your income regularly in this second stage, but you can spend less than what you earn. You can then turn the extra over into a pool of savings. You want to get into this stage to build up good savings; otherwise, you will end up working forever because your lifestyle will depend on all the money you earn. As you start to save some of your income, even if that amount is small initially, consider investing your savings into a diversified investment that will provide you with a stream of income when it grows. Or, you have the possibility of starting a business on the side so that you can create a second source of income.

You will find that your freedom is going to grow along with your savings. Over time, you will have saved enough money so that you are comfortable. You may decide to take some time to travel for a year, go back to school, start your own business, switch jobs, or do other things that would be hard if you worked a full-time job. These are significant changes in your life, but these are not permanent changes. The freedom that comes with this stage is going to be temporary. Your income will usually exceed your expenses with this one, and you will not be able to remain free for too long.

Permanent Freedom

When you get to the third stage, the non-employment income you make will be higher than your total expenses. You would be able to quit working your regular job and still have enough from your business or your investment that you are still able to pay all your bills. Have a reliable income that keeps coming in so that you can enjoy life and gain permanent freedom, not one that will be gone quickly.

If you have a side business, you will still put in some labor to make it work. You will still be trading your time for money. But it is much different compared to what you would do working for someone else. The side job that you take over should represent your passion, and be something that you enjoy doing. It means that while you may be working at a side job, you will enjoy it, and you will feel like you are free.

Having fulfillment is the entire point of financial freedom. It's all about having the independence to choose how your daily routine will go, and it will allow you to design a better life while being able to spend your energy, money, and time in a more meaningful way. This could include investing, starting a side business, or doing something else that you enjoy that brings in money.

Luxurious Freedom

This is a stage that is not going to be achieved by very many people. This is where you can have enough of a passive income that you can spend it freely. Your income will exceed the expenses that you have by a large margin to live the lifestyle that you would like without putting in much more work.

It is a challenging time to accomplish. You will have to work hard at your passive income, and perhaps have a few different sources so that you can earn enough to make this work. You have a choice. You can choose to get your passive income to a point where you can cover the bills and then stop, and hope you don't go backward. Or you can work a bit longer and end up with the luxurious freedom that we just talked about.

Do you want financial freedom?

There are three main questions that you should ask yourself. These include:

- Are you happy with the lifestyle that you have right now?

- Have you found a job that has good work to life balance?

- Do you enjoy the job that you do and enjoy the purpose of your daily routine?

These are hard questions that you have to answer, but they will help you determine your thoughts about gaining financial freedom. There are three categories that you can split these into. First, you have to check whether your work is meaningful. Some individuals like their jobs and see no reason why they should stop working. This is just fine because you can work while also being financially free.

The second category is that work is okay for you. You do not particularly enjoy the job, but it is something that you do because it is something that you don't completely despise, which will pay the bills.

If you are in this second situation, your preferred level of freedom financially should be inversely related to the amount of disdain that you have for your work. It is up to you to work harder to increase the amount of savings you have to have more control, and even change careers if you would like.

And finally, you could fall into the third group where you find work boring and somewhat terrible. For this group, financial freedom should be high on your priority list. If you hate the job you are in, it should be easy to make sacrifices to find a way to escape. This would include working a second job, moving somewhere with a lower cost of living, and cutting unnecessary expenses. Spend this time saving all the money that you can so that you can change jobs.

By focusing on this freedom, the perspective that you have is likely to change. You will go from sludging through many more years at a job you don't like to design the life that you would like to have. Remember that you will be more likely to see success when you can devote all your energy, time, and money to that goal.

During this point, time, rather than money, is the most valuable asset that you have. If your time at that job makes you miserable, it is time to save money to quit your job.

CHAPTER 2:

Habits and Mindset of The Financially Free

Financial freedom is coming from within you. It is why you need to invest in yourself. You need to take care of your mind and body because it is where the energy to get financial freedom comes from. Our self is what has the conscious and subconscious mind.

Certain things in your life will need to change in your life to make sure you are communicating positively with your subconscious mind.

Positive Thinking

As much as having positive thoughts seems easy, it is not. As human beings, we have the tendency always to think the worst of any situation. Our minds are geared towards seeing the faults rather than seeing the right things. Most times in our lives, we have missed out on many good things because we're focused on the wrong things. Be sure that your mind will always look for what you are used to. If you are used to seeing the wrong and harmful side of every situation, then when things happen, the negative results will hit you first. And most of the time, you will be so consumed by these negative thoughts that you will not take time to review the positive results.

Habits

If you have bad habits like always thinking negatively and procrastinating, then you need to change immediately. The good thing about a bad habit is it can be replaced with a good one. It will be easy to replace bad habits if you are willing to work towards replacing them. The best way to replace these bad habits is to start practicing good habits regularly. With time you will find yourself practicing these good habits as a norm.

Cultivate good habits like:

- Having positive thoughts about yourself, your money, and your work

- Setting goals for yourself

- Being accountable for your actions

- Learning to engage with people well

- Working on getting results and not just for the sake of it

- Living within your means

- Having savings

Remember that these habits are what the subconscious mind is going to record. Many financially free people are described to be people with good habits. They always have habits that set them apart and make them attain their success. You will find all of them have goals and always think positively. They have taught themselves and commissioned their minds and bodies only to perform these tasks, and never allow themselves or anyone around them to pick up bad habits because they know their impact.

Self-discipline

Being self-disciplined means having control over your life to do what you are required to do. At the time, it should be done whether you feel like doing it or not. To achieve good results in life, you need to be disciplined. Cultivating good habits and having good thoughts requires a lot of discipline.

You are also working towards financial freedom, which means you will be handling a lot of money. If you are not disciplined, you will squander all the money and have even more debts than before.

You know how life works. The more money you make, the more needs you get. Most times, the needs increase because we want to change our lifestyle.

As much as our lifestyles change, we need the discipline to take care of the money we are making and the assets we are acquiring.

Discipline will help you stick to your goals and make sure you achieve them. When you look at people with poor mindsets, you see no discipline in what they do. They do not meet their goals and deadlines, and they are not accountable for the things they do.

But people with a wealthy mindset are very disciplined. You will see them cultivating good habits in their lives, and they live by them. They set reasonable goals and deadlines, and are disciplined to make sure they achieve them. Their minds are set towards achieving something, and they know that discipline will keep them on track. Most of these people, when asked, will tell you that they have a daily schedule that they follow, and no minute of their day is wasted.

Knowledge

People geared toward financial freedom are always looking to learn something new. They are aware that the world is dynamic, and things change from time to time. So, they make sure they always know what the new version of something is. They always want to know what other methods they can employ to make their business successful.

As they keep learning and upgrading, their subconscious mind will register their interest in what they are doing, and they will be successful in it.

Poor mindset people will always stick to one way of doing things. They are lazy, so they do not want to think of better ways of changing the system they have in place. Investing in better equipment, and personnel to them is a lot of work that is money-wasting. They remain with the same methods even after they are outdated, and with time their businesses no longer produce quality products that consumers are looking for.

Invest in Your Health

You cannot enjoy your financial freedom if your health is failing. Do not lose yourself in your work and compromise your health. Donkey work is not what will get you to financial freedom. It is all in mind. How you set your mind will determine your success. You can be working hard, and your mindset is in the wrong place, so you do not achieve results.

You need to take enough rest and be physically active. Watch what you eat and what information you consume. Do not allow yourself to be stressed. Go for regular check-ups, and follow the directives of the doctor. Financial freedom requires a lot of energy. Having a positive mindset also requires a lot of energy. Always look out for your health so you can have this energy you need to grow.

Be Your Own Cheerleader

Cheer yourself on as you go. When you start new projects as you progress in achieving a goal, each time you have a win when pitching ideas, cheer yourself on. Congratulate yourself when you have won, no matter how big or small.

Be your biggest supporter. This is going to help you tune a positive mindset. Your senses will be helping you to progress in your life. The subconscious mind will pick on your enthusiasm and manifest success in your life. It will help when you see yourself as a winner in your own eyes.

People with poor mindsets often tend to be their number one hater. When things do not go well, they think things like, "I knew I wasn't going to make it," or "I am not good enough to do that." They hinder their growth themselves with their own thoughts and actions, and the subconscious mind manifests their thought failure.

Be Goal-Oriented

Always set goals for yourself. Goals will help you know what you want to achieve. Without goals, you will be working blindly because you will not know what you want to have achieved by the end of a specific time or project. The best way to set goals is to have long-term and short-term goals.

Be assured that your subconscious mind is going to note your goals. It is going to feed on your conscious mind what you are planning to achieve. Then it will begin to manifest these goals in your life. They will come to pass one after another.

But it will be hard to achieve anything if you have no idea what you are working towards. Setting goals will help you envision what you want, and the subconscious will record it. Your mindset will also be set towards achieving the goals.

There is no good feeling like that of achieving goals. See salespeople congratulating themselves and celebrating when they meet their weekly or monthly goals. Meeting their goals means earning more money because of commissions and other benefits. Now imagine how much you can achieve if you set reasonable goals and work towards them. Your path to financial freedom will be clearer now that you visualize how you want to get there.

Have a Plan

A plan will help you organize your thoughts, and know precisely how you will manage your financial freedom. You are going to avoid being confused and stagnant, not knowing what move to make next.

By the time you are making a plan, you will already have your goals written out. The plan is your execution strategy. How you intend to achieve your goals. With a plan, you will also have the opportunity to visualize how you are going to achieve your goals. You can map out your strategies and see how you want to work. All this will be registered in your subconscious mind. And with the right mindset, you will achieve them. Be good and generous to people

You may have the right attitude towards getting your financial freedom, but you will not reach far if you are not good to people. No man is an island. You will need people to hold your hand and help you on this journey. They could be the people that will help you with the finances you need. Or the people that will help you produce and sell your products. Either way, it is essential to be fair and generous to all of them.

Always have a generous heart. Have the conviction in you to help others succeed. This goodwill is not going to go unnoticed. It is like you are sowing a good seed in your life, and it will reap good things.

Be Accountable

Always account for everything you do. Account for money used to fund a project, money received from salaries and assets. Be a good manager. Know that you will be blessed with more when your subconscious notes that you are working at managing the little that you have.

Find someone that has achieved financial freedom or is working towards it. These are the best people to help you because they know what you need to work on to attain financial freedom.

Organization

Organize your thoughts and your plans. This is the best way to make sure you are not confusing your subconscious mind. You will not have different thoughts and ideas that are not in a particular order. It is good to organize them by writing them down. When you are looking at them, your mind will now pick up the points. Before, when they are just thoughts, they may sound and feel technical. But when you write them down, you will be able to understand them better. And you will not forget about an idea or a goal you had.

You can write them in your journal, diary, or vision board. Draw diagrams, use different colors, have graphs. Make your work exciting and colorful, so when you look at it, you get excited. The subconscious mind will note this excitement. It will change your mindset to your plans and goals.

They will stop feeling bulky and unachievable, and you will have confidence that you can do it. But make sure the thoughts flow from what you want to achieve first to last.

CHAPTER 3:

Stocks Vs Options

There is a big difference between options and stock.

S tock represents partial ownership of the company, implying that you are usually a part of the company when you purchase a stock. On the other hand, options trading is merely any ownership of a particular company; it is a contract involving a trader and another party that allows the trader to purchase or sell a certain amount of stock at a specific price within a particular period. The market may be so volatile, but the strike prices are so high, and when the market activities are depicted to be calm, the strike prices may eventually be so down.

The following are some of the major differences between options and stock:

- Options tend to expire, as detailed by the expiration dates. While stocks are much long-lasting since they are properties of the company and bear no expiration dates. Therefore, stock trading is likely to happen for a longer period as compared to stock trading.

- Options derive the actual value from the value of the other assets involved during options trading. In contrast, stocks have a definite actual value that is fully recognized by the company in question.

- In the options trading activities, traders have the full rights of the value amount. On the other hand, stock trading gives the traders full ownership of the property involved during trading activities.

- In options trading, the market predictability does not necessarily depend on the rates of supply and demand levels than stock trading. With this in mind, the options trader is unlikely to predict what happens to the market, but he/she can, however, check on the market's volatility.

- Options are much cheaper than stock. Money is so fundamental in trading and is always the biggest motivation in any trading activity. Options are less expensive since the trader gets to acquire 100 shares of the equity during trading. Moreover, the cost of grasping an option contract is much cheaper as compared to purchasing and the underlying stock, and the trader acquires more amounts of benefits as compared to stock trading.

- Options are usually a great leverage tool in maximizing the amounts of profits gained during a particular trading period compared to stock trading. This is evident in the collection of various amounts of premiums during the issuance of contracts hence increasing the amounts of profits collected in options trading compared to stock trading.

- Options trading is much good at flexibility compared to stock trading, as evident in its tactical operations that frequently happen in various trading activities. Traders can make smaller investments that lead to good amounts of profits, and fewer risks involved during a particular period. On the other hand, stock trading calls for good investments with multiple amounts of risks over an unspecified period.

- Another point is that options have a great chance of limiting the risks that are likely to be involved during trading than stock trading, where risk is pretty much unlimited during the unspecified period of trading.

- Options trading can better for you if your timing is okay, and as an options trader, you will be able to acquire larger amounts of profits during the contract compared to when you would be involved in options trading.

- Options trading allows a particular option trader to bet where the market will not go, an activity that is not allowed in stock trading. The advantage of this opportunity is that there are higher chances of success than betting on where the market will go.

CHAPTER 4:

Basics Of Options

The call option offers the holder the right to purchase the stock, and the put option offers the holder the right to sell the stock. See the call option as a down payment for a futuristic purpose.

Example of a Call Option

A prospective homeowner sees the rise of new development. That person may want the right to buy a new house in the future but will only want to exert that right once other developments in the area have been made.

The prospective home buyer will gain from the option of buying or not. Imagine they can purchase a call option from the developer to purchase the home at probably $400,000 at whatever point in the following three years. Oh, they can, because it's a non-refundable deposit. Usually, the developer wouldn't offer such an option for free. The prospective home buyer has to contribute a down-payment to keep that right locked.

As far as an option is concerned, this cost is referred to as the premium. It is the price of an option contract. In the home example, the deposit may be $20,000 paid by the purchaser to the developer. Assume two years have gone by, and new developments are underway, and zoning has been approved. The home buyer exerts the option and decides to buy the home at $400,000 because that's the contract he has bought.

The market value of the home may have been doubled to $800,000. The buyer pays $400,000 because the down payment is locked at a pre-determined price. In an alternative scenario, let's say zoning approval doesn't come through till year four. This is one year after this option has expired. Now the home buyer has to pay the market price since the contract is expired already. In either case, the developer will keep the initial $20,000 collected.

Example of Put Option

If you own your home, you're probably familiar with buying homeowner insurance. Think of the put option as an insurance policy. A homeowner purchases a homeowner's policy to protect his home from damage. They pay a certain amount known as the premium for a particular period, let's say a year. The policy has a face value and provides security to the insurance holder if the home is destroyed.

What if your asset was a stock or an index investment instead of a home? Comparably, if an investor needs insurance on his index portfolio (S&P 500), he can buy put options. The investor might fear that the bear market is close and may not be willing to lose more than 10 percent of its long position in the S&P 500 Index. If the S&P 500 is currently trading at $2,500, he/she may buy a put option that gives the right to sell the index at $2,250, for instance, at any point during the next two years.

If the market collapses by 20% (500 points on the index) in six months, he or she would have made 250 points by being willing to sell the index at $2250 while trading at $2000, a total loss of just 10%. Even though the market hits zero, the loss will only be 10% if this option is retained. Again, buying the option will have a cost (the premium) and, if the market does not collapse during that time, the maximum loss on the option is only the premium that was spent.

CHAPTER 5:

The Time Value

Every options contract has a time value, but it's also subject to time decay. Time value is the option's price that comes from the amount of time remaining until the option expires. The time or extrinsic value is not exact and can change based on the option's price relative to the market. To give an example, the more an option goes into the money, the less it's impacted by time decay. But one thing is certain; all options are impacted by time decay. Simply put, this means that the price of the options will decline as time passes.

For sellers of options contracts, time decay is their best friend. That makes it more likely the options will expire worthlessly, and the option won't be exercised.

For buyers of options contracts, time is your enemy. You are looking to profit before time runs out. Whether or not you can do so will depend on whether or not the option is in the money or not.

Also, remember that time value is also called extrinsic value. The option also has intrinsic value. This is pricing derived from the underlying stock. Properties that can influence it include price and its properties like volatility. Extrinsic value comes from the outside.

When options are sold, they all have time value. They have time value because the more time there is until the option expires; the probability is increased that the option can go in the money at some point. And that is when the option is worth something. But as time passes and the expiration date starts getting closer and closer, the less time there is for a stock to make a move. Of course, stocks make significant moves over short periods and even over a day or two, but the shorter the time left to expiration, the lower the probability that this will happen.

Let's look at a few examples. It helps hold variables constant and isolate the variable you are trying to learn about to understand how things work. That is a fictitious example, but once you understand how things work by examining them in isolation, you will be far more capable of understanding how the pricing of real options is changing and why.

We will begin with a stock with a $100 share price with 30 days left before expiration in the examples. We will set the implied volatility to 15%.

Let's consider an option which is at the money. If the strike price was $100, the call and the put for this option are priced at $1.78 and $1.76, respectively (remember to multiply by 100 to get the actual price you would have to pay to buy the option or the price you'd get selling the option).

Now let's see how time decay impacts the option prices. Simply moving to 20 days left to expiration, we find that the price of the call and put options have declined to $1.45 and $1.44, respectively. Both have declined because the strike is equal to the market price, and the only thing impacting the price of the option is time decay. With only 20 days left to expiration, the options have less time value. At this point, 100% of the option value is extrinsic, determined by time value.

Now let's shift the clock again to 10 days to expiration. Now the call option has dropped to $1.03, and the put option is $1.02. At seven days to expiration, the call option is $0.86, and the put option is $0.85. Moving to 3 days to expiration, the call option and put option are both priced at $0.56. Finally, one day to expiration, the call and put option are both worth $0.32.

Time decay works exponentially. In practice, it means that the closer you get to the expiration date, the faster the option decays' extrinsic or time value.

But let us consider what would happen if the option went in the money, right at the last moment. First, consider what would happen if the stock price went up to $102 a share. In that case, it means the call option is "in the money." We find that the price of the call jumps to $2.00. The put would be virtually worthless.

On the other hand, the stock price dropped by $2; instead, it would be the put that would be priced at $2.00, and the call would be virtually worthless.

Time decay always impacts options, except toward the end, the intrinsic value (see below) can overwhelm it. The degree to which it does depends on how far in the money the option price has moved.

Now let us consider an in the money option. First, we'll consider a put option, and we'll say the stock price is $98 a share, with a strike price of $100. With 30 days left to expiration, the put option is $2.91. The call option is $0.94. So, the call option, which is out of the money, is a comparative bargain, and if you are expecting the stock to rise over the next 30 days, it could be a good move to buy that call option.

If nothing else changes at 20 days to expiration (the stock price of $98, strike price of $100), the call option is priced at $0.65, and the put option is $2.64. It is an important note, so even though the put option is in the money, we see a price decline. This happens as a result of lost time value.

At ten days to expiration, the prices of the call and put have dropped to $0.31 and $2.30, respectively. At seven days, the put option is $2.19, and the call option is $0.20. Finally, with two days left to expiration, the put option is $2.02, while the call option is a mere $0.02.

The same thing would happen to a call option in the money if everything, but time decay was held constant. The call option will still have some value before expiration, but it would steadily lose it. If the stock price were $102, and we had a call option that has a strike set at $100, the option price on the following remaining time frames: 30, 20, 10, 7, and 3 days to expiration, would be: $2.98, $2.68, $2.33, $2.21, and $2.05.

The takeaway lesson is that the time value of an option always decreases.

CHAPTER 6:

Time Decay

If an option is valued so that it is the same as the share price, or if it is out of the money, time decay will have a significant influence over the value of an option at any given time. For an option that can be said to be in the money, the influence of time decay will be much less. The closer you get to the expiration date; the time value exerts less influence on the option's overall price. In that case, it's going to be more influenced by implied volatility and the underlying share price.

Options prices are determined in part by the price of the underlying stock. But options prices are also influenced by the time left to expiration and some other factors. We will go over all the different ways that the price of a given option can change, and what will be behind the changes. It has 0 intrinsic values if an option can be the same as the market pricing or not be ideal. It would have to be priced in the money to have any intrinsic value.

- For a call option, if the market price is lower than the strike price or the same, the option will have no pricing at all from the intrinsic value. Once the share price is higher than the price used to trade shares via the option, it will have intrinsic value.

- For a put option, once the share price is at or above the strike price, it will have 0 intrinsic values. If the share price is lower than the strike price, then it will have some value from the stock. This is called intrinsic value.

Even when an option is at or out of the money, the underlying stock price has some influence that can change the value of the option. The amount of influence that the item's market price known as the stock has on the price of the option is given by a quantity called delta. You can read the value for delta by looking at the data for any option you are interested in trading.

For call options, a decimal number ranging from 0 to 1 is given and a negative value for put options. It's given as a negative value for put options because this reflects the fact that if the stock price is found to increase, the price of a put option will be reduced. In contrast, if the stock price declines, the value of the put option will increase. It's an inverse relationship, and thus, the delta is negative for put options.

To understand how this will play out, let's look at a specific example. Suppose that we have a $100 option. That is, the strike price is set to $100. If the underlying stock price is $105, the delta for the call option is 0.77.

That means that if the dollar value of the stock increases by $1, the option's value will rise by approximately 77 cents. This is a per-share price change. So, for the option that you are trading, there are 100 underlying shares. So, a 77-cent price rise would increase the value of the option by $77.

For a put option with the same strike price, the option would be out of the money because the share price is higher than the strike price. In this case, for the put option, the delta is given as -0.23. That means that the put option would lose approximately $23 if the share price went up by $1. On the other hand, if the share price dropped by $1, the put option would gain $23.

The intrinsic value of the call option described in this theoretical exercise would be $5 per share. The option's total cost would be $6.06 per share, reflecting the fact that the call option has $1.06 in extrinsic value. In contrast, the put option has zero intrinsic value. It has almost the same extrinsic value, however, at $1.03.

Mathematical formulas govern option prices, so it's possible to estimate the option price ahead of time. Some many calculators and spreadsheets are available free online for this purpose.

To take an example, at four days to expiration, a $100 strike price on an underlying stock when the market price is set equal to $110 per share will have $10 in intrinsic value with $0.56 in extrinsic value and a total price per share of $10.56. So, the price is heavily weighted to the underlying price of the shares. However, theta is -0.23, meaning that on a per-share basis, the option will lose $0.23 in value at the market open the following day, all other things being equal. Of course, all other things are not equal, and changes in share price and implied volatility may wipe that out or add to it.

The important thing to do is check theta every afternoon so you can estimate what the cost is going to be for holding the option overnight. Time decay is an exponential phenomenon, so it decays faster the closer you get to the expiration date. The trader's important path is knowing when other factors are going to be more important than time decay. You are not only going to sell off your option because it's going to lose value from time decay the following morning.

You will also see the risk-free rate quoted for an option. This is the interest rate that you could earn on an ideal safe investment. Generally speaking, this would be the interest you could earn from a 10-year U.S. treasury throughout the option. In regular times, this is an essential factor to consider. Rising interest rates (that is significantly rising) can lower the value of options. In recent years, interest rates have been very low, and changes in interest rates have been small and very conservative. So, at present, at least, this is not something to worry about.

CHAPTER 7:

Volatility Strategies

As an options trader, you need to learn about the variables that can affect an option's price and the INS, and outs of implementing the right strategy. A stock trader who is familiar and good with predicting future stock price movement might think that shifting to options trading is easy, but it's not. There are three changing parameters that an options trader must deal with: the underlying stock's price, the time factor, and volatility.

The price of an option is also called the premium, and the pricing is per share. The option seller receives the premium, which gives the buyer any right that comes with the option. The buyer is the one paying the premium to the seller, and they can exercise this right or allow the option to expire without any worth in the end. The buyer is obliged to pay the premium whether the option is exercised or not, which means the seller will keep the premium, in the end, no matter what.

Let's have a simple example. A buyer paid a seller for purchasing rights to stock ABC for 100 shares, and a strike price at $60. The contract expires on June 19. If the option position becomes profitable, the option will be exercised by the buyer. If it does not seem to bear profit, the buyer can just let the contract expire. The seller then keeps the premium.

There are two sides to the premium of an option: its intrinsic and time value. You can compute an option's intrinsic value by getting the difference between the strike price and the stock price. For the call option, it is the stock price minus the strike price. For the put option, it is the strike price minus the stock price.

To value an option, at least theoretically, you will need to consider multiple variables such as the underlying stock price, volatility, exercise price, time to expiration, and interest rate. These factors will provide you with a reasonable estimate of the fair value of an option that you can incorporate into your strategy for maximum gains.

The value of puts and calls are affected by underlying stock price movements straightforwardly. That means when the price of a stock rises, there should be a corresponding rise in call value as well since you can purchase the underlying stock at a reduced price compared to the market's, while there is a price decrease input.

There should be an increase in the value of put options when the stock price dives, and a decrease in call options since the put option holder can sell the stock at above-market prices. This pre-set price you can sell, or buy is called the option's strike price or its exercise price. If the option's strike price gives you the advantage of selling or buying the stock at a cost that gives you immediate profit, that option is considered 'in the money.'

Volatility affects most investment forms to some degree, and as an options trader, you should be familiar with this element and how it affects options pricing. Volatility is the tendency of something to fluctuate or change significantly. In general investment, volatility refers to the rate a financial instrument price rises or falls.

A low volatility financial instrument has a relatively stable price. Conversely, a high volatility financial instrument is prone to dramatic price changes, either way. In general, financial market volatility can be broadly measured. So, when the market becomes difficult to predict, and prices keep on regularly and rapidly changing, the market is volatile.

Volatility can affect option pricing significantly. Many beginning options traders tend to ignore the implications, which can lead to huge investment losses.

Historical Volatility

Historical or statistical volatility is used to measure the changes in the price of the underlying option, so it's based on actual and real data. Let's refer to it as HV for the rest. HV shows how fast the stock price has moved. The higher HV is, the more the stock price has moved during a specific period. So, when a stock has a high HV, the price is more likely to move, at least theoretically. It's more of a future movement indication and not a real guarantee.

On the other hand, a low HV might indicate the stock price hasn't moved much, but it might be going in one direction steadily.

You can use HV to predict somewhat how much a security's price will change based on how fast it changed in the past, but you can't use it to predict an actual trend.

HV is measured over a certain period, such as a week, month, or year and you can compute for it in various ways.

Implied Volatility

Another type of volatility that options traders should be aware of is implied volatility or IV. Whereas HV measures a security's past volatility, IV is more of an estimate of its future volatility.

IV is a projection of how fast, and how much the stock price is likely to change in price. Many beginning traders focus on the profitability (difference in strike price and stock price), and the contract expiration when considering an option's price, but IV also plays a significant role.

You can determine an option's IV by considering factors such as the stock and strike prices, length of time before expiration, current interest rate, and HV. Since an option's IV may indicate how much the stock will change in price, the price gets higher when the IV itself increases. Because theoretically, more profit can be gained when there are dramatic movements in the price of the underlying stock. The price of an option can also change significantly even when the stock price remains the same, which is usually caused by its IV.

For example, ABC is about to release a new product, and speculations build-up that the company is about to announce it. The options' IV for stock ABC can be very high since there are expectations of significant movement in the underlying stock price. The announcement might be received well, and the stock price might go up, or the audience will be disappointed with the new product, and stock prices can drop quickly. In this scenario, the stock price might not move since investors will be waiting for the press release before buying or selling stocks. There will then be an increase in extrinsic value for both puts and calls rather than the stock price movement. This is one way that IV can affect option pricing.

If you're betting that a stock's price will dramatically increase once that announcement has been made, you may purchase 'at the money' call options to maximize probable gains for that increase. If ABC announced and was received well, causing the stock prices to shoot up, there would have been significant gains in the call options' intrinsic value. After the press release and the stock price movement, IV will be lower since it's predicted that the stock price won't change very soon. There will then be a substantial fall on the calls' extrinsic value, which would offset most of the profit you gained with the increased intrinsic value.

CHAPTER 8:

Four Primary Greek Risk Measures

Greeks is a term utilized in the options market to portray the various risk associated dimensions with taking an options position. Each risk variable is a sign of a flawed presumption or relationship of the option with another underlying variable. Traders use Greek qualities, for example, Theta, Delta, and others, to evaluate options risk and oversee option portfolios.

- The 'Greeks' allude to the different components of risk that an options position entails.

- Greeks are utilized by options portfolio and traders' managers to hedge the risk and comprehend how their profit and loss will carry on as prices move.

- The most regular Greeks incorporate the Gamma, Delta, Vega, and Theta, which are the first partial subsidiaries of the options pricing model.

Greeks entail numerous factors. Every last one of these factors/Greeks has a number related to it, and that number enlightens traders concerning how the option moves or the risk related to that option.

The value or number related to Greek changes after some time. Modern options traders may ascertain these qualities every day to survey any progressions that may influence their outlook or position or check if their portfolio should be rebalanced. The following are a few of the primary Greeks traders take a look at.

Theta

Theta means the rate of change among the time and option price - in some cases known as an option's time decay. Theta shows the sum an option's price would diminish as the time to expiration diminishes, all else equivalent. For instance, assume an investor is long an option with a theta of -0.50. The option's price would diminish by 50 cents daily, all else being equal.

Theta increments when options are at-the-money, and diminish when options are in-and out-of-the-money. Options closer to lapse likewise have quickening time decay. Long puts and long calls will normally have negative Theta; short puts and calls will have positive Theta. By contrast, an instrument whose worth isn't dissolved by time, for example, a stock, would have zero Theta.

Vega

Vega implies the rate of change between the underlying assets' implied volatility and an option's value. It demonstrates the sum of an option's value changes, given a 1 percent change in implied volatility. A Vega of 0.10 shows the option's worth is relied upon to change if the implied volatility changes by 1 percent.

Because expanded volatility infers that the underlying instrument is guaranteed to meet extreme values, a rise in volatility will consistently build an option's value. Alternately, a reduction in volatility will adversely influence the value of the option. Vega is at its most extreme for at-the-money options that have longer times until expiration.

Greek-language nerds will call attention to that there is no genuine Greek letter named Vega. Different hypotheses about how this symbol, which takes after the Greek letter nu, found its way into the stock-trading language.

Delta

Delta means the rate of change between the option's cost and a $1 change in the underlying asset's price. The price sensitivity of the option comparative with the underlying. The Delta of a call option has a range somewhere in the range of zero and one, while the Delta of a put option ranges between zero and a negative one. For instance, assume an investor is long a call option with a delta of 0.50. In this manner, if the underlying stock increments by $1, the option's cost would hypothetically increment by 50 cents.

For options traders, the Delta likewise represents the hedge ratio for making a delta-unbiased position. For instance, if you buy a standard American call option with a 0.40 delta, you should sell 40 shares of stock to be hedged entirely. Net Delta can also be used to get the portfolio's hedge ratio.

Less basic utilization of an option's Delta is the present probability that it will terminate in-the-money. For example, a 0.40 delta call option today has an implied 40% probability of completing in-the-money.

Gamma

Gamma means the amount of change between an option's Delta and the underlying asset's cost. This is called second-derivative price sensitivity. It shows the sum the Delta would change given a $1 move in the fundamental security. For instance, assume a financial specialist is a long one call option on speculative stock XYZ.

If stock XYZ increments or diminishes by $1, the call option's Delta will increment or decrease by 0.10.

Gamma is utilized to determine how steady an option's Delta is. A higher gamma shows that Delta could change extremely even little movements in the underlying's price. It is higher for options that are at-the-money, and lower for options in-and out-of-the-money and quickens in size as expiration draws near. Gamma values are commonly littler the further away from expiration dates; options with extended expirations are less sensitive to delta changes. As expiration draws near, gamma values are ordinarily more significant, as price changes have more effect on gamma.

Rho (ρ)

Rho implies the rate of change between an option's price, and a 1% change in the interest rate. This estimates sensitivity to the interest rate. For instance, expect a call option that has a rho of 0.05, and a cost of $1.25. If the interest rate ascends by 1%, the call option's estimation will increment to $1.30, all else being equal. The inverse is valid for put options. Rho is most prominent for at-the-money options with long times until termination/expiration.

Minor Greeks

Some different Greeks, which are not discussed often, are epsilon, vomma, lambda, speed, vera, ultima, color, and zomma.

These Greeks are second-or third subordinates of the pricing model and influence things, such as the change in Delta with a change in volatility. They are progressively utilized in options trading strategies as computer programming can rapidly process and record for these complex and sometimes obscure risk factors.

CHAPTER 9:

Options Contract

We will now introduce the concept of options contracts, and how they are used in the stock market. The most basic way to get involved in option involves buying options contracts based on bets you make on whether future stock prices will rise or fall.

An options contract is a pretty simple concept.

- It's a contract. That means it's a legal agreement between a buyer and a seller.

- It allows the purchaser of the contract to purchase or dispose of an asset with a fixed amount.

- The purchase is optional, so the buyer of the contract does not have to buy or sell the asset.

- The contract has an expiration date, so the purchaser must make the trade before the expiration date once they choose to exercise their right.

The purchaser of the contract pays a non-refundable fee for the contract. Some options contracts take place in all aspects of daily life, including real estate and speculation. A simple example illustrates the concept of an options contract.

Suppose you are itching to buy a BMW, and you've decided the model you want must be silver. You drop by a local dealer, and it turns out they don't have a stock. The dealer affirms he can get you by the end of the month. You say you'll take the car if the dealer can get it by the last day of the month, and sell it to you for $67,500. He agrees and requires you to put a $3,000 deposit on the car.

If the last day of the month arrives and the dealer hasn't produced the car, you're freed from the contract and get your money back. In the event he does deliver the vehicle at any date before the end of the month, you have the option to buy it or not. If you wanted the car, you could buy it, but of course, you can't be forced to buy the car, and maybe you've changed your mind in the interim.

The right is there but not the obligation to purchase. In short, no pressure if you decided not to push through with the car's purchase. However, if you choose to let the opportunity pass since the dealer met his end of the bargain and produced the car, you lose the $3,000 deposit.

In this case, the dealer, who plays the contract writer's role, must follow through with the sale based upon the agreed-upon price.

Suppose that when the car arrives at the dealership, BMW announces it will no longer make silver cars. As a result, the prices of new silver BMWs that were the last ones to roll off the assembly line skyrocket. Other dealers are selling their BMWs for $100,000. However, since this dealer entered into an options contract with you, he must sell the car to you for the pre-agreed price of $67,500. You decide to get the car and drive away, smiling, knowing that you saved $32,500 and sell it at a profit if you wanted to. The situation here captures the essence of options contracts, even if you've never thought of negotiating with a car dealer in those terms.

An option is a kind of bet. In the car's example, the dealer can deliver the particular vehicle you want within the stated period and at the agreed-upon price. The dealer is betting too. He bets that the pre-agreed cost is a good one for him. Of course, if BMW stops making silver cars, then he's made the wrong bet.

It can work the other way too. Let's say that instead of BMW deciding not to make silver cars anymore when your vehicle is being driven onto the lot, another car crashes into it. Now your silver BMW has a small dent on the rear bumper with some scratches. As a result, the vehicle has immediately declined in value. But if you want the car, since you've agreed to the options contract, you must pay $67,500, even though with the dent, it's only really worth $55,000. You can walk away and lose your $3,000 or pay what is now a premium price on a damaged car.

Another example that is commonly used to explain options contracts is purchasing a home built by a developer under the agreement that certain conditions are met. The buyer will be required to put a non-refundable down payment or deposit on the home. Let's say that the developer agrees to build them the house for $300,000, provided that a new school is made within 5 miles of the development within one year. So, the contract expires within a year. During the year, the buyer can go forward with the construction of the home for $300,000 if the school is built.

The developer has agreed to the price no matter what. So if the housing market in general and construction of the school, in particular, drive up demand for housing in the area, and the developer is selling new homes that are now priced at $500,000, he has to sell this home for $300,000 because that was the price agreed to when the contract was signed.

The home buyer got what they wanted, being within 5 miles of the new school, with the home price fixed at $300,000. The developer was assured of the sale but missed out on the unknown, which was the skyrocketing price due to increased demand. If the school isn't built, and the buyers don't exercise their option to buy the house before the contract expires at one year, the developer can pocket the $20,000 cash.

In the car case, the buyer is hoping to get the vehicle they want at what they perceive to be a bargain price, although if BMW stopped making silver cars, they might sell it to a third party and then get a white one from the dealer. However, in most cases, the buyer wants the car. That isn't the case when it comes to options with stocks.

On the stock market, we are betting on the future price itself, and the shares of stock will be bought or sold at a profit if things work out. The critical point is the buyer of the options contract is not hoping to acquire the shares and hold them for an extended period like a traditional investor. Instead, you're hoping to make a bet on the stock price, secure that price, and then be able to trade the shares on that price no matter what happens in the actual markets.

CHAPTER 10:

Securities

Everyone who wants to avoid being broke or living from payslip to payslip must have the right investment strategy. An investment strategy is a plan for making the money you already have to multiply to more money.

Suitable investments have to have liquidity, meaning that whatever you invest in has to be easily convertible into cash at hand. Investments are risky, though, meaning that it's not guaranteed to always get your intended profits because, at any time, your assets can devalue. Therefore, it is essential to carefully examine your investments and see how much it's likely to yield; this is called looking at the potential returns. Looking through all these possibilities will help a person determine what type of investment to go for.

An investment strategy is best if it works to meet your needs. Do not go for investment only because it's trending; it may not work for you. Going for what works for you will ensure that you stick to your investment for long, and swayed away by other trends. The best way to find an investment that works for you is by getting something that defines you, and that would be something you patient about.

It is good for young people to take more risks in investments by going for high growing stock investments. While someone who is about to retire, they must take fewer risks and distribute their assets to bonds.

A security type is the kind of investment you hold, and it should always be diverse.

Cash and Bank Security

This type has very high liquidity because you are dealing with cash at hand that you take to the bank and withdraw at will. It has a low risk because unless you need the money, it is safely kept at the bank. However, this means that it has no potential for growth, and can even lose its value if there is inflation. The most significant advantage with this, however, is that you have access at any needed time. Banks also offer emergency funds, and therefore in case you urgently need money, you do not have to wait for long.

Certificate of Deposit

The liquidity in this is low because you cannot withdraw cash whenever you want. You can only get the money after the agreed time with the bank. The risk is low because the money is safely kept at the bank. However, its growth potential is very minimal since it has a specified rate of interest. This means that your money is lying in a bank waiting for a specific interest rate instead of taking chances elsewhere. The growth rate is so low and not worth the time you waited to get the interest.

Stocks

Whenever people think about investments, they think of stocks. The liquidity is high because you get to buy shares from a company and share their profits. You can purchase shares from one or as many companies as possible, and therefore get to enjoy a certain percentage of their earnings. The risk is medium because you are also involved with their losses as much as you want the profits. Thus, this means that you should not expect to be paid when the company you have shared with is not making profits. However, all investments go through this uncertainty; no single investment won't have a loss risk. The potential for growth in this is very high as you grow, the more the company grows. Every company's objective is to yield profits, and therefore companies will continue putting their best foot forward to make sure they do not incur losses. The more they work on this, the more their profits. The more the company's profits, the more your shares, therefore, why the potential growth is high.

Bonds

The liquidity in this is medium because it involves getting to give some of your money as a loan to a company or government. Then after the agreed time, your money is returned to you along with the interest you agreed on. The interest rates may be very high or low, depending on whom you have loaned. If you lend big companies or treasury, you are much secured, and therefore the returns in this are small. The risk comes in because you may give loans to what is known as junk bonds, and you risk not being paid or having partial payments. However, since junk bonds do not guarantee security, they make sure to offer a little higher return than a large corporate that ensures security. The growth potential is medium because it depends on the profits you make from the payments.

Real Estate

The liquidity is low because it involves lands and buildings. Converting lands and buildings is dependent on the value the assets have accumulated over time. If you need to have cash from these investments, you have to make sure you are selling at a better price than you used when buying them. This makes the risk medium because they are assets, and may either maintain their value or grow. If they fail, it is a disadvantage to the investor, but if the assets increase in value, then the investor has made it. Growth potential is medium because of how long it takes to generate value finally.

Precious Metals

The liquidity is very high because it involves buying precious metals like gold and silver. When you buy precious metals, you can easily convert them into cash by selling them at an even higher price than you bought them. The risk is medium because the metals need a lot of proper handling to ensure that they do spoil, and also most buyers tend to buy at very low prices. The potential growth is medium because it depends on the available market and the demand as well.

Derivatives

The liquidity is medium. You can either convert your earnings quickly, depending on how accessible the stocks you bought are. Here you get to purchase stocks from another stock instead of making a direct purchase. And for this to happen, you have to believe that the stock you are buying will increase its value. The risk is very high because you depend on another stock to earn your profits without being directly involved. If the stock does not allow you to buy in a more valuable stock, then you are unlikely to make any value out of it. However, the growth potential is very high since you only get to buy from stocks with value.

It is important to be diverse in your investments; this means you do not settle on a particular type. If you can split your assets, you are in a better secure position. When there is a downfall in one sector, you can count on another industry. But if you hold all your assets in one industry and the sector goes down, you will significantly suffer as an investor because you will lose everything. Something else worth noting is that one should be careful with their investment as they get older. One mistake from such a person can lead them into a very desperate life after retirement.

Investing Strategies

Buy and Hold

This calls for thorough research before entirely going into any investment. After the research, you should settle for a long-term investment of like ten years. You should then buy this investment, and hold it irrespective of how many temptations that you may come through along the way to sell them. Sometimes it may be so tempting to sell it because the price you are being offered is a little tempting, but you should be able to resist. An investor should only sell if the rules for sticking to the stock are no longer favorable.

This may happen in that either there is a sign that the stocks are no longer maintainable. This could be because the company is taking a different strategy than what you signed up for, and there you get uncomfortable to continue. You may also sell only. If you have had enough before the end of the long-term and you want to opt-out. It should never be out of greed, thinking that what you are being offered is too good to resist because you do not know how much better you will get.

You may do significant research and have everything correctly figured out. You may yield your investments after the long-term you had invested in. However, when retirement sinks in, you need the money urgently because that's your only survival hope. The other downside is that you may have made the wrong choice all along. With a buy and hold strategy, you may make a lot of loss that will kick you out of the market even if unwilling to.

Value Investment

This means that you go for stocks that are more underestimated than the other stocks. In short, it means going for stocks that most people are unlikely to go for. This is risky but brave because you are not following the crowd. In doing this, you go for companies that are just beginning to grow, and have not attracted the big fish in the market; you can also go for only recently established companies. You can stick to this investment until you feel that you are doing quite well or have achieved more than you expected before eventually selling. This, however, does not come without a possible risk, as explained below.

Being an active trader makes you have easy, quick access to more significant returns. However, that also means that it's also very easy and fast to make losses as quick as it is to make profits. Therefore, it is usually recommended that you use small investments instead of putting in too much for this kind of trading because anything can happen. It is better to lose little than to lose hugely, and therefore, not taking the risk is very important.

Growth Investing

This means going for stocks in well-established companies; companies are already doing well and attracting many potentials. This means that everyone is already running for these investments, and they are doing pretty well. There is even evidence of how well the companies are doing. People investing in this have a lot of faith in this investment because they expect that it only keeps growing. People buying in this type of investment do not mind buying at a high price because they know that they will sell even more significantly than they bought it. Therefore, what happens here is that you go for big and well-known companies. These are companies that are well known and have been in the market for a long time.

The right investment strategy, however, still goes back to an individual. What works for an investor is very important instead of relying on what worked for others. It may have worked for others, but not work for you. However, it is good to involve all the strategies as you make decisions as an individual investor.

CHAPTER 11:

Debit And Credit Spreads

Debit Spread

A debit spread entails buying a high premium choice while offering a low premium choice in the same category and the same protection, which leads to debit from the trader's account.

Alternatively, a debit spread (usually utilized by beginners to option techniques) requires purchasing an option with a more significant premium and selling an alternative with a reduced premium. The place that the premium settled for the lengthy choice of the spread is much more than the premium gotten from the written choice.

A debit spread leads to a high quality debited, or maybe given, out of the trader's or perhaps investor's account whenever the position is opened compared with a credit spread. Debit spreads are used mainly to offset the expenses related to owning long feature positions.

For instance, a trader buys, one could place a choice with a strike price of $20 for $5, and also instantly sells one could put an option with a strike price of $10 for $1. Thus, he paid $4 and $400 for the swap. In case the trade is from the money, the max loss of his is lowered to $400 instead of $500.

Types of Debit Spreads

- Bear put spread requires two transactions and a bearish strategy, which are buying one at the money put option, and the selling of 1 on the money put option. This is done because the trader is betting that the associated asset's price movement will go down. Profit is earned when the associated asset's price is the same as the put option's strike price.

- Bull call spread, a bullish strategy that includes two transactions: buying one at the money call option, and selling 1 out of the money call option. A trader implements this strategy when they think that the associated asset's price movement will go up modestly. Profit is gained when the associated asset's price is the same as the short call option's strike price.

- Butterfly spread, a neutral strategy that involves three transactions whereby the trader buys 1 in the money call option, sells two at the money call option, and buys one on the money call option. Profit is gained when the price of the associated asset remained the same on the date of expiration.

- The reverse iron butterfly is a volatile strategy that involves four transactions. These transactions are selling 1 out of money put option, buying one at the money put option, buying one at the money call option, and selling 1 out of money call option. Profit is gained when the price of the associated asset falls.

Credit Spread

Spreads can be classified in different ways. Credit spreads are distributed strategies that involve total receipts of premiums, while debit spreads include total payments of premiums. It entails promoting a high premium choice while buying a low premium choice in the same category or the same security, which leads to a credit on the trader's account.

The premium got from the written choice is higher than the premium settled for the long option, leading to a high quality credited into the trader or maybe the investor's account whenever the position is opened. When traders or investors utilize a credit spread program, the maximum revenue will be the total premium. The credit spread leads to an income once the options' spreads narrow.

For instance, a trader tools a credit spread program by composing the 1st March call option with a strike price of $30 for $3 plus concurrently purchasing the 1st March call option with $40 for $1.

Since the typical multiplier on an equity choice is a hundred, the web premium received is $200 because of the swap. Moreover, the trader is going to profit when the spread tactic narrows. A bearish trader expects stock prices to reduce, therefore, and buys call choices (long call) in a particular hit cost and offers (short call) the same amount of call options inside the same category, and the same expiration in a reduced hit selling price. In comparison, bullish traders expect stock prices to increase, and consequently, purchase call options in a particular hit cost and promote the same call options.

Types of Credit Spreads

- Bear call spread, which is a beginner-friendly strategy. It employs a bearish outlook that relies on the price of the associated asset decreasing modestly. Profit is gained by finding the difference between the option premium and the commissions paid. Loss occurs when the asset price increases below the strike price.

- Bull put spread is a beginner-friendly strategy with a bearish outlook that substantially decreases the associated asset price. Loss occurs when the asset price drops below the strike price.

- Iron butterfly spread, which involves four transactions. The options trader is buying 1 out of the money call option, selling one at the money call option, buying 1 out of the money put option, and selling one at the money put option, all with the same expiration date and associated asset. This is a complex strategy that is not recommended for beginners.

- A short butter spread entails three transactions. The transactions are buying 1 out of the money call/put option, selling 1 out of the money call/put option, and buying one at the money call/put option with the same expiration date and associated asset. This is also a complex strategy that is not recommended for beginners.

CHAPTER 12:

Options Strategies: Going Long vs. Going Short

A s an options trader, you will often hear the terms going long or having a long position and going short or taking a short position. The positions are opposites. Both terms refer to what the investor owns, and what they need to own to be effective at options trading.

Having a short position means that the investor does not own the assets being associated with the option. For example, there may be an option for 100 shares, but the investor doing the selling does not own the shares.

Long Position

On the other hand, having a long position means that the investor owns the option's asset. For example, an investor who bought and added 100 shares to their portfolio has a long position. This investor likely bought this asset, which can be stock, commodity, or currency, expecting that the value will rise. This is known as having a bullish view. A bullish view describes an investor's characteristic of pursuing an asset with the feeling that it will appreciate because they wish to limit any potential losses.

There is another view that can affect if an options trader decides to hold a long position. The trader may try to make a profit, but the fall of an asset's value. This can be advantageous because the trader can obtain an option to sell that asset at a price that is advantageous to them.

The long position refers to whether or not the trader will hold a long call or long put option as it relates to options trading. This is dependent on the associated asset attached to that contract. Having a long call option means that the trader expects that the asset's price will go up so that he or she can benefit in that regard. The option allows the trader to buy that asset at the strike price to fulfill the upward trend.

With a long-put option, the trader expects the asset to depreciate so that he or she can purchase the right to sell that asset at a predetermined price.

In both cases, the long position does not in any way refer to the period. The focus is entirely on the associated asset and who owns it. The person who owns the asset is called the long position holder.

One of the biggest benefits of a long position is an option of this nature locks in the strike prices. Losses are limited because the trader can base his or her bets on historical market performance.

Unfortunately, there are disadvantages to going long. Firstly, the financial market may become volatile and cause abrupt price changes. This may not be for the benefit of the options trader. Secondly, the option may reach its expiration date before the advantage the options trader hopes to achieve is realized.

Simple Going Long Strategies

Of course, there are very complicated, going long strategies that can be employed, but it is best to start and get a lay of the land as a beginner.

Long Call

This strategy is considered by options traders who want to make a profit from an asset that increases in the price above the strike price. This is often considered so that the trader does not have to buy the asset outright to potentially profit without having to take on the significant risk of owning that asset.

This option can also afford the trader access to assets he or she cannot afford to purchase at that time. This is a common practice in accessing stock. Having the option to purchase is less expensive than purchasing the stock outright.

Here is a summary of how a long call works:

Outlook: Bullish.

Risk: The premium paid.

Potential profit: Unlimited. It increases as the price of the asset increases.

Break-even price: The sum of the strike price and premium paid (strike price + premium paid).

An example of a successful long call is as follows:

An option trader buys 100 shares of stock that he believes will increase in value within the next few months. Each share costs $20. He believes the shares will go up by at least $10. Therefore, he buys the option at a strike price of $20 plus a cost of $2 for each stock, which totals $22 per stock.

As long as the stock goes above $22, this long call option is profitable to the trader. For every dollar the stock goes higher, the trader will profit $100. As the stock price increases, so do the option value. Therefore, the trader can sell the option to lock in his profit.

The best thing about such an option is that the asset can infinitely increase in value, leading to massive profits. This is why long calls are a popular way to bet on rising stock prices.

In this case, this is also a risk that the trader will lose their investment in the cost of the premium and associated fees. The asset may not become advantageous before the expiration date arrives, and thus, the option becomes worthless to the trader.

Long Put

This type of option gives the trader the right to sell the associated asset at the strike price on or before the expiration date. The options trader makes a profit from the asset, decreasing to a price below the strike price. As you can see, this is very similar to the long call, and only differs in that the trader is betting on the fact that the asset's value will fall below the strike price on or before the expiration date.

Long puts are a great way of protecting the value of assets that you already own.

Here is a summary of how a long put works:

Outlook: Bearish (Falling prices).

Risk: The premium paid.

Potential profit: Unlimited. It increases as the price of the asset decreases.

Break-even price: The difference between the strike price and premium paid (strike price - premium paid).

An example of a successful long put is as follows:

A company is trading stock at $50 per share. An options trader feels that the price of this will fall to at least $30 per share within the coming months, and so seeks a put option with a strike price of $50 that had an expiration date of 2 months. He buys 100 shares and pays $150 to purchase each $50 share. The option is priced at $5 per share, and so the trader pays $500.

The trader was right, and the stock's price depreciated to $25 per share before the expiration date. With the current stock price, the trader with the put option will be in the money because the stock's intrinsic value has risen. Let's say that this value is now $1500. The trader can sell the stock for that price. The trader will make a profit of $1000 after removing his investment of $500.

This scenario's great advantage is similar to the advantage in the long call, hence why this too is a popular way of betting on declining stock values. As a result, a long put is a great option if the trader expects the asset's price to fall significantly before the expiration date arrives. If the price falls only a little or not, the trader may be in the money only slightly, which is not profitable, or worse, it may not even return the premium the trader spent.

Short Position

The second position in Options Trading is the short positions. It is the opposite of the long position explained. The investor anticipates a decrease in the price of the option to gain profit. Executing a short position is not as easy as when you buy an asset.

Using a short stock position as an example, the investor expects profit if the stock drops price. This is possible by borrowing some shares from a particular company's stakeholders while selling it at the current price.

With this, the investor has an open position for the number of shares they bought with the broken. Remember, this stock has a particular timeframe before it will be closed.

By chance, the stock price drops, the investor has the right to buy the number of stock shares lower than the total price he sold them.

The excess cash for this trade is the profit of the investor.

Most investors find it hard to understand the idea behind short selling; however, it shouldn't be complicated. To clarify this, the example below can make things clear for you.

Assuming the stock of NCE is currently sold for $50 per share. For some reason, you anticipate a fall in the stock price and decide to sell short of making a gain from your anticipation. How then should your short sale look like?

- You place a margin deposit as collateral to your broker to give you a loan of 100 stock shares.

- With the loaned shares given to you, you sell them at the price of $50 per share. With this, the share isn't yours anymore; however, in your account, you have $5,000 ($50 x 100 = $5000). In this situation, you are short of stock because you are in debt of 100 shares to your broker.

- Assuming your expectation that the price would fall happens gradually. After some weeks, the price dropped to $30 per share. Furthermore, you expect the price not to go any lower, so you decide it's time to close the sale.

- You then bought the 100 shares at the price of $30, amounting to $3,000. You decide to repay the 100 shares of stock you borrowed from your broker.

- With the 100 stocks, you could make a profit of $2,000 by activating a short trade. When your broker loaned you the shares, you received $5,000 ($50 x 100 = $5000), and after buying, you were able to pay back your loan amounting to $3,000. Amount received ($5,000) − Amount Paid ($3,000) = Profit ($2,000).

Short positions are usually given to accredited investors because it requires a high level of trust between the broker and the investor to execute this deal. It doesn't matter if the short is executed; the investor must place collateral that the broker will use in exchange for the loan you want to take.

Short Call

A short call position is activated when an investor sells a call option. The position is the opposite of the long call. The seller is in a better position to profit short call position is activated, and the value of the asset or stock drops.

Alternatively, when the investor triggers a put option, the seller profits if the option traded is higher than the predetermined option price.

Options trading comes with varieties of long and short positions for you to adopt during trading. A knowledgeable investor who understands all individual positions' advantages and disadvantages will always be ahead of the market.

However, if you are a new trader, don't rush to apply for these positions. Understand each position before making an effort to combine it into your trading strategy.

CHAPTER 13:

The Flexibility Of Options

Flexible trade options, or FLEX options, are non-standard choices that permit both the essayist and buyer to arrange different terms. Terms that are debatable incorporate the activity style, strike value, lapse date, just as different highlights and advantages. These alternatives also offer financial specialists the chance to exchange for a more significant scope with extended or disposed position limits.

- FLEX alternatives are a particular sort of choice contribution outrageous debatable adaptability.

- FLEX represents an adaptable trade choice.

- These alternatives don't have standard statement streams yet distribute cites just according to popular demand.

Understanding Flexible Exchange Option (FLEX)

FLEX alternatives were made in 1993 by the Chicago Board Options Exchange (CBOE). The other options focus on the counter (OTC) market of file choices and give clients greater adaptability. It currently exchanges on different trades just as the CBOE.

Besides permitting both the purchaser and vendor to tweak contract terms precisely as they would prefer, FLEX alternatives give different advantages. These advantages incorporate security from counterparty hazards related to over-the-counter exchange. The Options Clearing Corporation ensures exchanges (OCC), as are other trade exchanged choices.

The market is additionally increasingly severe and straightforward for expanded liquidity. An optional market permits purchasers and dealers to counterbalance positions before termination. This optional market evacuates a portion of the dangers of exchanging off-trade markets.

A huge contrast between FLEX alternatives and conventional choices is that FLEX options don't have a consistent statement stream. Subsequently, the age of a statement for FLEX options happens just when a solicitation for a quote (RFQ) is made.

In 2007, The CBOE propelled CFLEX, an Internet-based, electronic exchanging framework for file and value FLEX options. Merchants enter day by day arranges into the FLEX electronic book.

Parts of a FLEX Option Contract

The base size for a FLEX alternative is one agreement. Strike costs might be in penny increases, and may likewise be in what could be compared to a level of the hidden stock.

The portrayal of premiums might be in the estimation of explicit dollar sums and are ordinarily in penny increases or basic stock rates.

A termination date can be any business day and can be future-dated similar to 15 years from the exchange date. Lapse styles might be American or European. American lapse takes into consideration practice whenever before the agreement closes. European lapse grants practice just at the termination date.

Value FLEX choices, the two puts, and calls settle with the conveyance of stock portions whenever worked out. Record FLEX choices will settle in real money.

Position Limits for Flexible Exchange Options

There are no position limits for FLEX alternatives on important market files, including the Dow Jones Industrial Average, Nasdaq-100, Russell 2000, S&P 500, and S&P 100. Be that as it may, there are revealing prerequisites if position sizes surpass sure edges.

As far as possible for expansive based Index FLEX Options, other than those recorded above, are 200,000 agreements, with contracts being on a similar side of the market for each given list.

There are no position limits for value or ETF FLEX alternatives, even though there are announcing prerequisites.

CHAPTER 14:

Strangles Strategies

The strangle strategy will help you benefit from the trade no matter the direction of price movement. Here too, you will buy put and call options of an equal amount, and both of them should have the same expiration date. The only difference between strangle and straddle is that in the straddle strategy, both the options' strike prices were the same, whereas, in the case of strangle, the strike prices are different. The trader believes that there will be movement in a specific direction, or there is a greater chance for the stock to move in that direction. Still, even then, the trader wants to protect his position if there is a negative move. The two types of strangle strategies are the long strangle, and the other is the short strangle.

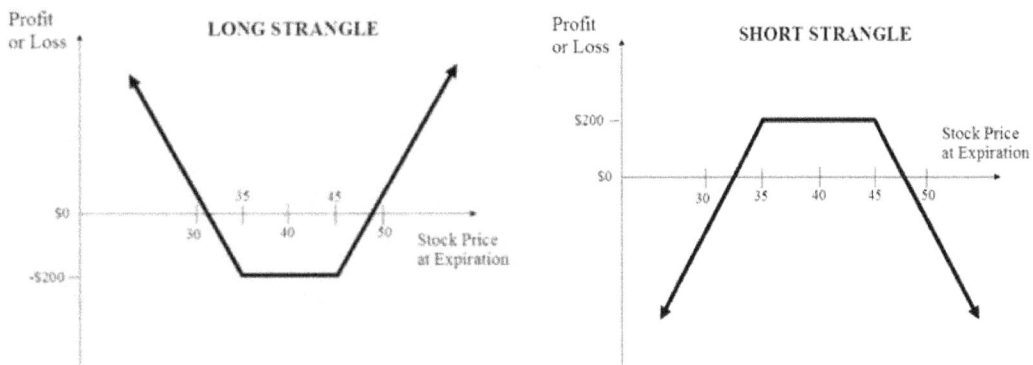

The long strangles main aim is to help you make a profit whenever the stock undergoes a huge change in price in either direction.

This strategy comprises one long put that has a lower strike price, and a long call with a greater strike price. The expiration dates of these options' underlying assets are the same, whereas the strike prices are different. This type of strategy is based on net debit, and it will be profitable if the price of the underlying stock decreases, and goes below the lower breakeven point or goes above the upper breakeven point.

On the upside, the potential for making profits with this strategy is unlimited, and on the downside, it is substantial. On the other hand, the potential loss in this type of strategy is capped by the strangles total cost and any commissions that you had to pay.

You will incur a loss with this strategy if you trade fewer volatile stocks because for the stock price to move beyond the put or the call, there has to be high volatility. Only seasoned veterans and higher-ups should approach using this strategy because it might seem relatively simple to you initially, but executing it in the right way is not everyone's cup of tea. Your forecasting ability should be sharp and advanced for you to profit from this strategy.

Traders usually implement this strategy when they think that there will be an abnormally huge move in the stock price because of a significant event or news. For example, if an earnings announcement is approaching, then you can consider running this strategy before that. But unless you are dead sure about that huge swing in price, I think you should stick to long straddle instead of long strangle. I know that it is costlier to run a straddle, but the breakeven points are closer than that of the strangle, and so the stock can outrun those points even when the move is not that huge.

What Are the Advantages of This Strategy?

Look at some of the advantages that this strategy has to provide you:

- The first advantage of the long strangle is that it is less expensive than the long straddle. Now, this strategy deals with out-of-the-money options, which you already know have a lower premium than the options that are at-the-money.

- The second advantage is that the maximum loss that a trader can incur with this strategy is limited. This maximum loss situation happens when at the time of expiration; the price of the underlying stock is trading in a range between the strike price of the call option, and the put option you just bought. In such a scenario, the options will reach their expiration, and they will expire worthlessly. The initial debit that you had to pay to enter the trade will be lost.

- The potential for profit in this strategy is unlimited, which is one of the most significant advantages. This happens when there is a huge move in the price of the underlying stock to crosses and goes beyond the strike price of either option.

One disadvantage associated with this strategy, and that is, to make a profit from this strategy, the movement has to be quite huge. Consider also the time decay because, with time, both the options lose their value, and the factor of time decay is double because of the involvement of both call and put options.

This strategy is quite similar to that with just one difference because a slight adjustment has been made to make this strategy cost-effective. To ensure that you bring home profits from this strategy, the increase in the call options' value has to be more than the decrease in the value of the put options. You can also make a profit when the increase in the value of the put options is more than the decrease in the value of the call options. The strike prices you choose for this strategy can be of any desired combination, but it is usually established near an at-the-money option towards the mid-point of the strike price.

You should also ensure that the stock has low implied volatility so that the price of the options is low, but there should be a probability for the stock to make an explosive move in a direction. Suppose you consider from your intuitive point of view. In that case, you will realize that implanting the strangle strategy is a very lucrative option because you will make a profit irrespective of the stock's direction of movement. But both of your selling and buying decisions have to be perfectly timed to benefit from this strategy truly.

In simpler terms, volatility expansion is one of the main things on which the strangle strategy's success depends. The sharp price movement can be brought about by anything like earnings reports, important announcements, or even a lawsuit's verdict. In some cases, the traders prefer to benefit from a low volatility situation and purchase the strangle at that time so that when after the announcement, the volatility increases, they can sell the option and make a huge profit.

But you have to decide whether you have to implement a long straddle or a long strangle, and the decision will have to be made after judging the probability of the stock to make a huge movement and the amount of the cost you want to bear.

The maximum risk is the net debit invested at the beginning of the strategy. The maximum reward is unlimited because the underlying stock can show downward or upward movement without any limits. To calculate the upside breakeven, add the net premium paid with the strike price. For the downside breakeven, subtract the net premium paid from the strike price.

CHAPTER 15:

Straddle Strategies

T his is a strategy you could use to profit if the stock rose high, and you also earned profit if the stock crashed. The strategy used to accomplish this is called straddles. These strategies are great for use in volatile markets.

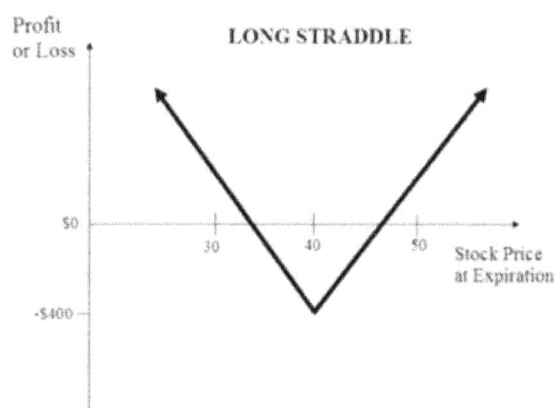

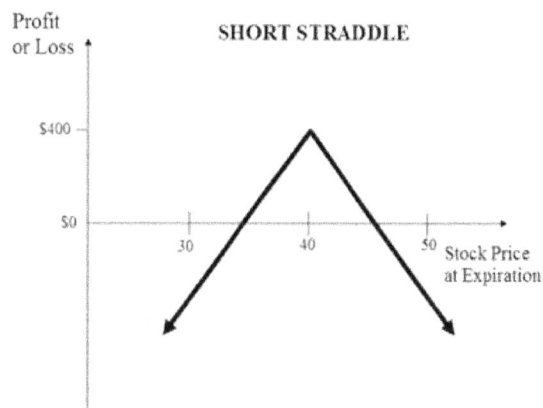

This is also a two-legged strategy designed to take advantage of price breakouts of stock, without regard to the breakout's direction. Like a strangle, a straddle will also involve buying a call option and a put option on the same stock, and with the same expiration date, simultaneously.

However, a straddle differs from a strangle in one key aspect. To set up a straddle, you will also set up the trade so that the call option and the put have the same expiration date. The chart for a straddle is shown below. This narrows down the range over which there are losses. Maximum loss on the trade would occur if the stock price were equal to the strike price at option expiration.

The same type of strategies should be employed when using straddles rather than strangles. This means you want to enter your position over a week's time frame up to maybe three or four weeks before a big event like an earnings call. Over the period between your purchase and the earnings call, the straddle will gain value from stock movements, regardless of whether the stock's price moves up or moves down.

If the stock price increases, the straddle's value will increase because of the call option that is a part of the trade. However, it could also lose value due to the put option that is a part of the trade. The price has to move one way or the other so that the share price is higher than the strike price + cost of the position or lower than the strike price minus the position's cost. Remember that for a straddle, the call option and the put option have the same strike prices.

For our example, we are entering the trade 21 days before expiration. The call is $6.93, and the put is $7.89, so the total cost to enter the position would be $14.92. Let's say that there is an earnings call when the option is five days to expiration.

Now, by 15 days to expiration, in anticipation of the upcoming earnings call, the share price might have moved a bit. Let's suppose that the market expects a good earnings call, so share prices are going up. If the share price went up to $237, this is a modest gain that, despite time decay, will help the value of the call option. It has risen from $6.93 to $7.36. However, the put option has lost some value due to time decay combined with the modestly higher stock price, and it's now going for $5.33.

Our plan, however, is to hold the position until the earnings call. Remember that earnings call also impact volatility. We are setting the implied volatility at 33% for this exercise, but as we get closer to the earnings call, that value will rise.

Now ten days to expiration, which would be five days to the earnings call in our scenario. The share price has risen to $240 share since the markets are expecting good news. Implied volatility has also increased to 37%. The call has jumped to $8.37, but the put is now down to $3.63.

There are only two days left until the earnings call, moving forward to just seven days to expiration. Now implied volatility has risen to 45%. The share price has increased steadily with the passing days and now stands at $245. Under these conditions, the call is $12.26, and the put is $2.25. The total value now is $14.51, and it cost $14.92 to enter the position, so we have a mild loss at this point, but it should be ignored. We need to hold the position until the earnings call.

Later that day, the stock is at $247, and the implied volatility has risen to 50%. The call is now $14.32, and the put is $2.30, so our position is now worth $16.62. Since it cost $14.92 to enter the position, we are now at a point of profitability to the tune of $16.62 - $14.92 = $1.70. If you wanted to, you could sell it now for a profit of $170. You'd find an eager buyer without a doubt because most traders would be anxious to get in on the trade before the actual earnings call.

Finally, we reach the earnings call. It beats expectations by a surprising margin, and the price of the stock jumps $23 a share in after-hours trading. At market open, the call option is worth $36.01, and the put is worth pennies on the dollar. At this point, the put option is worthless, but the call option has gone up so much in value that we are looking at a profit of $36.01 - $14.92 = $21.09 per share, putting us in a position where we can sell for a total profit of $2,109.

If the stock continued climbing the morning after the earnings call, which sometimes happens, we could earn even more profits. If it went to $280 a share by the afternoon, the call option would be worth $45. In that case, we'd have another $900 in total profits on the trade. Of course, you are taking some risk. The longer you hold the position. The stock might start declining a bit or stop rising. And if you hold it overnight, you are going to get hit with time decay. The put option is entirely worthless at this point, but it doesn't matter.

Suppose that instead, the price had plummeted. Our hypothetical company might have missed expectations by a large margin, and rather than rising by a huge amount, it could drop to $210 a share instead. The beauty of the straddle is that in this scenario, we make a profit as well. This time, the call option would be completely worthless on the trading day after the earnings call, but the put option would be worth $24.99, giving us about a $1,000 profit. The more the stock drops, the more profit we would earn. The same holds for a strangle, but remember that the call and put options have different strike prices, and there might be a wider range over which the stock needs to move to earn profits.

CHAPTER 16:

Covered Call

I t is a trading strategy for beginners, which is an excellent way to get started selling options. By covered, we mean that you've got an asset that you own that covers the potential sale of the underlying stocks. In other words, you already own the shares of stocks.

The basis of this strategy is that you don't expect the stock price to move very much during the options contract's lifetime, but you want to generate money over the short term in the form of premiums that you can collect. This can help you develop a short-term income stream; you must structure your calls carefully.

Setting up covered calls is relatively low risk, and will help you get familiar with many options trading aspects. While it's probably not going to make you rich overnight, it's an excellent way to learn the trade tools.

Benefits of Covered Call Options

- A covered call is a relatively low-risk option. The worst-case scenario is that you'll be out of your shares but earn a small profit, a smaller profit than you could have made if you had not created the call contract and sold your shares. However, you also get the premium.

- It allows you to create income from your portfolio in the form of premiums.

- If you don't expect any price moves on the stock in the near term, and plan to hold it long term, it's a reasonable strategy to generate income without taking much risk.

Risks of Covered Call Options

- Covered calls can be a risk if you're bullish on the stock, and your expectations are realized, and there is a price spike. In that case, you've traded the small amount of income of the premium with a voluntary cap of the strike price for the possible upside you could have had if you had held the stock and sold it at the high price.

- If the stock price falls, even though you still get the premium, it will be worthless unless they rebound over the long term. You shouldn't use a call option on stocks that you expect to be on the path to a significant drop in the coming months. In that case, rather than writing a covered call, you should sell the stocks and take your losses. Alternatively, you can keep the stocks to see if they recover over the long term.

Covered Calls Involve A Long Position

To create a covered call, you need to own at least 100 shares in one underlying equity. When you make a call, you will be offering potential buyers a chance to buy these shares from you. Of course, the strategy is that you're only going to sell high, but your real goal is to get the premium income stream.

The premium is a one-time non-refundable fee. If a buyer purchases your call option and pays you the premium, that money is yours. No matter what happens after that, you've got that cash to keep. If the stock doesn't reach the strike price, the contract will expire, and you can create a new call option on the same underlying shares. Of course, if the stock price does pass the strike price, the contract buyer will probably exercise their right to buy the shares. You will still earn money on the trade, but the risk is you're giving up the potential to earn as much money that could have been earned on the trade.

If the stock price doesn't exceed the strike price over the contract's length, you get to keep the premium, and you get to keep the shares no matter what.

In reality, in most situations, a covered call will be a win-win situation for you.

Covered Calls Are A Neutral Strategy

It is also known as a neutral strategy. Investors make covered calls for stocks in their portfolio, where they only assume small moves over the contract's lifetime. Moreover, investors will use covered calls on stocks that they expect to hold for the long term. It's a way to earn money on the stocks during a period in which the investor expects that the stock won't change much at a price and have no earning possible from selling.

How to Create a Covered Call Option

To create a covered call, you'll need to own 100 shares of stock. While you don't want to risk a stock that is likely to take off shortly, you don't want to pick a total dud. There is always someone willing to buy something, at the right price. But you want to go with a decent stock so that you can earn a decent premium.

You start by getting online at your brokerage and looking up the stock online. When you look up stocks online, you'll look at their "option chain," which will give you information from a table on premiums available for calls on this stock. You can see these listed under the bid price. The bid price is provided on a per-share basis, but a call contract has 100 shares. You have an option with the premium you want to charge. You can set any price you want. Of course, that requires a buyer willing to pay that price for you to make money. A more reasonable strategy is to look at prices people are currently requesting for call options on this stock. You can do this by checking the asking price for the call options on the stock. You can also see prices that buyers are currently offering by looking at the bid prices.

To sell a covered call, you select "sell to open."

An Example Of A Covered Call

Let's say that you own 100 shares of Acme Communications. It's currently trading at $40 a share. Over the next several months, nobody expects the stock to move very much, but you feel Acme Communications has solid long-term growth potential as an investor. You sell a call option on Acme

Communications with a strike price of $43 to make a little bit of money. Suppose that the premium is $0.78 and that the call option lasts three months.

For 100 shares, you'll receive a total premium payment of $0.78 x 100 = $78. You pocket the $78 no matter what happens.

Now let's say that the stock drops a bit in price over the next three months so that it never comes close to the strike price, and at the end of the three months, it's trading at $39 a share.

The options contract will expire, and it's worthless. The buyer of the options contract ends up empty-handed. You have a win-win situation. You've earned the extra $78 per 100 shares, and you still own your shares at the end of the contract.

Now let's say that the stock does increase a bit in value. Over time, it jumps up to $42, and then to $42.75, but then drops down to $41.80 by the time the options contract expires. In this scenario, you're finding yourself in a much better position. In this case, the strike price of $43 was never reached, so the buyer of the call option is again left out in the cold. On the other hand, you keep the premium of $78, and you still get to keep stock shares. This time since the shares have increased in value, you're a lot better off than you were before, so it's a win-win situation for YOU, even though it's a losing situation for the poor soul who purchased your call.

There is another possibility that the stock price exceeds the strike price before the contract expires. In that case, you're required to sell the stock. You still end up in a position that isn't all that bad, however. You didn't lose any actual money, but you lost a potential profit. You still get the premium of $78, plus the earnings from the 100 shares' sale at the strike price of $43.

A covered call is almost a zero-risk situation because you never actually lose money even though you missed out on an opportunity if the stock price soars. You can minimize that risk by choosing stocks you use for a covered call option carefully. For example, if you have shares in a pharmaceutical company rumored to be announcing a cure for cancer in two months, you probably don't want to use those shares for a covered call. A company with more long-term prospects but probably isn't going anywhere in the following months is a better bet.

CHAPTER 17:

Strategies for Selling Covered Call

Bear Put Spread Strategy

The bear put trade seeks to take advantage of bearish markets. In contrast to bullish markets with varying degrees, bearish markets tend to have far lesser degrees of strength. While a bullish market can be classified on many levels ranging from slightly bullish to extremely bullish, bear markets would lend themselves to only two or three such classifications.

The reason for this is straightforward. The general public and the large majority of institutional activity is focused on the long side of the market. Therefore, when these institutions conduct their buying campaigns, you will see a greater degree of fluctuation within a stock as it goes up. The very fact that a larger number of traders are involved produces more price behavior scenarios, resulting in a more significant number of trend strength levels.

In contrast, bear markets have far lesser traders involved, and they tend to quickly get to the point. You won't find a bear market trying to make up its mind as it leans towards moving downwards. Distribution movements that often occur before a bear trend don't last very long and bear trends run faster and exhaust themselves sooner than bull trends.

The point of this is to say that you need to be on your toes with bear markets. The bear aims to do the same thing, but there are slight differences in the way they play themselves out.

Execution

The bear put his two legs to it:

- Long put at or near the money.

- Short put out of the money below the long.

The primary profit here is the long put, which will appreciate as the stock price decreases. The short put aims to reduce the cost of carrying the long put via the premium earned upon writing it.

AMZN is currently trading at 1833.51, and let's assume that the bear trend in this stock is beginning to show signs of slowing down, and it is approaching a strong support level that it is unlikely to go past. You'll learn the signs of identifying all these things later. For now, commit them to memory, and make a note to refer to them later.

The closest at the money put in the 1835 strike price near month put, which asks $53.80 per share. This is a large portion of our trade. Now, we need to determine which level is appropriate for the short. Well, we've seen from our chart that a strong support level is close by that is unlikely to be breached. Why not use this as a low level?

Let's say this is $1800. The bid for this put is $39.85 per share. Here's how the math works out:

Cost of entry = Cost of long put - Premium earned from short = 53.8-39.85 = $13.95 per share.

Maximum gain = Difference between long and short put strike prices = 1835-1800 = $35 per share.

The maximum loss is the same as the cost of entry since the changes in the premiums of both puts will offset one another. As the price rises, the long put will decrease in price while the short will decrease by the same rate, thus giving us a profit that offsets the loss on the long leg of the trade.

By this point, hopefully, you're familiar with working out the math of spread trades and can see how the dynamics of it work. In terms of adjustment, it works the same way with the bear put as it does with the bear call. If the price rises and takes your long put out of the money, you need to determine whether your analysis was correct.

If you think it holds, you can close out the short, which will give you a profit to offset the large portion, which will also be closed out. Establish a new spread or keep the short at the same level.

Note that you can close out your long put, and go long again at a higher price without touching the short if you wish to keep it at the same level.

The criteria you need to follow for adjustment are the same as with call spread trades. Your decision will be based on the technical analysis factors you see, and how well you can deduce conclusions from them. There is another choice you face, now that you've learned how the bear put works, and that is whether you should choose a bear call spread or a bear put spread.

Both strategies seek to take advantage of similar market conditions, so which one should you choose? Before we get into the evaluation of this, we need to look at bull put spreads first.

Bull Put Spread Strategy

Bull put spreads are useful to take advantage of sluggish uptrends or sideways movements with an upward tilt to them. In doing this, they're pretty similar to bull call spreads, and the mechanics of this trade is pretty straightforward, as you'll see.

Execution

Two legs make up the entirety of this trade:

- Short in the money or at the money put

- Long out of the money put a few levels below the short

The short put is the leg that takes advantage of the rise in prices. The long put covers your downside in case market sentiment doesn't work out in your favor. Once you enter the trade, you'll earn the put premium, and will have to pay to enter the long put. The difference between the two is your cost of entry, as well as your maximum gain.

Your maximum loss is the difference between the strike prices of both legs. If the stock price falls and brings your long put into the money, your downside is capped at that level. Therefore, when you enter this trade, you will receive money or a net credit. Contrast this with the bear put, which is a net debit. In other words, you pay money to be in the trade.

Let's look at an example to flesh this out further using AMZN. The market price is the same, but this time, our environment is different. It is a bullish environment that is sluggishly moving upwards. Our closest at the money put to short is the 1835 level, which puts $53.30 per share in our pocket.

Let's assume the support level below is at 1800, so the cost of going long here is $40.40. Thus, our cost of entry is:

Cost of entry = Cost of long put - Premium from short put = 40.4-53.3 = -12.90 per share (we receive this much as credit). This is the maximum gain as well.

Max loss = Short put strike price - long put strike price of = 35$ per share.

As you can see here, just like the bear call, the reward to risk ratio is skewed, but the reasons for entering this trade despite this are the same as in the former case. In case you wish to adjust your trade, your criteria are the same as before; that is, it depends on your faith in your technical analysis.

Put Calendar Spread Strategy

In direct contrast to the call calendar spread trade, the put calendar spread trade seeks to take advantage of a decline in a stock's price. This is less widely used than the call calendar spread. Either way, it works in the same manner by creating a horizontal spread between the same strike prices but different expiration dates.

If you anticipate AMZN to decline to 1800 after a month, you can buy the put of the near or far month, which will cost you $40.40 per share. Since you reason that AMZN is not going to hit this mark within this month, you can buy the front-month put at the same level, which will net you $21.95 per share.

This creates a net debit of $18.45 per share and is your maximum loss. Your maximum gain is subject to the same conditions as with the call calendar spread. That is to say, it is unlimited, and depends on whether the price hits your shorter-term put before it expires. Either way, this horizontal spread is a great way to take advantage of bearish market movements.

Choices

While the horizontal spreads offer us pretty easy choices between the two of them, with the call spread for bull markets and the bear spread for bear markets, things get a bit murkier with the vertical spreads. Two sets of strategies exist to take advantage of similar market conditions, so which one is better?

Usually, such a question is often answered by looking at which one makes more money. The reality of the situation is a bit different, however. The money you make on the trades can be affected by the strike price levels, and you can manipulate a net debit spread trade to yield more than a credit spread by just fiddling with the strike prices, and hoping for some luck. No, a more sophisticated set of rules is needed.

Thankfully, risk management principles give us the way out. Volatility is the most significant risk that plagues option traders. It isn't volatility itself but changes in volatility. You'll often find options traders abandon vertical spreads before major announcements because option prices go haywire thanks to current fluctuations in the markets. This is, in fact, true for directional traders as well, but they at least have the choice of betting in a particular direction and profiting from a huge move.

Ideally, options traders seek to enter at times of low volatility, and exit during high times. This is because the volatility factor in the option price produces significant increases in premiums. It is this precise number that gives us hints as to which strategy to choose.

Purpose

Despite looking to take advantage of similar market conditions, the net credit and debt strategies' underlying principles are very different. A net debit strategy seeks to reduce the premium a trader pays to enter the trade. As premiums shoot up during periods of high volatility, a net credit strategy will end up with the trader footing hefty bills for inflated option premiums.

Sure, they will be able to make a greater profit on a credit spread. However, if volatility results in them paying a huge amount in the first place, the decrease in volatility will reduce the extent to which the premium will move. This is where debit spreads are so useful. They take the volatility out of the equation, with one leg canceling the other.

CHAPTER 18:

Iron Condor

The Iron Condor (IC) is a strategy that requires you to have some prior knowledge of the Greeks, and how you can go about taking advantage of them.

This is why before trading this; it helps to simulate this strategy extensively and to never go live with it unless you know everything to do with it inside out.

The most important education you will receive in this strategy will be when you deal with live prices.

The trade itself has four legs to it:

- An out of the money (OTM) short put

- An OTM long put with a lower strike price

- An OTM short call

- An OTM long call with a higher strike price

The income-generating portions of this trade are legs 1 and 3.

These will earn you a premium, and subtracting the premium paid from the premium received will define your maximum profit. In terms of structuring the trade, it works like this.

Around your market price that is on top of it, and to the bottom you'll write an OTM call and an OTM put. Above the call and put, you will buy an even further OTM call and put.

Thus, you short the lower OTM strikes and buy even more OTM strikes.

Iron Condors

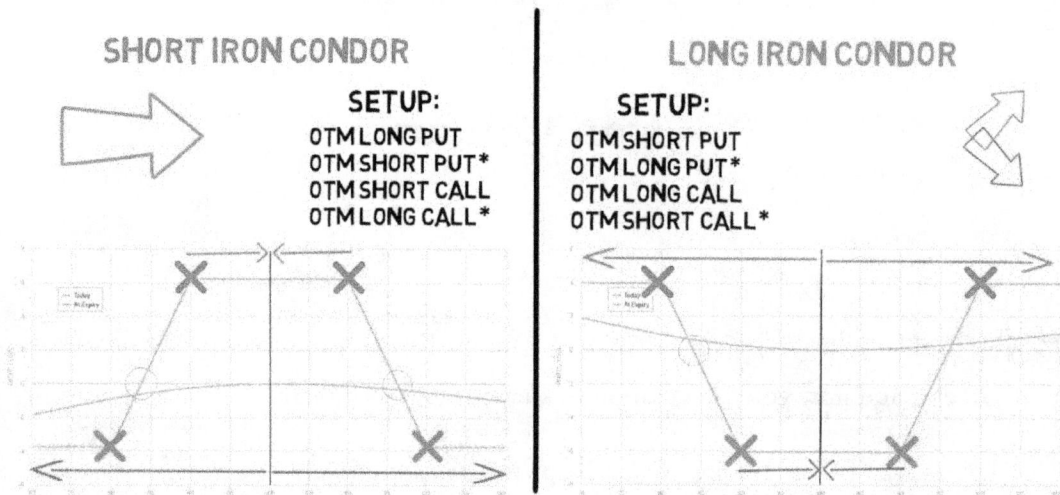

SHORT IRON CONDOR

SETUP:
OTM LONG PUT
OTM SHORT PUT*
OTM SHORT CALL
OTM LONG CALL*

LONG IRON CONDOR

SETUP:
OTM SHORT PUT
OTM LONG PUT*
OTM LONG CALL
OTM SHORT CALL*

Execution

Before jumping in and placing your orders, you need first to identify possible candidates. More than anything else, this is what will define your trade's success. The idea is to set up an IC when volatility is low. In other words, you're sure that the price is going to be within a tight channel, and isn't going to break out in a particular direction.

Hence, when searching for stocks, you need to look for those in a ranging environment. The ideal stocks are entering a tight range, preferably in the middle or towards the end of a trend. Stay away from ranges that occur at the end of trends because they produce many upswings and downswings, and increase the implied volatility.

The implied volatility is a good measure for you to use. Do not rely on this directly since it is merely a measure of what other traders think will happen to volatility. So, if you enter based on a low implied vol but see that the price is headed into a trend, stick with what the chart says. Let the other traders have their implied volatility numbers and suffer with them.

When speaking of implied volatility, it is about comparative values. So, you need to look at the current values to the historical ones and determine whether they're on the higher or lower side.

Next comes the timing of the trade. How long should you target to keep this open? Unlike the last strategies, you should seek to open an IC at least fifty to sixty days out from expiration. You want to give yourself this much time because as the option moves closer to the expiry date, its gamma is going to increase. Gamma increasing implies a volatility increase, which will reflect itself in how the option is priced.

When you trade close to expiry options with this strategy, the option prices will reflect a fast-moving gamma and volatility. Thus, it will take just a small change in prices for the option premiums to go against you. You're liable to find yourself in a position where the underlying price has decreased, but your short call has increased or stayed at the same premium.

This makes it difficult for you to adjust the trade. Any subsequent small increase in the underlying will put you in the red, and the subsequent movement from the short put will not compensate for the value lost.

A good method to adopt is to look at all the Greeks to see how they're printing relative to their historical values. All four are related to one another, so if there is a truly low volatility situation, you're in for a great chance at a profit.

This is why traders love the IC. It is complicated enough to put off any newbies who couldn't be bothered to spend the time learning it. It is just easy enough to present the intermediate to advanced trader with good and high probability opportunities.

The IC is called a net credit trade, meaning you receive money when you enter the trade. This also happens to be your maximum gain, while your maximum loss is far more significant. Estimating your maximum loss is the key to figuring out how much of a position you need to take. This is where it gets a bit tricky since option pricing requires you to take volatility into account. How can you predict what volatility is going to be in the future to predict a price?

You'll see what I mean when we look at an example using numbers. For now, understand that you need to establish the long legs of the trade before the short legs. If you set the short call and put it before the other two, you're likely to trigger all sorts of warnings from your broker, and they might even suspend your account for some time since it looks like you have no idea what you're doing.

So, take it slow and easy. Most important of all is determining that the volatility conditions are good for entering and executing the IC.

Example

Let's stick with GOOG for this, assuming it is in a range and that all the indications are for it to enter a low volatility period for the following month or so, or the near future at the very least. The current market price is 1229.

For our long legs, let's say we buy the November 15th, 1245 call. This will cost us 41.40. Next, we set up the long-put leg for November 15th. Let's choose a strike price of 1215. This costs us 38.50 to purchase.

Now, it's time to set up the short legs of the trade. Remember, each leg's strike prices need to be closer to the market price than the long ones. For the put, we choose 1220 as the strike and earn 38.6, and for the call, we choose the 1240 call. This yields us 39.20.

So, our cost of entry is:

Cost of entry = sum of premiums received - the sum of premiums paid = 2.10 per share.

Now to figure out our maximum loss. The trade works in our favor as long as the price remains between the two short legs' strike prices. If it exceeds the strike price of either one of the long legs, that is, if it moves either long into the money, we're faced with our worst-case scenario.

To figure this out is to estimate the intrinsic value in such a situation. So, if GOOG were to rise past 1245, the long option will gain at least a dollar in intrinsic value per unit rise. Furthermore, the short call will now be in the money, and its premium will have decreased by at least $5 (since that's the spread between the two legs).

Our short put and long put will still be out of the money, but both will have lost their values by at least the difference between their strike prices and the current worst-case market price. In this case, they will decrease by at least $29 in total. This is your minimum worst-case scenario level. Keep in mind that this is just an estimate.

There are volatility factors that will affect the price of the options. Therefore, it is a good idea to apply a safety factor of some sort to this value and then use that to determine your position size. How much of a factor should you apply? This is difficult to say because every stock has its volatility history. So, you ought to play around with it on simulation before going live.

Now that we've set up the trade, we need to think about the exit. Our goal is not to let these expire or hold them until the two-month period is up. After all, it will be tough to find a stock that remains in a range for that long. Besides, the volatility will go all over the place if it stays in a range for that long. No, we aim to capture the decay of time value.

The usual exit point is when the options have thirty days remaining on their expiration dates. Since you're starting, targeting far month options (sixty days or more left till expiry) is your best bet. When you become more comfortable executing these trades, you can take weekly options that expire a month plus a week away. Thus, your trade will be active for a week.

Easy Formula

Many traders will target half of the maximum profit level to fix an exit point. For example, if your trade was projected to earn you a maximum of 10%, traders will make a profit when it hits the 5% mark. This method has its advantages and disadvantages.

The biggest advantage is that it makes it very easy to monitor your trade. Using an online option calculator or even the one in your trading terminal, you can input the prices and calculate your current profit. When your net gain moves to half of what you received as credit, you take the trades off the table and exit the position entirely.

The biggest disadvantage is that beginners are prone to take this far too early. Remember, you need to stay in the position to capture the greatest time value decay. If your position moves into a loss early, you need to adjust it, and this is a whole other ball game.

A lot of traders are intimidated by adjustment, and this is why they'll exit quickly. From a reward to risk standpoint, taking half of your intended profits over and over will reduce your winnings because you'll be leaving too much on the table. However, take enough trades, and this even out. So, it's a tradeoff at the end of the day.

CHAPTER 19:

Options Pricing

O
ptions traders need to comprehend extra factors that influence an option's price, and the complexity of picking the right technique. When a stockbroker becomes acceptable at foreseeing the future price movement, the person may believe it is a simple change from options, but this isn't accurate. Options traders must deal with 3 shifting parameters that influence the price: the underlying time, volatility, and security. Changes in any of these factors affect the option's value.

Option pricing hypothesis utilizes factors (exercise price, stock price, interest rate, time to expiration, volatility) to value an option hypothetically. It estimates an option's reasonable value, which traders join into their techniques to maximize profits. Some ordinarily utilized models to value options are Black-Scholes, Monte-Carlo, and Binomial Option Pricing. These speculations have wide margins for error because of deriving their values from different assets, typically the cost of an organization's basic stock. There are scientific formulas intended to compute the fair, reasonable value of an option. The broker inputs known factors and finds a solution that depicts what the option should be worth.

The essential objective of any option pricing model is to compute the probability that an option will be worked out or be in-the-money (ITM) at lapse. Basic asset value (stock value), interest rate, exercise price, time to expiration, and volatility, which is the number of days between the computation date and the option's exercise date, are usually utilized variables that are input into logical models to derive an option's hypothetical fair value.

Here are the general impacts that factors have on an option's cost:

Strike Price and Underlying Price

The value of puts and cuts are influenced by changes in the fundamental stock cost in a generally clear manner. When the stock cost goes up, calls should gain value since you can purchase the underlying asset at a lower cost than where the market is, and puts should diminish. In like manner, put options should increase in value, and calls should drop as the stock value falls, as the put holder gives the right to sell stock at costs over the falling market cost.

That pre-determined price to purchase or sell is known as the option's exercise price or strike price. Suppose the strike price permits you to purchase or sell the basic at a level that allows for a quick profits purchase, discarding that exchange in the open market. In that case, the option is in-the-money (for instance, a call to purchase shares at $10 when the market cost is currently $15, you can make a prompt $5 profit).

Like most other monetary resources, options costs are affected by prevailing interest rates and are affected by interest rate changes. Put option and call option premiums are affected contrarily as interest rates change lose value while calls benefit from rising rates. The inverse is genuine when interest rates fall.

The impact of volatility on an option's price is the most difficult concept for beginners to comprehend. It depends on a measure called statistical (also known as historical) volatility, SV for short, looking at past value developments of the stock over a given timeframe.

Option pricing models necessitate the trader to go in future volatility throughout the life of the option. Normally, options traders don't generally know what it will be, and need to guess by working the pricing model "in reverse". The merchant knows the cost at which the option is trading and can inspect different factors, including dividends, interest rates, and time left with a bit of research. Subsequently, the main missing number will be future volatility, which can be evaluated from different information sources.

Factors That Affect An Option's Price

You cannot price an option until you realize what makes up its worth. An options trade can turn into a mind-boggling machine of legs, numerous orders, Greeks, and adjustments. However, if you don't have the foggiest idea about the essentials, what are you attempting to achieve?

When you take a look at an option chain, have you considered how they generated every one of those prices for the options? However, these options are not created randomly, but rather calculated out utilizing a model, for example, the Black-Scholes Model. We will dive further into the Black-Scholes Model's seven components, and how and why they are utilized to determine an option's cost/price. Like all models, the Black-Scholes Model has a shortcoming and is a long way from perfect.

History Of The Black-Scholes Model

The Black-Scholes Model was distributed in 1973 as The Pricing of Options and Corporate Liabilities in the Journal of Political Economy. It was created by Myron Scholes and Fisher Black as an approach to evaluate the price of an option after some time. Robert Merton later distributed a subsequent paper, further extending the comprehension of the model. As with any model, a few assumptions must be comprehended.

- The rate of profit for the riskless asset is constant.

- The more the option will be worth, the underlying follows, which expresses that move in an unpredictable and random path.

- There is no riskless profit, arbitrage, opportunity.

- It is possible to lend and borrow any amount of money at a riskless rate.

- It is possible to purchase or short any amount of stock.

- There are no charges or costs.

The model has seven factors: strike price, stock price, interest rates, types of option, dividends, time of expiration, and future volatility.

Stock Price

If a call option permits you to purchase a stock at a pre-determined cost later on, then the higher that cost goes, the more the option will be worth.

Which option would have a higher worth:

- A call option permits you to purchase TOP (The Option Prophet) for $100 while it is trading at $80 or

- A call option will enable you to buy TOP for $100 while it is trading at $120

Nobody will pay $100 for something they can purchase on the open market for $80, so our option in Choice 1 will have a low worth.

All the more alluring is Choice 2, an option to purchase TOP for $100 when its worth is $120. In this circumstance, our option worth will be higher.

Strike Price

The strike price follows the same lines as the stock price. At the point when we group strikes, we do it as in-the-money, at-the-money, or out-of-the-money. When a call option is in-the-money, it implies the stock price/cost is higher than the strike cost. The stock price is not exactly the strike price when a call is out-of-the-money.

A TOP call has a strike of fifty while TOP is presently trading at $60. This option is in-the-money.

The stock price is not exactly the strike price when a put option is in the money. A put option is out-of-the-money when the stock price is greater than the strike price.

A TOP put has a strike of twenty while TOP is presently trading at $40. This option is out-of-the-money.

In-the-money options have a greater value contrasted with out-of-the-money options.

Type Of Option

This is likely the easiest factor to comprehend. An option is either a call or a put, and the option's estimation will change appropriately.

- A call option gives the holder the option or right to purchase the basic at a predefined cost within a particular timeframe.

- A put option gives the holder the option or right to sell the hidden at a predefined price within a particular timeframe.

If you are long a call or short a put, your option value increments as the market moves higher. Suppose you are short a call or long a put your option value increments as the market goes lower.

Time To expiration

Options have a constrained life expectancy; thus, their worth is influenced by the progression of time. As the time to expiration upturns, the value of the option increments. As the time to termination draws nearer, the value of the option starts to diminish. The value starts to quickly diminish within the last 30 days of an option's life. The additional time an option has till termination/expiration, the option needs to move around.

Interest Rates

The interest rate has a nominal effect on an option's value. When interest rates rise, a call option's value will rise, and a put option's value will decrease.

To drive this idea home, how about we take a look at the dynamic procedure of investing in TOP while trading at $50.

- We can purchase 100 shares of the stock altogether, which would cost us $5,000.

- Instead of purchasing the stock altogether, we can get long an at-the-money call for $5.00. Our all-out expense here would be $500. Our underlying cost of money would be littler, and this would leave us $4,500 leftover. Also, we will have a similar prize potential for half the risk. Presently we can take that additional money and invest it somewhere else, for example, Treasury Bills. This would create a guaranteed return on our investment in TOP.

The higher the interest rate, the more appealing the subsequent option becomes. In this manner, when interest rates go up, calls are a superior investment, so their cost likewise increments.

On the other side of that coin, if we look at a long put versus a long call, we can see an impediment. We have two options when we want to play an underlying drawback.

- You can short a hundred shares of the stock that would produce money into the business, and earn interest in that money.

- You long a put which will cost you less money by and large, but not put additional money into your business that produces interest income.

The higher the interest rate, the more appealing the primary option becomes. Accordingly, when interest rates rise, the value of put options decreases.

Dividends

Options don't get dividends, so their value varies when profits are discharged. When an organization discharges dividends, they have an ex-dividend date. If you own the stock on that date, you will be granted the dividend. Additionally, on this date, the estimation of the stock will diminish by the number of dividends. As dividends increment, a put option's value likewise increments, and a calls' value declines.

Volatility

Volatility is the main evaluated factor in this model. The volatility that is utilized is forward. Forward volatility is the proportion of implied volatility over a period later on.

Implied volatility shows the "simplified" development in a stock's future volatility. It discloses to you how traders think the stock will move. Implied volatility is constantly communicated as a percentage, non-directional, and on a yearly premise.

CHAPTER 20:

Dividends

With dividend stocks, you only invest once and earn forever! Passive income refers to the type of income that you create even when sleeping it is something desired by many. This income generation method can build your wealth either by helping cover your monthly expenses or reinvesting. Dividends are the best fit as a passive income source. This is because the income is sustainable, requires little maintenance, grows faster than inflation, and can also be tax-advantaged. It might take you time to get a reasonable amount of dividend income, but time is always on your side in this case.

What Are Dividends?

Dividends, just like many other financial subjects, are simple on the surface but very complicated underneath. From a surface point of view, dividends are paid to give out a company's earnings to its shareholders. You must be aware that being a shareholder in a company that pays dividends `entitles you a share of its profits. A perfect dividend policy is beneficial to both the company and the shareholder. Many investors chose to invest in great dividend-paying companies as the basis of their portfolio. This technique is referred to as dividend growth investing. In this case, growth refers to the growth of dividend payments over some time. Since the 1990s, the average annual dividend increase is always around 6%. This, however, is not a fixed rate; it isn't unheard of for companies to have a yearly dividend of 10% or more!

Dividend Investing

If you are not sure about dividend investing is, this topic is for you. As mentioned earlier, dividends refer to the way companies share success with their shareholders. It is like a portion of the total earnings paid out you as the shareholder. You can choose to get your dividends in the form of cash or more shares. You might want to know what dividend dates are? For instance, a company can declare a dividend of Y dollars. The day this information was relayed is known as the declaration date, the time is, however not that important.

When looking at a dividend, there are two significant dates you should know. Ex-Dividend Date: you must own a stock before this date so that you can receive the bonus. Payment Date: This is the day money is paid to shareholders. The Record Date is technically the date you need to be recorded as a shareholder to be entitled to dividends. This date is always two business days after the ex-dividend date: this is solely because trades take two days to settle. It has lesser importance to an investor than the ex-dividend date. It is, however, good to know what the record date is. Additionally, pay more attention to the ex-dividend date!

Comparing Stocks for Dividend Investing

There are two ways you can look at dividends and determine how good they are. Both of them are pure math. The dividend yield is a certain percentage showing the amount of money the profit is compared to the share price. The higher the amount, the better: this means you earn more passive income out of your investment. For example, if the average dividend amount of the company is 3.46%, it means you earned $3.45 in dividends for every $100 you invested.

The second you can use to determine whether the dividend ID proper is the dividend payout ratio: this refers to the paid dividends and divided by the company's total earnings. You should ask yourself if the company makes sufficient profit to cover for the dividends, they promised you. Look at the dividend growth rate. Most companies tend to increase their dividends over time, and this metric establishes the rate at which they do so.

When to Reinvest or Not to Reinvest

Remember, when we deliberated the two options when it comes to when acquiring your dividend? You should consider that in this situation. It can be easier two chose to base on that because you will know what your investment objectives are.

Considering your age, this could be the best decision as you will take advantage of the compounding magic.

Dividend Growth Investing: Case Study

In this case, we make up a situation to show you just how great dividend growth investing can be. Let us assume you bought $10,000 worth of Toyota shares on the New York Stock Exchange in early 1999. Below is how much you will have at the moment. 243 share of Toyota worth $41.02 each $4296.34 in passive income in the following 12 months ($1.22 per share annually) 2.96% dividend yield ($296.45/$10,000).

You should note that the example had to be set in the USA Stock Exchange because all these financial calculators online-only support American tickers. Fast forward to 2019; you made five times your initial investment mainly due to capital gains. Interestingly, your passive income grew even more, multiplying itself more than seven times the initial amount. The outcome (passive income growth) was due to two factors: dividend reinvestments and dividend pay raise.

How to Start Chasing Dividend Income

Below are the three steps you can take to start chasing your dividend income.

Pick a Type of Account

The first thing you need to do is pick a type of account you prefer to work with. Dividends are taxable in some countries, meaning you could benefit from keeping them legally registered accounts like RRSP or TFSA. Deciding where to place your investments can be a very confusing thing. Below is what you need to take away from this subtopic. TFSA: applies Canadian, American, and other international stocks, and ETFs RRSP: Refers to Canadian, American, and other foreign stocks, and ETFs.

Unregistered Accounts: Canadian, American, and other international stocks, and any margin trading engagements (paying maximum taxes on dividends, and handle riskier investments to get capital investments just in case an investment goes wrong). Generally, the fee charged on profits is lower than that charged on a regular income. There are, however, many rules and exceptions, especially regarding US Stocks.

Choose a Stockbroker

As you might know, the broker needs to provide the type of account you required in Step 1. You will also want a broker that offers a DRIP when chasing dividends. You should, therefore, be careful with the kind of broker you are opting for. Preferably, go for brokers that support registered accounts like RRSPs and TFSAs.

Decide between ETFs and Stocks

The essential dividend growth investing pertains to picking individual stocks using the metrics we deliberated earlier. There are plenty of ETFs in different countries that mainly focus on dividend income, and have little management expenses. While ETFs charge a fee that digs into the returns, it is a shallow maintenance strategy. You don't need to look at individual companies and their payout ratios. Instead, what you need to focus on is the distribution you earn and the yield it provides you.

Keep on Contributing and Investing

This is a continuous process that does not stop once you purchase your first stocks. The case study we used above focused only on a one-time investment tracked over 20 years far along. You should, therefore, be making regular deposits, and slowly be picking up even more ETFs, and dividend stocks. This will result in your passive income stream growing even at a faster rate. Ideally, you can use a DRIP where possible for most of your investment life to accelerate growth.

CHAPTER 21:

Technical Analysis For Options Trading

Traders often use a set of tools known as technical analysis to help them make better trades. Specifically, it can help you detect developing trend reversals in stock charts. This information can help you get into, and out of your trades at the best possible time. Technical analysis involves a wide range of tools.

Studying Trends with Moving Averages

The most important thing on a stock chart that a trader will look for on a stock chart is a trend reversal. If you are looking to profit from call options, then what you will look for is a relatively low stock price or a stock price in decline, and then wait for it to show signs of a reversal. This is going to help you buy low and sell high. Once you have entered a position, the technique is to study the charts looking for the coming reversal once the price has peaked, so you can exit your position.

Moving averages are the easiest tools to use for this purpose. It takes several periods of stock data, and at each point, it calculates the average out to a fixed number of points. The definition of a "point" is up to the individual trader, and it could be an hour, four hours, a day, or a week. It could even be five-minute intervals. If you plan on trading an option over 30 days, you will probably be looking at using days for your time frame. In that case, a 9-period moving average would calculate the average of the closing price at each day, using the past nine days to do the calculation.

To spot trend reversals, traders rely on moving averages with different periods (but they will use the same definition of the period, be it a day, week, or five minutes). You could use a 9-period moving average, and a 20-period moving average. Alternatively, you might use a 50-period moving average, and a 200-period moving average.

A longer-period moving average will give you more information on the historical pricing level of the stock in question. Different types of moving averages are going to treat this in different ways. A simple moving average will do a standard mathematical average of all data points. So, if we had a 9-period simple moving average for closing prices of Apple, on a particular day, it might calculate:

SMA = (212.41 + 213.11 + 212.50 +214.29 + 215.72 +216.01 + 217.22 + 217.50 + 216.95)/9.

Many traders are completely content to use the simple moving average, but if you look at how it's calculated, you should note that all prices are treated the same. This is objectionable because if you are looking to make a trade, recent prices will be more important than history, older prices. We certainly want information from the stock's historical pricing level, but it is more recent prices that are going to have the most impact on our trading decisions. Many traders use weighted moving averages that give more weight to recent closing prices, and less weight to closing prices in the past. Two very popular weighted moving averages are used, the Hull moving average, and the more popular exponential moving average.

To detect a trend reversal, you will use two moving averages on your stock chart of the same type, but with different period lengths. You can use nine days exponential moving average with 20 days exponential moving average.

The first rule is known as a golden cross. This happens when the short-period moving average curve crosses above the long-period moving average curve. This tells you that the stock is likely to be entering an upward trend. In the example below, a 50-day simple moving average, and a 200-day simple moving average are used. Notice that after the golden cross (the 50-day moving average crossing above the 200-day moving average); the stock enters a relatively long-term upward trend.

This tool's beauty is that it is very simple to use, it is also something that a beginning trader can understand quite easily.

Of course, stocks are not always going up. Otherwise, everyone would be rich. So, we have to know how to spot the development of a downward trend in prices. A so-called death cross indicates this. In a death cross, the short-period moving average curve crosses below the long-period moving average curve.

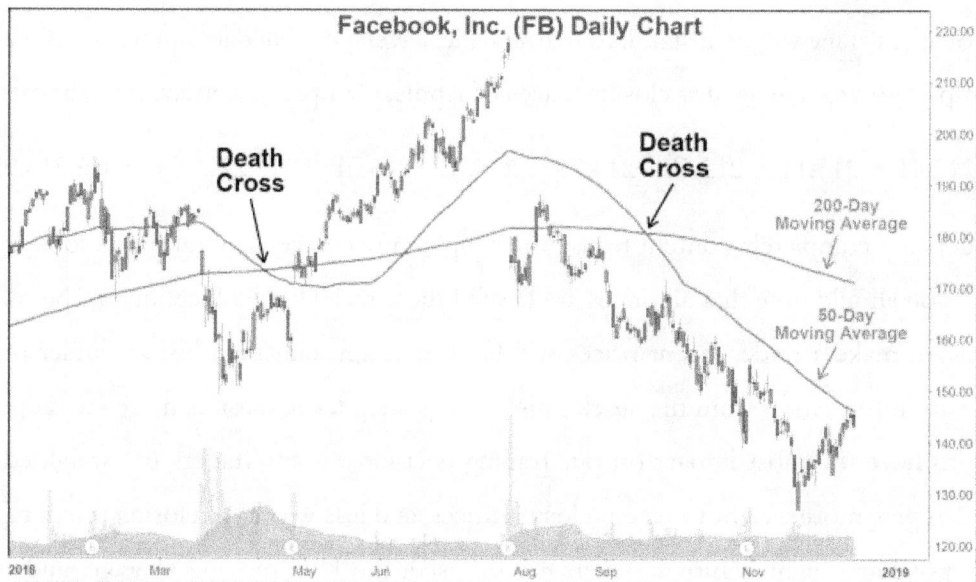

The question now is how to use crosses of moving average curves with options trading. When you are looking to get into a trade, you should add the appropriate moving averages to your charts, and then use a golden cross or a death cross as a signal to enter or exit trades.

For call options, you want to enter a trade when there is a golden cross. Then, when the chart shows a death cross, exit your positions. It's that simple.

For put options, you will do the opposite. That is, you will wait to enter your trade until you see a death cross. For options traders, since you can profit, either way, a "death" cross is also a signal for profits, but with using put options. Then you hold your position until you've either reached a level of profit you are comfortable with or you see a golden cross, indicating a coming trend reversal.

Remember that with options, the expiration date and time decay are always lurking in the background, so you don't necessarily want to wait for another crossing to occur before exiting your positions.

Momentum

One of the most essential concepts that stock traders look for is momentum. Price momentum occurs when many traders are either buying or selling a stock, pushing prices strongly in one direction or another. The tool you can use to study the momentum of a stock price is called the Relative Strength Indicator. You can add this to your stock charts to help you study the best times to get into and out of positions to maximize possible profits.

The relative strength indicator will be displayed below your stock chart. It is a curve that can go between 0 to 100. Typically, the values 0-30 and 70-100 are what traders are looking for on the chart. When the curve goes into the range of 0-30, this means that a stock is "oversold." That is, traders have sold off too many shares, pushing prices down to a level that makes it likely that new traders will find the stock now an attractive buy, so they are likely to start loading up on the stock and pushing prices upward again. The lower the RSI gets, the stronger this signal is.

When the RSI goes into the range of 70 and above, this indicates overbought conditions. In this case, frantic purchasing of the shares has pushed prices up too high, and traders are likely to start getting out of the stock because they want to get out before the price drops when there is a large selloff.

The RSI should not be taken in isolation. A good way to use it is to use it in conjunction with the moving averages. So, if you see oversold conditions with the RSI, together with a golden cross, that indicates that stock prices are likely to start moving upwards. If the RSI shows overbought conditions, and you also see a death cross, this can be taken to indicate that stock prices are likely to be pushed in a downward direction soon.

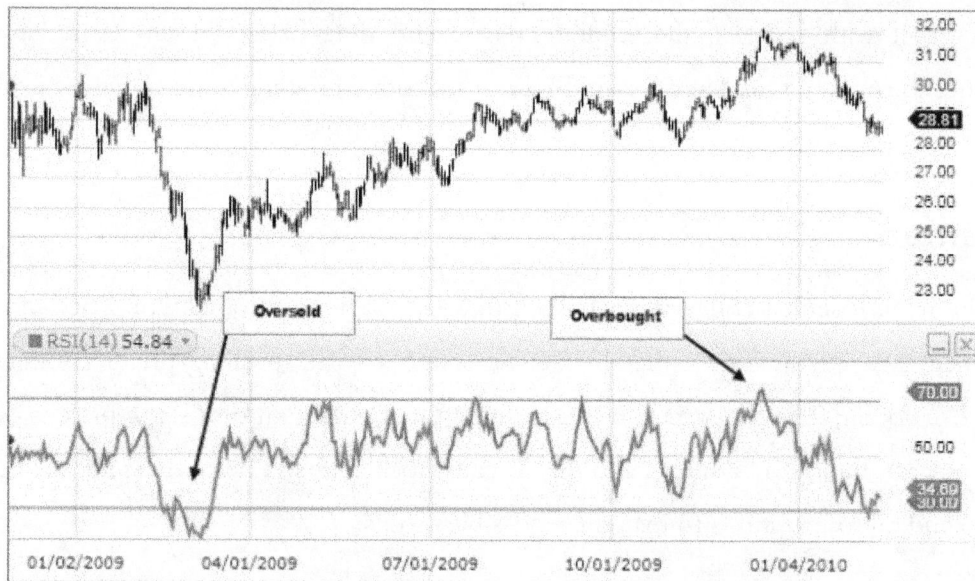

Support and Resistance

The concepts of support and resistance are important for options traders to understand, especially if you are interested in trading iron condors. These concepts are not complicated, so most readers will have no problem grasping them.

In many cases, a stock is not going to be shooting up or crashing to the floor. In fact, over most periods of the stock market, stocks will be bouncing around in the same price range, and possibly gradually increasing or maybe decreasing, but over relatively short periods staying the same. When this happens, we say that the stock is "ranging." The values that the stock prices range between are called support and resistance.

Support is the low-price level. So, while the stock is ranging, it will dip down to the support price level but not go below it. After it drops to support, it will probably start rising again. You want to look for a price that the stock reaches at least twice over the time frame you are looking to declare a support price.

Resistance is the upper price level that the stock cannot break above. Again, you want to look for the stock price to move up to the resistance price at least twice over the time frame. So, while the stock is ranging, it will drop down to support, then bounce around, go up to resistance, drop back down to support again, and keep repeating this process. Stocks can do this for extended periods.

For options traders, when the price drops to resistance, this is a time for those trading call options to enter their positions. Put option traders would sell their positions at this point. When the price goes up to a resistance level, then traders investing in call options should sell their positions, while this is a point that you would be looking to enter a position if you were interested in trading put options. The rules are pretty simple.

Breakouts

Breakouts occur when a stock suddenly gains momentum in one direction or the other, so the stock price will break out above resistance or drop below support. In this case, you are likely to be looking at forming a new, long-term trend that can help you make profits either with call options or with put options. If there is a breakout above resistance, you want to invest in call options, and ride the upward trend for as long as possible. To take advantage of breakouts, an options trader should be paying close attention to the financial and economic news. In particular, keep an eye on any news about specific companies that you are interested in investing in.

Trendlines

A simple method of analysis that you can use to "trade with the trend," whether it is up or down, draws trendlines on your charts. A trendline will help you determine where the stock price is going to end up in the future. You cannot take this to be an absolute fact, and it is only a guide for what might happen. To draw a trendline for an upward moving stock price, start at a local low price, and then draw the line upwards, touching the local dips in the curve up. At least 2-3 minima should touch your line. The end of the line (which we are assuming extends past the current price) will give you an estimate of where the price will be at a future date. To draw a trendline for a downward trending price, use the same procedure, but use the local peaks in the price to determine your line.

CHAPTER 22:

Trading Psychology

We associate trading psychology to some behaviors and emotions that are often the triggers for catalysts for decisions. The most common emotions that every trader will come across are fear and greed.

Fear

At any given time, fear represents one of the worst kinds of emotions that you can have. Check-in your newspaper one day, and you read about a steep selloff, and the next thing is trying to rack your brain about what to do next, even if it isn't the right action at that time.

Many investors think that they know what will happen in the following few days, which makes them have a lot of confidence in the trade outcome. It leads to investors getting into the trade at a level that is too high or too low, which in turn makes them react emotionally.

As the trader puts a lot of hope on the single trade, the level of fear tends to increase, and hesitation and caution kick in.

Fear is part of every trader, but skilled traders can manage the fear. There are various types of fears that you will experience:

The Fear to Lose

Have you ever entered a trade and all you could think about is losing? The fear of losing makes it hard for you to execute the perfect strategy or enter or exit a strategy at the right time.

As a trader, you know that you need to make timely decisions when the strategy signals you to take one. When fear guiding you, the level of confidence drops, and you can't execute the strategy the right way, at the right time. When a strategy fails, you lose trust in your abilities as well as strategy.

When you lose trust in many of the strategies, you end up with analysis paralysis, whereby you can't pull the trigger on any decision you make. Making a move becomes a huge challenge.

When you cannot pull the trigger, all you can think about is staying away from the pain of loss while you need to move towards gains.

No trader likes to lose, but it is a fact that even the best traders will make losses once in a while. The key is for them to make more profitable trades that allow them to stay in the game.

When you worry too much, you end up being distracted from your execution process, and instead, you focus on the results.

To reduce the fear of trading, you need to accept losses. The probability of losing or making a profit is 50/50, and you need to get this fact and accept a trade, whether it is a sell or a buy signal.

The Fear of a Positive Trend Going Negative (and Vice Versa)

Many traders choose to go for quick profits, and then leave the losses to run down. Many traders want to convince themselves that they have made some money for the day, so they tend to go for a quick profit to have the winning feeling.

So, what should you do instead? You need to stick with the trend. When you notice a trend is starting, it is good to stay with the trend until you signal that the trend is about to reverse. It is only then that you exit this position.

To understand this concept, you need to consider the history of the market. History is good at pointing out that times change, and trends can go either way. Remember that no one knows the exact time the trend will start or end; all you need to do is wait upon the signal.

The Fear of Missing Out

For every trade, you have people that doubt the capacity of the trade to go through. After you place the trade, you will be faced with many skeptics that will question the whole procedure and leave you wondering whether to exit the strategy or not.

This fear is also characterized by greed because you aren't working on the premise of making a successful trade rather the fact that the security is rising without you having a piece of the pie.

This fear is usually based on information that you missed a trend that you would have capitalized on.

This fear has a downside, you will forget about any potential risk associated with the trade, and instead, think that you can make a profit because other people benefited from the action.

Fear of Being Wrong

Many traders put too much emphasis on being right that they forget that this is a business they should run the right way. They also forget that being successful is all about knowing the trend and how it affects their engagement.

When you follow the best timing strategy, you create many positive results over a specific time.

The uncanny desire to focus on always being right instead of focusing on making money is a great part of your ego, and to stay on the right path, you need to trade without your ego for once.

If you accommodate a perfectionist mentality when you get into trades, you will be after failure because you will experience many losses. Perfectionists don't take losses the right way, and this translates into fear.

Ways to Overcome Fear in Trading

As you can see, it is evident that fear can lead to losses. So, how can you avoid this fear and become successful?

Learn

You need to find a way to get knowledge so that you have the basis for making decisions. When you know all there is to know about options, you know what to buy and when to sell, and learn which ones to watch. You are then more comfortable making the right decisions.

Have Goals

What are your short-term and long-term goals? Setting the right goals helps you to overcome fear. When you have goals, you have rules that dictate how you behave, even in times of fear. You also have a timeline for your journey.

Envision the Bigger Picture

You always need to evaluate your choices at all times and see what you have gained or lost so far for taking some steps. Understanding the mistakes, you made guides you to make better decisions in the future.

Start Small

Many traders that subscribe to fear have lost a lot before. They put many funds on the line and ended up losing, which made them fear to place other trades. Begin with small sums so that you don't risk too much to put fear in you. Once you get more confident, you can invest more considerable sums so that you enjoy more profit.

Use the Right Strategy

Having the right trading strategy makes it easy to execute your trades successfully. Make sure you look at various options trading strategies to know which one is ideal for your situation and skills.

Many strategies can help you succeed, but others might leave you confused. If you have a strategy that doesn't give you the returns you desire, then adjust it to suit your needs over time. Refine it till you are comfortable with its performance.

Go Simple

When you have a simple and straightforward strategy, you will be less likely to lose confidence along the way because you know what to expect. The easier the strategy, the faster it will be to spot any issues.

Don't Hesitate

At times you have to jump into the fray even if you aren't so comfortable with the way it works. Once you begin taking steps, you will learn more about the trade.

You always need to be prepared when taking any trade. The more prepared you are, the easier it will be for you to run successful trades.

Don't Give Up

Some things might not go as you expect them to do. Remember that mistakes are there to give you lessons that will make you a better trader. When you lose, take time to identify the mistake you made and then correct it, then try again.

Greed

This refers to a selfish desire to get more money than you need from a trade. When the desire to get more than you can usually make takes over your decision-making process, you are looking at failure.

Greed is seen to be more detrimental than fear. Yes, fear can make you lose trades, but the good thing is that you get to preserve your capital. On the other hand, greed places you in a situation where you spend your capital faster than you return. It pushes you to act when you shouldn't be acting at all.

The Danger of Being Greedy

When you are greedy, you end up acting irrationally. Irrational trading behavior can be overtrading, overleveraging, holding onto trades for too long, or chasing different markets.

The more greed you have, the more foolish you act. If you reach a point at which greed takes over from common sense, you are overdoing it.

When you are greedy, you also risk much more than you can handle, and you end up with a loss. You also have unrealistic expectations from the market, making it seem as if you are after just money and nothing else.

When you are greedy, you also start trading prematurely without any knowledge of the options trading market.

When you are too greedy, your judgment is clouded, and you won't think about any negative consequences that might result when you make certain decisions.

Many traders that were too greedy ended up giving up after making this mistake in the initial trading phase.

How to Overcome Greed

You need a lot of effort to overcome greed. It might not be easy because we are talking about human emotions here, but it is possible.

First, you have to know that every call you make won't be the right one at all times. There are times when you won't make the right move, and you will end up losing money. At times you will miss the perfect strategy altogether and you won't move a step ahead.

Secondly, you have to agree that the market is way bigger than you. When you do this, you will accept and make mistakes in the process.

Hope

Hope is what keeps a trading expectation alive when it has reached reversal. It is usually factored in a trader's mind that has placed a huge amount on a trade. Many traders also go for hope when they wish to recoup past losses. These traders are always hopeful that the next trade will be the best, and they end up placing more than they should on the trade.

This emotion is dangerous because the market doesn't care about your hopes and will take your money.

Regret

This is the feeling of disappointment or sadness over a trade that has been done, especially when it has resulted in a loss.

Focusing too much on missing trade makes the trader not to move forward. After you learn the lessons after such a loss, you need to understand the mistakes you made then move ahead.

When you decide to let regret rule your thinking, you start chasing markets, hoping that you will make money on a position by doubling the entrance price.

CHAPTER 23:

Risk Management in Options Trading

Trading is generally not without risk, and options pose a higher risk than other forms of securities. The risk is mostly due to its speculative nature. As a trader, you need to protect yourself and trading capital from unnecessary losses, and any potential losses that can be prevented.

We do not engage in trades to lose money. A lot of beginners lose money in their early days. Some believe that this is an inevitable process. However, it does not have to be this way. With proper planning and especially proper risk management, you should not unnecessarily lose money trading the markets.

Your number one focus should be risk management rather than winning trades or strategies to be successful as a trader. A good trader is one who does not unnecessarily lose money. The most successful traders manage their funds so well they always know how much to spend or hold back. To do this, you have to watch your every move and countercheck every decision that you make. For instance, if you want to enter a market position, you need to ask yourself if that move is necessary and what amounts you stand to lose should it not work out.

Effective Risk Management

The options trading process does carry some risks with it. Understanding these risks and taking mitigating steps will make you not just a better trader but a more profitable one as well. Many traders love options trade because of the immense leverage that this kind of trading affords them. Should an investment work out as desired, then the profits are often relatively high. You can expect returns of between 10%, 15%, or even 20% with stocks. However, when it comes to options, profit margins of more than 1,000% are possible.

We are familiar with bad investments and losses emanating from individuals or organizations that were hoping to be profitable. Numerous traders make huge errors when they trade, resulting in significant losses. This only happens when they know not what they are doing and when they do not take sufficient steps to protect themselves.

Remember that profits do not just show up. It takes plenty of hard work and, most of all, proper risk management techniques. Without risk management techniques, there is no need to enter the markets because you will be risking your funds. Keep in mind that trading options are a highly risky venture because it is speculative. As such, you cannot trade without protecting yourself. Here are ways you can protect yourself and your trading capital.

Have a Trading Plan

This cannot be mentioned enough times. One of the most important things is to have a trading plan. This plan details exactly all the steps that you will follow from market entry to exit. You should sit down and consider all possible scenarios.

There is no need to take any risks. Once you learn as much as you can about options and trading, you should learn how to plan your trades. Wise traders say anyone who fails to plan is planning to fail. If you want to succeed, you should develop a trading plan that you should then abide by. Again, there is no need to develop a trading plan if you will not implement it fully.

A trading plan's primary purpose is to ensure that you manage your money wisely and place it only well-planned and well-executed strategies. This way, you will avoid reckless moves and only put your money in strategies well worked out.

All too often, a trader will enter a trade without understanding exactly how it will play out. In such instances, the chances of losing money are incredibly high. If you are unsure about any move, then please do not make it. A single move could imply a risk. With a good plan, all moves will be calculated, and no unnecessary risks will be taken.

Understand Trading Psychology

Trading options largely revolves around three significant factors. These are money management, trading strategies, and psychology. Keep in mind that the markets can be a very emotional place, so you must remain focused and disciplined. If you do not stay disciplined, you will lose out, and others will likely take advantage of you.

You need to trade successfully to have a solid strategy, follow the strategy, and stick to it. If the strategy does not follow the intended plan, then quit and develop another strategy.

If you have a strong mindset, you will understand when to pursue a losing trade and when to quit. If you lack discipline, then one of two emotions will take over. These are greed and fear.

Sometimes traders trade on a whim and keep posting random trades. Rather than take this approach, you really should focus on a successful strategy which you will pursue until you need to exit. You should also have good trading skills and a proper money management plan. With these in place, you will focus better and think in terms of probabilities, and risk-reward ratios. This way, you will not leave room for emotional trading.

There are other things that you need to also keep in mind. For instance, you need to develop and stick with good trading habits.

As a trader, you need to note that a winner is one who is persistent and consistent. You should develop the habit of closely studying the markets, conducting your analysis, and position sizing.

Position sizing is crucial, especially in a volatile market. As such, you need to take care of your downside risks and ensure that your position size appropriate. You should also envision the end game. See a vision of where you want the trade to head, and then prepare to make any necessary adjustments.

You also need to accept any possible failures. Sometimes your strategies will not work out, and you will lose some trades. This happens to all traders, even experienced ones. If you assume that you must succeed on each attempt, you will set yourself up for failure.

Risks are Inherent

All types of investing opportunities carry a certain level of risk. However, trading options carry a much higher risk of loss. Therefore, ensure that you have a thorough understanding of the risks, and always be on the lookout.

Also, these kinds of trades are possible due to the nature and leverage offered by options. A savvy trader realizes that they can control an almost equivalent number of shares as a traditional stock investor but at a fraction of the cost. Therefore, when you invest in options, you can spend a tiny amount of money to control a large number of shares. This kind of leverage limits your risks and exposure compared to a stock investor.

Time is not on your side

All options have an expiration date. When you invest in stocks, time is on your side most of the time. However, things are different when it comes to options. The closer an option gets to its expiration, the quicker it loses its value and earning potential.

Options deterioration is usually rather rapid, and it accelerates in the last days until expiration. As an investor, ensure that you only invest dollar amounts that you can afford to lose. The good news, though, is that there are a couple of actions that you can take to get things on your side.

Therefore, try and always or at least mostly to choose options whose expiry dates lie within your investment opportunity. Also, identify options that are at the money or very close. These increase your chances of profitability while minimizing risks and exposure. Ensure that you sell options whenever you believe that high prices are due to volatility. Instead, choose to purchase options when you believe that volatility is undervalued.

Naked Short Positions Can Result in Substantial Losses

Anytime you decide to short options naked, this presents a high likelihood of substantial and sometimes even unlimited losses. Shorting put naked means selling stock options with no hedging of your position.

When selling a naked short, it simply implies that you are actually selling a call option or even a put option but without securing it using an option position, stock, or cash. It is advisable to sell a put or a call-in combination with other options or with stocks. Remember that whenever you short sell a stock, you are, in essence, selling borrowed stock. Sooner or later, you will have to return the stock.

Fortunately, with options, there is no borrowing of stock or any other security.

Prices can Move Pretty Fast

Options are highly leveraged financial instruments. Because of this, prices tend to move pretty fast. Options prices can move huge amounts within minutes and sometimes even seconds. This is unlike other stock market instruments like stocks that move-in hours and days.

When structuring your options, you should ensure that you use the correct strike prices, and expiration months to cut out most of the risk. You should also consider closing out your trades well before the expiration of options. This way, the time value will not dramatically deteriorate.

CHAPTER 24:

Trading Option to Gain Financial Freedom

The path of options trading is simple but not easy. However, you can make it work in significant ways. All you need is the discipline, determination, skills, and ambition that will enable you to navigate this journey.

You must develop the qualities that all successful options traders have. Qualities such as patience, perseverance, flexibility, meticulousness, optimism, discipline, and you must be capable of managing risk. You need to know your numbers and never allow yourself to become complacent. Complacency is the enemy of financial success in this game. You also need to have clear specific financial goals and keep your eye focused on the end goal.

The seven stages of financial freedom:

Stage one: Gain clarity

You need to know where you are and identify where you want to be. What are your expenses like? Can you cut back on certain things so you can have more to invest in? What's the current state of your credit card statement? Financial experts recommend having a particular budget for your life.

Having a budget for your life and options trading activities, so you monitor each closely. Track all your expenses, and once you're clear on what you owe, where you will cut back, and where you want to be soon, you're ready for the second stage.

Remember, you need to be specific with the exact amount of money you want to have in your account at the end of this year, five and ten years from now.

Stage two: Self-sufficiency

The next step is to learn to provide for yourself. There's no attaining financial freedom if you don't know how to earn enough so that you can live on your terms and cater to your needs. This level requires many sacrifices, but if you have that big picture driving you, it won't be too hard to make it work.

Stage three: Breathing room

This is the stage where you earn enough to provide and start saving some money. After you have saved up for months' worth of expenses, you can finally begin to have enough room to breathe.

Stage four: Stability

This is where you increase your savings to a year and knowing that you'll be good for a year helps you feel grounded and secure.

Stage five: Flexibility

It is the last level of saving that you'll need to do. Go ahead and save up two years' worth of expenses so you can feel completely protected and free enough to live how you want. You now have the flexibility you've always dreamed of, and you can start reassessing your priorities.

Stage six: Financial independence

Life is delightful at this stage because you know you have enough money to last you for the rest of your life. Sabatier recommends investing in income-producing assets to achieve financial independence or saving a million dollars then living off your investment interest. Of course, as options traders, we know investing in options can get us to financial independence faster than any of his methods.

Stage seven: Abundant wealth

At this stage of your financial journey, you are not only free, but you also have the means and power to be, do, have, and give whatever you want to share with the world. It's where you can start thinking about your legacy, and the difference you want to make in the world. If you have a favorite cause that you wish to support or create a foundation of your own or whatever your dream is, this is where it all turns into reality. If you're on a mission to do something meaningful in this world, having an abundance of wealth is an advantage that will guarantee you achieve that mission. The moment money stops being a source of stress in your life, you will unlock more potential, resources, and creativity from within you that you never thought possible.

If you play the game right in the long run, and you stick to your vision, mission, and plan options, trading can help you manifest your dream life sooner rather than later.

At the end of the day, although there are many different paths to get to the top and no one-size-fits-all strategy or plan can work across the board for all traders, they all have one thing in common is the right mindset. All successful traders work hard to keep upgrading and maintain the right mindset.

We must continuously work on our mindset to withstand and rise above the daily challenges of options trading. Certain qualities are inherent and nurtured by all successful traders. Still, you also need to remember that putting in the work and keep a level head are equally as important as having those qualities such as discipline, persistence, perseverance, etc.

Work on upgrading your mindset. Feed your mind good food just as you feed your body good food. Work on your weaknesses; get to know the habits that hinder you and those that foster success. Double down on your strengths and developmental resilience. You need to manage your mental activity and energy better if you want to master this trading game. So be mindful and watchful of your behavior as you study and start trading.

Once you identify your thought patterns and start course correction, everything else you do will begin to pay off in a big way.

CHAPTER 25:

LEAPS

L EAPS (Long-term Equity Anticipation Security) are long-term options with expiration dates of up to 3 years, commonly expiring in January.

Ex-Dividend Date/Ex-Date

This term is the day before the date on which the investor had to buy the stock to gather the dividend. On the ex-dividend date, the earlier day's price is decreased by the amount of the premium because the purchaser collects the dividend payment on the ex-dividend date, and it will not receive it. This date is usually referred to as an ex-date and should apply to many other situations (e.g., splits, distributions). If you purchase a stock on the ex-date for a stock or a distribution, you will not be entitled to the split stock or distribution. Nevertheless, the stock's opening price would be decreased by a large amount, as at the ex-dividend date.

Exchange-Traded Funds (ETFs)

These are index funds or trusts enlisted on an exchange and traded in a manner almost like that of single equity. The first ETF came into being in 1993 with the AMEX's concept of a tradable stock basket: Standard and Poor's Depositary Receipt (SPDR). The numbers of ETFs that trade options grow continuously and diversify today. Investors can buy or sell shares within the whole stock portfolio (or bond portfolio) as one security. Exchange-traded funds help investors enjoy a number of the more desirable stock trading features, just like the simple equity style and liquidity, in a more conventional index investing setting.

Fence

Options could have the same or different strike prices. The months of expiration may or might not be the same. For example, if the investor had formerly purchased ABC Corporation at $46 and increased to $62, the investor would be ready to create a collar involving the buying of a put for May 60, and the writing of a call for May 65 as a way of preserving a number of the unrealized profits in the stock position of ABC Corporation. An investor can also use the reverse, i.e., a long call combined with a written put if he has initially established a brief stock position in ABC Corporation.

Holder

A holder is one that has made a gap purchase transaction, put or call, and holds that position in a brokerage account.

Mark-To-Market

This manner implies an accounting mechanism whereby the price of securities held in an account is valued daily to represent the price or market quotes. As a result, the equity within the account is updated daily to represent current security prices appropriately.

Market Order

This word is a trading order issued to a broker to immediately purchase or sell a stock or an option at the best price available.

OTC Option

The over-the-counter option is traded on the OTC market. These options are not listed on an exchange of options and do not have standard terms. These are to be differentiated from the exchange-listed and traded standard equity options.

In-The-Money Option

The term is used to define an option with an intrinsic value. When the stock price is above the strike price, a call option is said to be in-the-money. The put option is in-the-money if the stock price is a smaller amount than the strike price.

Out-Of-The-Money Option

This word is a term used to describe an option that does not have an intrinsic value. The premium for the option is value. In ordinary contracts, the call option is out-of-the-money if the stock price is below its strike price. The put option is out-of-the-money when the stock price is above its strike price.

Naked or Uncovered Option

This word is a short option position that is not entirely protected if assignment notification is received. A short call position is claimed to be uncovered when the author does not have a long stock or deeper in-the-money long call position. A short put is uncovered when the author does not have a brief stock or an extended deeper in-the-money position.

The Role of Underlying Stocks

The underlying asset is a financial asset on which the price of the derivative is predicated. Options are examples of a derivative. A derivative is a financial tool that has a price that is based on a particular asset.

Underlying assets give value to derivatives. For example, the stock ABC option gives the holder right to buy or sell ABC at the strike price up till the expiration date. The stock of XYZ is that the underlying asset for the option.

The underlying asset could also be used to identify an item within the agreement that adds value to the contract. This way supports the security involved in the contract, in which the parties involved make a covenant to exchange as a part of the derivative contract.

Derivative Contracts

This product is an option price or derivative instrument springs of the underlying asset. In an option contract, the author has got to either purchase or sell the underlying asset to the purchaser on the required date at an agreed price. The buyer is not obliged to buy the asset, but they can use their right if they need to do so. Suppose the option is about expiring, and the underlying asset has not progressed favorably enough to render exercising of the option worthwhile. In that case, the purchaser may allow it to expire and lose the amount paid for the option.

A future is an obligation to the buyer and the seller. The longer-term vendor decides to provide the underlying asset at the expiration, and the buyer agrees to get the underlying asset at the expiry. The price they earn and pay is when they have entered into a futures contract. Many futures traders chose to close their positions before the expiration date. But they will buy or sell a contract at a specific price, and if it changes favorably, they will get out of the trade and earn a profit that way. A future is a derivative since, for instance, the price of an oil derivative instrument depends on the movement of oil prices.

Example of Underlying Assets

The underlying asset is the stock, in the case of stock options. For example, with an option to purchase 100 shares of Company A at $100, the underlying asset is that the stock of Company A. That determines the option's price up to its expiration date. This value could change, influencing the cost of the option before the contract expires. At any given time, the underlying asset's price helps traders know whether or not the choice is worth exercising.

A stock market index (or currency like S&P 500) can also be an asset. In the stock indexes, the asset consists of common stocks in the stock exchange index.

CHAPTER 26:

Methods of Buying Options

Buyers of call options view the marketplace cost of a specific stock and are looking to benefit from this predicted increase in market price.

The most well-known technique for buying call options is speculating on a boost in the underlying stock market. It is an essential strategy that is more popular than purchasing put options, as it is more easily comprehended.

Purchasing Options

When buying call options, you hypothesize that the underlying stock rate will increase substantially within the restricted time duration to produce revenue. The percentage returns on your trade if you are proven proper are enormous. If you are incorrect, you can lose some or all of the premium initial you paid.

Buying the right to you is to purchase 100 shares of the underlying stock at the strike cost before the expiry date. You pay a premium for this right. Once you have bought your option, you have three options:

- Sell your options before expiry.

- Exercise your options before expiration.

- Allow the option to expire worthlessly.

The action you take will rely on the movement in the market rate of the hidden share, your expectation of any future motion before expiry, your factors for purchasing the call, and your danger tolerance.

Time is a substantial aspect of figuring out how you manage your options trade. Everyday options that you hold, the value time of your option will decrease. And it will reduce at an increasing rate as you approach the expiration date. In truth, even if the market price of the underlying stock increases before expiry, you might still lose cash on your option due to the impact of time decay, counteracting any increase in intrinsic value.

Methods for purchasing call options

How can you have the money lost on your option when the underlying stock's market cost has risen?

When you bought your option, it was at-the-money. As a result, the overall option premium of $3.50 consisted of time worth. Even though the stock cost increased by $2.00, and your option's intrinsic worth increased by $2.00, this was offset by a time decay of $3.50.

- Increase in intrinsic value$ 2.00.

- Decline in time value ($ 3.50).

- Your net loss on the options *($ 1.50).

This estimation does not consist of deal costs. The above example shows that to earn a profit on buying a call OPTION, the marketplace worth of the underlying stock requirements to increase by enough to both:

- Balanced out the time decay.

- Create development in the intrinsic value of the option.

There are several factors why you may think about buying call options as your trading technique. These include the following:

Method 1: Gain Use

Purchasing call options give you an advantage in your profit. You only need to provide small capital to purchase call options compared to buying the stock entirely. It also allows you to increase the portion of your returns.

Method 2: Limit Your Danger

Instead of acquiring the stock directly, getting call options also allows you to limit your losses if the stock cost falls. You might wish to speculate on a boost in the market worth of a specific stock; however, you might also not want to be exposed to prospective losses if the marketplace value falls considerably. If the stock you purchase, you are exposed to the full quantity of any fall in the stock cost. Nevertheless, with call options, you can ever lose the premium you paid, despite how far the stock rate might fall.

Method 3: Postpone A Stock Purchase

Once you buy a call option, you are purchasing the right to buy 100 shares of the primary stock at the strike price before the expiry date or anytime. Therefore, you are securing the rate you will pay for the shares if you decide to work out the option and buy it before the options' expiry date.

You may want to invest long term in a specific stock as you feel it will increase in worth; nevertheless, you wish to delay your purchase for some factor. Or perhaps you want to buy the stock; however, it wishes to increase in worth to confirm your analysis of an anticipated price boost. Buying a call option permits you to postpone your purchase but still lock in the price you will acquire the stock. The marketplace has experienced some substantial falls in value recently, and you wish to take advantage of the price depression. There is a stock single you have been watching before the fall, was trading over $30 per share, and is now trading at merely $18 per share. You think that the cost will rebound; however, you do not have the funds offered.

You choose to buy a $19 call option that has five months to expiry. The premium is $1. This purchase lets you acquire the stock at $19 per share whenever in the following five months. You have five months to raise funds to purchase the shares, and still purchase them at $19. Based upon what the stock rate does over this time, you can choose to offer your call options or exercise your call options, and buy the stock at $19.

Method 4: Hypothesize for Profit

A significant factor for buying call options is hypothesizing to generate short-term revenue. You are just speculating on the cost of the underlying stock rising by enough totals up to make earnings on your options. You are not acquiring the call options with any intent to exercise them.

Time decay will trigger the call options worth to fall as long as you are holding the option. For this factor, you need to be mindful of selecting the call options you wish to trade. You will require to stabilize the time you need for the stock to move in your instructions against the time value (expense) in the options premium.

You likewise require considering the strike price concerning the current market price of the stock underlying. You need options to be in-the-money to produce a boost in intrinsic worth. Call options will be more affordable when they are out-of-the-money, as more extensive price motion is needed to generate the option's inherent value. Conditions you should search for in selecting a call option for speculation consist of:

The strike price needs to be close to the current market value of the stock. When they are in-the-money options, this will ensure that the boost in the underlying stock cost will be shown in your option's price.

The expiry time must be extended enough for your stock cost to increase adequately to balance out the time decay and create a profit on your call options.

CHAPTER 27:

Financial Leverage in Options Trading

W hen you engage in options trading, you participate in what is called financial leverage. Financial leverage refers to the concept that instead of buying the stock outright and paying the full share price amount, you can put up an initial less capital. Based on the type of your options trade, you can enhance the return on your equity within or after the set time frame. Often, the amount of capital you leverage is lower than the actual share price of the stock. This apparent less capital is what gives options trading its appeal.

Advantages of Financial Leverage in Options Trading

1. You have rights. There are two types of options, both of which have rights: call option and put option. Call options allow you to buy shares at a given strike cost before the duration's expiry. On the other hand, put options will enable you to sell a specific amount of your stock at an agreed price any time within the trade contract's stipulated period.

2. You will own a given number of shares as stipulated in the options contract. We call it the option contract multiplier (most options have a multiplier of x100), which means you get to own 100 stock per option. Any return on your prospect is factored into this multiplier, giving you an accurate figure on your overall investment return. This multiplier is the number of shares that your option contract can be converted into if you exercised that option. You can use your right to sell your trade contract at any time within the stipulated time frame if it is before the expiry date.

3. Your profit margins are highly magnified when compared to directly buying stocks and selling them at a profit later. In an options trading scenario, you leverage your investment at

a given strike price against a future rise in the share price of that same stock price. Now, if the stock price rises as per your speculation, the return on your investment will be much higher than direct stock trading. Your profit margin ratio is much higher, as shown by this example:

Let us assume a current stock price of $20. A broker predicts the stock price to rise to $30 in a month. The trader issues a call option to buy the 20call for a $5 strike price, which expires in 1 month.

Given an option contract multiplier of 100, you can see below the marked difference in profit margin between direct stock trade of 100 shares, and options trade at the specified strike price.

If the final stock price is $30 in a month:

- Direct stock trade gives you a profit of $1000, 50% of the original investment.

- Options trade gives you a profit of $500, which is 100% of the initial investment.

If the final stock price is $35 in a month:

- Direct stock trade gives you a profit of $1500, which is 75% of the original investment.

- Options trade gives you a profit of $1000, which is 200% of the original investment.

4. Your initial cost is low. Buying options are less expensive than buying stock since it depends on the strike price at which you purchased the option. Buying stock depends on the stock price, which is usually markedly higher than the strike price. Therefore, it becomes favorable for you to buy a stake in the stock at a discounted rate.

5. Your call option value goes up whenever the share price rises above the stipulated initial cost.

6. Your put option value goes up as the share price falls below the stipulated initial cost.

7. You have an extra revenue stream. Profits from options trading are a source of income for your business. Given the potential for much higher returns than conventional profit revenues, it gives you the ability to engage in more ambitious business endeavors.

8. Financial leverage in options trading allows you to settle debts incurred during the business. Your business may have a margin account used to accrue debt and leverage the debt in an options contract in anticipation of receiving markedly higher returns. Once you have taken care of liabilities, options trading gives you room to invest in other business opportunities.

Disadvantages of Financial Leverage in Options Trading

1. You have obligations when you sell, depending on your options. You are obligated to sell a specified number of shares for the determined amount whenever any call buyers trigger their contract when you are selling a call option. As a put option seller, you must buy a given number of stocks for a listed amount whenever any put buyers use their commitment. Your obligations force you to buy and sell at strike prices with much higher loss margins than if you had traded at the final stock prices.

2. Your get magnified losses. As much as your returns may have a higher profit margin, the same margin also applies to stock prices, which move in the opposite direction to the ones initially speculated. These losses have a significantly higher margin compared to losses incurred in cases of direct stock trading. You end up with disproportionate losses, which can leave you in financial ruin.

3. You are exposed to higher risks. Losing on your leverage does not depend on an unfavorable final stock price. In case your final stock price remains the same as the initial strike price by the end of the options period, you lose the whole of your initial investment. Using the earlier example, you can see this situation:

   Given an option contract multiplier of 100, you can see the difference between the direct stock trade returns from 100 shares, and the effect on options trade when the stock price remains the same.

   If the final stock price is $20 in a month:

- Direct stock trade gives you neither profit nor loss since the original investment remains unchanged.

- Options trade makes you lose your original investment of $500 since the call option becomes worthless at an unchanged final stock price.

It costs more to return to your original capital baseline. In cases where you incur losses, it will paradoxically cost you more to regain your initial investment. Look at the following example:

- If you had $1000 capital and lost 25%, you remain at $7500. Now, to regain your original money, you need to make a profit of $2500 from your existing $7500 (which means a return of 33% on $7500). You will need a much higher yield of 33% to cover an initial loss of 25%.

- Your put option loses value if the final share price rises above your specified initial value. Also, the closer you get to the option's expiration, the less valuable it becomes.

4. The value of your call option depreciates when the final share price goes below the initial cost amount.

5. Fear of the unknown. You depend on a chance or probability situation to go your way, and market forces have a nature of unpredictability. When leveraging high-risk accounts such as margin accounts, your debt liability increases significantly. You become overleveraged and possibly may lead you into bankruptcy.

6. You are contract-bound. The contract specifies the conditions and duration relating to the option. Terms become void once the expiration period has lapsed. When the market trend on stock prices is not going your way, you do not have the option of opting out to avoid further loss. You need to wait it out, and incur the full loss at the end of the specified period.

7. You may become addicted. Any situation in life, which promises the chance of a higher return from little or no input, is prone to be abused. When it comes to money, people's

greed knows no bounds. A loss leads to a tendency to try to recover what was lost. The cycle becomes self-propagating.

8. Options trading in valued stock is expensive. Stocks with lower strike prices will cost you more because they are valuable to traders. Whenever you engage in financial leveraging within options trading, you will prefer to buy options at a much lower stock price, increasing value. However, options that involve these highly volatile stocks are valuable and tend to cost you more.

9. You have a deadline. Every option trade has a specified time frame within which the financial leverage is of value. Beyond the expiration date, your options can no longer trade. There is a limited window for your stock to gain profit.

CHAPTER 28:

What is Forex

O n the whole, the FOREX market functions like any other financial market. You have a series of buyers and sellers looking to make a profit buying and selling currency. In these transactions, you hope to buy at a lower price while hoping to sell at a higher price. That's all there is to it in terms of the day-to-day transactions that you will be making.

Beyond that, the intricacies of the FOREX market are based upon the currencies you are dealing with. In short, you are pitting one country's currency against other countries. This is why you need to be aware of the economic, political, and social issues that influence a nation's currency value. As such, this understanding will help you figure out how you can spot a potential profit.

Thus, to make a profit, you need to know how a currency's value is determined.

The value of a currency is set by the market. However, it's important to note that there needs to be a second currency to express the first value. It's like establishing the price of a pair of shoes. You need to use the currency to express the value of the shoes. Otherwise, it's impossible to determine the price. Sure, you could express it in terms of sugar, automobiles, or bottles of water, but that would be impractical.

The value of a currency is set just like any other commodity, through the market. The market is what enables a currency to have a specific market value. In general, this market value is expressed in US Dollars, as the US Dollar is the world reserve currency. Nevertheless, it is possible to express currencies in terms of any other currency. However, this can be a complex calculation, and it almost always involves pegging one currency to the US Dollar unless there is a specific calculation done among currencies. This is generally done among neighboring countries, especially when there is a large trade among them.

Currency Pairs

FOREX is based on currency pairs. This means that you can only trade two currencies at any one time. While it is entirely possible to place as many trades as you like, individual trades can only be conducted in two currencies. What this means is that you start with one currency and trade in another.

Common currency pairs are the US Dollar and the Euro, the Dollar and the Japanese Yen, the Euro and the Chinese Yuan, or the Dollars and the Swiss Franc. The British Pound Sterling is a commonly traded currency, though it isn't quite as predominant as the US Dollar. Virtually all investors speculate for or against the Dollar at any point.

We will assume that investors are holding US Dollars and will start trading in US Dollars. You can build up a position in any currency you feel would make a good profit for you. So, there is no restriction in that sense.

The mechanism that's used to calculate trades is known as the "exchange rate." The exchange rate is the value of one currency expressed in another. This is what you commonly see when you travel to another country. You need to exchange currency to purchase the local currency that you can use to buy and sell. This is the pricing mechanism that FOREX uses to calculate the magnitude of a trade.

In general, the more valuable currency will translate into a greater amount of the less valuable currency. For instance, currency A is more valuable than currency B. The exchange rate would reflect this as 2 to 1, that is, 1 unit of currency A gets you 2 units of currency B. When there is a 1 to 1 ratio, you assume that both currencies are worth the same. While this rarely happens in today's economy, it should be noted some currencies are close to a 1 to 1 ratio. There is very little room to make a profit unless you either invest a large sum or make multiple transactions that add up over time.

Fundamental Mechanics of FOREX Trading

So, let's assume that you are holding 100 US Dollars (USD). Since this is your starting point, you need to analyze which currency you wish to trade. In this case, let's consider the Euro (EUR) as it is the most commonly traded pair.

Let's assume there is a 1 to 1.10 exchange rate, meaning that 1 EUR will get you 1.10 USD. Therefore, the EUR is more valuable than the USD. When you take 100 USD and purchase EUR, you will receive 90.9 EUR. Now, to make money, you would have to speculate that the USD falls in value. Suppose the exchange rate is now 1 to 1.15. Under this assumption, the 90.9 EUR you have is now worth 104.54 USD. In this example, you stand to profit from 4.54 USD when you convert the EUR back into USD.

This transaction is an example of an investor betting against the USD. This is important because had the USD and the EUR went to a 1 to 1 ratio, and the investor would have lost 10 USD.

Also, this example highlights how you are only flipping one currency for another and back. This can work when working in market conditions where there is a relative amount of volatility, that is, changes in the exchange rates. This is what can allow you to make short-term gains. When you have relatively stable currency pairs, you may have to hold out a bit longer to make money.

Alternatively, you could trade USD into EUR and then take those EUR, and make another trade pitting another currency against the EUR. You are guessing that this particular currency would drop in value against the EUR, thereby making the EUR much more valuable against it. As you can see, these transactions can be as complex as you would like them to be.

It should also be noted that these transactions which we have described are known as the "spot" market. This means that all positions are settled in cash, and are based on the 1 to 1 trade of currency. This is important as there are various amounts of derivatives based on currency. Derivatives are contracts in which special agreements are made involving the currency. One such example is a futures contract. A futures contract is a guarantee to buy or sell a currency at some point in the future. This is ideal for individuals and companies that may need a foreign currency point in the future but may not be certain of it. It helps them lock in a specific exchange rate, especially when there is a large degree of uncertainty in the global market.

How to Get Started with FOREX Trading

Virtually all trading is now conducted electronically. The days of brokers pounding the trading floor are not quite as predominant as they once were. This means that you can trade in FOREX from the comfort of your home or office. However, it isn't quite as simple as that. You need to gain access to the FOREX marketplace through a trading platform. A trading platform is a piece of software that is used to conduct trades. Duly licensed financial institutions develop this platform. As such, you are granted access to this platform by the financial institution to trade on their behalf. In essence, this makes you a stockbroker. The difference is that you are not paying a professional money manager a commission to handle your funds. You are doing that on your own.

To get started with a FOREX trading platform, you can do a quick online search to find the options available to you. That's why it's up to you to conduct your own research so that you can find the one that offers you the best overall choice.

That being said, gaining access to a trading platform generally consists of purchasing a subscription. Subscriptions vary in cost and services offered. Generally speaking, they offer access to the trading platform in addition to analytics services. These analytics are used to conduct technical analysis and fundamental analysis. These types of analysis help you base your decision on statistical models. Please bear in mind that guessing will only lead you to subpar, if not disappointing, results.

Also, please ensure that you get all of the information regarding the cost of membership, a fee per trade (or transaction), and any minimum account balance that you need to maintain. Please note that if transaction fees are high, these may end up zapping your profits.

Reasons Why FOREX Is a Good Investment Opportunity

Unlike other investment opportunities such as day and swing trading, FOREX offers a greater deal of flexibility, and the chance to make sizeable returns. Day trading generally consumes a lot of time in terms of research and actual trading. Day traders are subject to market hours and need to place trades at the beginning and the end of the day. Otherwise, they may leave positions open or risk losing on their deals due to overnight trading.

With FOREX, you don't need to invest a great deal of money. Most FOREX trading accounts have minimums of $300 to $500. While that's not chump change, it pales in comparison to the thousands of dollars that professional day traders move around on a single day. The best part of FOREX trading is that you can conduct trades for a few minutes at a time, cash out, and be certain that you know exactly where your money is.

Also, given the fact that FOREX is a 24-hour market, you can trade at any time. Most folks look into trading as a means of bringing in more money. Sure, it would be great to hit the jackpot and become a millionaire, but at least early on, that's not very likely. As such, looking to invest in FOREX early on as a part-time deal is a great way to find your footing.

There are plenty of folks who start in FOREX looking to earn an extra $200 or $300 a month. From there, you can increase your expectations, and perhaps bringing a couple of extra thousand dollars a month. If you put in the time and effort to become good at it, you can even make more than your regular salary. This is what enables some folks to become full-time traders. And while they may not become uber-wealthy, they make enough to earn a decent living.

CHAPTER 29:

Day Trading Options

Whenen trading straight calls and puts, one of the best ways to earn profits is through day trading. Although options are not stocks, the same day trading rules apply to trading options as they do with stocks. It means that you have to know the definitions of a day trade and the legal requirements and risks.

Day trading options can be both desirable and lucrative because small price movements in stock, which happen all the time, are magnified in options. You can use day trading to get into options when prices are relatively low. Then you can get out when they reach a pricing level that represents an acceptable profit level for you on the same day before prices begin moving in the other direction again.

A $1 move in a stock price can represent a $10 to $100 move in an options price is what makes this approach very attractive. However, understanding how options are treated is important, as well. If you cannot meet the requirements for day trade options, you can still do it a few times a week, as we will discuss in a moment.

Options Tickers

Remember that each option has its ticker. This is important because day trading involves day traders of the same financial security. Once you buy and sell Apple stock on the same trading day, that is a day trade. However, buying and selling two different options on Apple stock does not constitute a day trade when it comes to options. To understand why, note that an option is defined on the underlying stock, in addition to the predetermined factors (strike and expiration). It also depends on the type of option. To continue our example above, a call option set at $240, with a deadline of 12/12/2019, is not the same financial security as a call option set at $240, with a deadline of 12/30/2019.

In the same breath, a call option with a strike price of $240 and an expiration date of 12/12/19 is not the same financial security as a put option expiring on 12/12/2019 with a predetermined $240 strike price.

So, the first thing to keep straight in your mind if you want to day trade options is the same financial security for day trading and what is not.

Day Trading: Defined

A day trade involves buying a stock or option and then selling that same stock or option before the close of the same trading day. Anyone is allowed to do a limited number of day trades, but what brokers and regulators are looking for is known as a pattern day trader. A pattern day trader, by definition, is someone that makes 4 or more day trades in any five days. A five-day period means five consecutive trading days, so a weekend does not reset the counter. These days, most brokers will track the number of day trades you have in your account for you. So, when you are looking to make some trades but don't want to be labeled as a pattern day trader, you can make up to three-day trades, and then wait for the counter to drop to 2 or below.

Day Trader Requirements

Federal regulators consider day trading to be a high-risk activity. So, while it is legal, there are rules in place designed to keep day traders from causing brokers too much financial trouble should their trades go badly. The main rule you have to be aware of is that a day trader must have $25,000 deposited in their account. You also have to open a margin account. This is a large sum of money to put up for many people so that they might be effectively cut off from day trading. But if you can open a margin account and deposit the required sum, then you are free to enter into as many day trades as you like.

Of course, we hope that you won't be running out of the $25,000 if you choose this path, but becoming a day trader on an official basis will open up a lot more opportunities for you. Stocks are constantly moving up or down by small amounts, with trends that last a few hours or throughout the day that will generate large changes in options prices.

Getting rid of the day trade limitation not only lets you frequently trade, which will let you take advantage of more of these trends when you can spot them, but it will also allow you to make high-volume trades. Suppose you are subject to the day trading limitation, meaning you do not have a margin account with $25,000 in value in the account. In that case, you may get notices about day trading limitations if you try to trade multiple options in a single trade.

In other words, if you try trading 10 Apple options, all with the same strike price and expiration date, you might be told that you will not be allowed to sell all ten options on the same trading day. If you become an official day trader, then these restrictions would be lifted, giving you a lot more flexibility when trading.

Day Trading Without Becoming a Day Trader

If you cannot deposit $25,000 in a margin account or want to avoid becoming a pattern day trader, you can still use day trading as a part of a larger options trading strategy. In this case, you might want to trade options in a way that utilizes three or fewer-day trades in every five-trading day period. This can allow you to make three lucrative day trades per week to boost your overall trading revenues. The only issue with this type of trading activity is that you must avoid making too many day trades over a given five-business day period. If you are careful about avoiding this problem, this will not be an issue for you.

You can also effectively day trade by letting your trades run overnight. Technically speaking, this makes you a so-called "swing trader." A swing trader holds their positions overnight, for a few days, or even weeks. In practice, any options trader is a swing trader because all options contracts expire. So, in reality, there isn't any other way to be when trading options, except a day or swing trader.

If you are looking to day trade but want to avoid adding to your day trade account, there are two ways to go about doing it. The first way is to start in the morning looking for trends to trade on. Then you enter your trade and hold it overnight, provided that the profit you are going to make will account for the losses that could occur from theta or time decay.

So, if you've made $100 during the day, and theta is -0.12, you know that your profit is going to be automatically reduced by $12, but you might be willing to accept that small decline in profits. You can wait for the markets to close, and then enter an after-hours sale order, which will be executed at the market open. Or you can wait until the market opens before actually placing your order.

Alternatively, you can enter your positions just before the market close if you suspect a trend will carry through the following day. You will do this knowing that you will take a hit on the price of the option at the market open due to the theta or time decay.

This procedure can be very tricking, of course. The reason is that a lot of action can happen at the market open, and this can wipe out your positions if it is not something that works in your favor. For this reason, day traders of stocks don't hold positions overnight. But the risk with some options contracts will be lower than it would be trading a highly volatile penny stock the way that day traders of stocks do.

Remember the activity that takes place at the market open. Sometimes, even if you have placed an after-hours sale order, you might not be able to sell your option because prices are moving so fast at the market open. This may or may not happen, but you have to be aware of the possibility. That means that this is not a set-it-and-forget-it is a trading strategy. You will have to be on top of things, and actively following your trades at the market open if you need to cancel and replace an order.

Day Trading Options: The General Strategy

Now, let's consider this from the perspective of a trader who is going to straight-up day trade options. In this case, you will start in the morning and look for stocks that are entering a trend. Since you are trading options, which direction the trend is going is completely irrelevant. If the trend is down, buying put options is a legitimate way to earn profits.

You are going to want to look for signals that a new trend is forming. Sometimes, this can be after a trend reversal. A trend reversal can occur after a large selloff of stocks occurs, and the stock enters oversold conditions. This is a time to buy shares as the stock will probably reverse and start increasing in price. Or, in the case of trading options, you are going to want to buy call options.

Of course, the trend that is forming may be a reversal of an uptrend. So, the stock may be overbought, and there might have been a long upward trend in price, but now, it's showing signals of declining. In that case, you are going to want to buy put options.

A large trend reversal isn't necessary either. Look for signs in the stock charts that an upward trend is forming. This can be high risk, and it's awfully hard to predict when a trend is forming accurately, but with practice, many traders can get quite good at it. When the signals are there, you can then buy options that fit the trend you are looking for.

CHAPTER 30:

Binary Options Trading

A Binary Option is a method for investing in an asset price that has just two closing positions. A wise investment can be made if the closing area is estimated precisely.

The most widely recognized option is the "High" or "Low" option. To begin, an understanding of the time length is fixed before making the expectation. The trader can anticipate a fixed return if, toward the end, the price lies on the right side of the started price.

The trader will lose the entirety he invested when the trade was opened if predicted incorrectly.

With an itemized investigation into buying and selling stocks, the straightforwardness at which one can place trades using Binary Options ends up visible.

An investor starts trading by selecting and purchasing a measure of a stock or an asset. By calculating the offer price individually, we can ascertain what the price of the asset is.

A trader can produce a decent return by selling his asset when the price has risen from the asset's price at the outset. In like manner, the investor will encounter a loss if the asset's selling price is not the exact price it was acquired.

Complete learning and experience of numerous outcomes are fundamental to invest in these lines — an intensive understanding of how the financial market capacity is critical. The investor would need to examine the asset's price movements, how price-changing occasions influence the asset in the market, and how the asset's price will change in the future.

To effectively bring these components together, the investor who routinely creates gainful returns identifies and understands asset price switches, and is sponsored by trading strategies and methods that can be actualized when the circumstance requests it.

Having no technique or understanding of assets, and the market may leave you in your very own private sorrow what you have saved for investing will before long vanish. You won't have adequate assets to buy presents for the children at Christmas, and your accomplice may keep running off with somebody more proficient at investing their money than yourself!

What is appealing in the examination is that there is no compelling reason to buy into anything when investing with Binary Options. Binary investments highlight prices of assets, and if the price of an asset will rise or fall. For this situation, you are trading exclusively on an up or down movement in an asset's price. Consequently, it is an impressively less unsafe investment opportunity.

Likewise, it is deserving of note that Binary Options Trading enables potential investors to get up, and running without putting down enormous entireties to begin because the required investment sum can be a lot smaller.

If an investor were looking to start trading on gold, which depended on the present estimation of gold, it would make it exceptionally difficult for many people to make it an advantageous asset to invest in. In Binary Options Trading, nobody is genuinely buying any gold; instead, traders invest in price changes of gold over a set time frame.

Assets Available to Trade with Binary Options

Before we talked about gold, now would be a good time to dig into the sorts of assets regularly utilized for Binary Options Trading.

- Indices: An index is simply the market. It is conceivable to invest in the markets themselves.

- Forex: Or Foreign Exchange is worried about trade rates between significant currency sets, for example, the USD, the GBP, or the JP. You can trade on combinations of all these real monetary forms.

- Commodities: A crude material or essential rural item that can be purchased or sold, for example, Gold, Copper, or Coffee.

Selecting which asset to trade is the starting point for a trader. The magnificence of Binary Options Trading is as natural as getting up and run.

Getting Started

Most trading stages give two necessary decisions regarding binary trading: The put option is chosen if the trader accepts that the cost will decline, while the call option is accessible. If they receive that, the price will rise. All traders need to choose their position depending on any number of market factors. There are various trading methods and calculations that can be utilized, which will be secured later.

Before choosing your position, you will be required to pick a trading stage to direct most of your trades. Selecting the correct broker to deal with your finances is essential to accomplishing your trades, particularly for new traders who need to benefit as much as possible from every single financial option. Not all brokers will most likely give you similar trading methods, much like not all brokers will have similar restrictions and profits accessible for their sites. New traders are prescribed not to stress over a portion of the more confounded binary trading methods. First, pick a decent brokerage that offers a high rate on their profits, and check whether there are any incentive projects offered that you can exploit.

Tips to Keep in Mind

There is a wide range of tips and deceives that beginning traders can remember to increase their odds of profiting. A considerable amount of these tips is additionally intended to enable individuals to be more open to the trading background, particularly if they need a couple of dependable guidelines to remember as they trade. As the trader becomes increasingly experienced, they will most likely build up their trading methods and frames of mind, which are explicitly structured to supplement their very own remarkable way of dealing with trading. Until further notice, in any case, merely remembering a couple of these essential tips can be enough to enable most traders to get a head start.

Let Emotions well enough alone for Your Trades

Maybe the most crucial suggestion to recollect is to never depend on hunches or natural desires. Trading binary options don't care for gambling or some other essential money-making process. While chance still assumes a job in determining your profits, most of them will be identified via deliberately examined indicators and adequately actualized strategies. Traders who depend on their instincts or any passionate associations with their finances will find that they will begin losing money in the long term, regardless of what inadvertent profits they may verify from the start.

Making genuinely determined trades is an extremely massive slip-up that, shockingly, numerous section level traders make. If your head isn't clear and you are not thinking objectively, you will wind up making trading botches. It is as straightforward as that. If you begin to feel baffled or irate with your trades or become too energized after successful ones, it is essential to take a step back, take a full breath, and think about taking a break.

Think About Yourself as a Trader

The best traders are simply the ones who know and realize what they need to escape their trades. These individuals have investigated different types of options, and have chosen to work with ones that match their characters as traders. Short-term trades are identified by brisk exchanges in unstable situations, such as sixty second and two-minute trades. Medium-term trades allude to any exchanges that can be made somewhere in the range of five and fifteen minutes. As the name infers, long-term trades depict more extended expiry periods, which can go anyplace from an hour to multi-day, depending on the broker.

As should be evident from the range, there is a way to deal with each type, which defines the trader. If you flourish in quick paced situations and enjoy the dangers of dealing with instability, you will be more qualified to work with short term trades. Then again, if you enjoy a lower level of risk, and plan on trading consistently if possible, you may profit from more extended expiry options.

CHAPTER 31:

How to Get Maximum Profits

You Can Profit from Any Market Situation

I t is to benefit from any market situation trading options. Most options strategies are carried out by combining different option positions, and sometimes even the underlying stock's position. A trading strategy can be used singly or in combination with others to profit from market situations.

You stand to make huge profits with options trading, yet your risk and exposure are limited. Ordinary stock trading does not afford you such opportunities. The most crucial aspects of options trading know when to exit a trade, and how to exit. Knowing how and when to exit is vital for successful trading.

Options strategies are the most versatile strategies in the financial markets. They provide traders and investors with numerous profit-making opportunities with limited exposure and risk. These strategies can be favorable whether the underlying security's stock price rises, remains the same, or falls.

Taking Profits with Options Trading

One of the best-known ways of profiting from options is through the purchase of undervalued options. You can even buy options at the right price and still benefit from them.

Options prices usually are extremely volatile. This provides an excellent chance to benefit from profit-taking. However, when you miss the right moment to take profits, you will have lost out on an amazing opportunity.

Take Advantage of Volatility and Collect Profits

Options are unlike stocks because they have a time limit. Stocks can be held indefinitely, but options can expire. This means that the time for trades is limited. As a trader, you cannot afford to miss this window. Should such a chance be missed, then it might not be seen again in a long while.

You should avoid long-term strategies when trading options. Strategies such as the average are unsuitable for options trading because of the limited time that options have. Also, watch out for margin requirements. Such requirements have to capacity to severely impact your trading funds requirements.

Watch out for multiple factors that may affect a favorable price. For instance, the price of the underlying stock may go up, which is a good thing. However, other factors, such as dividend payment, time decay, or volatility, may erode any accruing benefit. Such constraints make it imperative that you learn to follow profit-taking strategies. Here are some of these crucial profit-taking strategies that you can use as a trader.

Trailing Stop Strategy

When using this strategy, you will set a pre-determined percentage for a particular target. For instance, you can ten options contracts, each costing $80 with a profit target of $100 and a $70 stop-loss.

Set a Profit-Taking Stop-Loss

We can set a stop-loss at 5%, which means if our target price of $100 is attained, our trailing target will be $95. If the upward trend continues and our price gets to $120, then the trailing target of 5% becomes $114. Should the price movement continue to, say, $150, then the trailing target this time becomes $142.5.

Should the price now start falling, you will exit and collect profits at this $142.5. The trailing stop lets you enjoy protection as the price increases, and then exits a trade once the price turns around. The stop-loss levels should neither be too small nor too large. If they are too small, they will cause frequent triggers, whereas too large will make profit-taking unachievable.

Partial Profit Booking

Season traders have a routine that they follow to book partial profits. First, they set a target and take profits when it is attained.

Partial profit booking helps to protect the trader's capital to a large extent. This essentially has the effect of preventing capital losses in the event of a sudden price change. Such price reversals are commonly observed in options trading.

Book Partial Profits at Regular Time Intervals

As a trader, you can book partial profits at regular time intervals. However, you will need to pay close attention to the time limit. A massive portion of your options premium is made of its time value. As time runs out, then its value also goes down. As a trader, you should keep a keen eye on your options' time value as this erodes its value. Buyers should be careful about the time limit.

Sell Covered Call Options against Long Positions

Selling options is a lucrative income-generating process. This is not the only pathway to riches in the markets. You can also sell naked puts. This is like selling shares or stocks that you do not.

When you sell naked put options, you will free up your time to do a lot more. Stock trading allows you to sell stocks of shares that you do not have for a profit. This tends to free up your capital so you can invest it or trade with it indefinitely. It is advisable to stick to stocks that you understand very well, and those you would not mind. There is still hedging associated with options trading, so always be careful and watch about that. Most large investors who deal in options are often hedging.

Consider all the Options Available to You

We make assumptions that traders will hold their positions until the end. You can choose from several options to ensure that you can leverage any time you want to see its need.

Learn to Select the Right Options to Trade

You have to identify options that will see you earn a profit.

- Ensure you determine whether you are bullish or bearish on the market, sector, or just the stock. When you make these decisions, you will be able to identify the options you wish to buy.

- Consider volatility and think about how it would affect your options trading strategy. Think about the status of the market. Is it calm, or is it volatile? You may also want to consider the expiration date and strike price. If you only have a couple of shares, this would be a great time and opportunity to purchase more stock.

CHAPTER 32:

Stock Market

The stock market is the place you can purchase and trade stocks on any business day. It's also called a stock trade.

Why Companies Sell Stocks

Organizations sell stocks to get brokers to grow bigger. When individuals need to begin a business, they frequently pay for it with individual loans or even their credit cards. When they develop the organization enough, they can get bank loans. They can also sell bonds to individual investors.

In the end, they'll need a great deal of cash to take the business to the following stage. Around then, they will sell the main stocks, called an initial public offering. When that occurs, no single individual owns the organization since they have sold it to the stockholders. Since the U.S. stock market is so modern, it is simpler in this nation than in many others to take a company public. It enables the economy to extend since it gives a lift up to companies wishing to grow huge.

The requirement for organizations to raise money and investors to profit from them keeps the stock market up.

Why Invest in the Stock Market?

Stock market investing is the ideal approach to accomplish returns that beat inflation over time. There are four different advantages to investing.

1. Stock ownership exploits a developing economy.

2. Unlike brokers, it's anything but difficult to purchase stocks and just as simple to sell.

3. The best part is that you can make money in two different ways. A few investors like to let their stock appreciate over time.

4. Others favor stocks that deliver dividends to give a consistent income stream.

There different ways for you to invest in the stock market. The quickest and least expensive is to buy them online. If you need more direction at a sensible value, join an investment club. A full-service broker will cost all the more, however, would value the price. The person will give you proficient suggestions. A money manager charges the most yet will accomplish all the work for you.

Rather than purchasing singular stocks, you could get them as part of an index fund or a mutual fund. An index fund follows a guide, for example, the MSCI developing market index. A mutual fund has a manager that purchases the stocks for you. The most dangerous is the hedge fund. They invest likewise in derivatives, which could build the return and increase the risk.

Investing Risks

The most note value downside is that you can lose your whole investment if the stock value falls to zero. If the organization goes bankrupt, stock investors are paid after bondholders. Thus, stock investing can be an emotional rollercoaster. If you need guaranteed returns, stick to bonds. Be that as it may, stocks are a superior approach if you are in it as long as possible.

When stock market costs decay under 10% that is known as a stock market revision. When costs fall that much or more in one day, it's known as a stock market crash. When costs fall 20% or more, it's known as a bear advertise. These usually last 18 months. The inverse is a bull market, and they last two to five years.

The U.S. Stock market is the World's Financial Capital

The United States is in the area of the two biggest trades on the planet. The New York Stock Trade accounts for 2,400 organizations. The estimated value is at around $21 trillion in market capitalization. The NYSE is arranged on Wall Street. The NASDAQ companies with a market top of $11 trillion. It's arranged in Times Square. Both are in Manhattan, New York.

The stock market works by coordinating buyers and dealers. The two significant trades do it any other way from one another. The NYSE is a genuine auction house. It coordinates the most note Value offer at the least sales price. A market producer for each stock will fill in the hole to guarantee exchanges go without any problem. At the NASDAQ, purchasers and merchants exchange with a seller as opposed to each other. It's done electronically, so exchanges happen in split seconds.

The United States is the world's monetary capital since its financial markets are so advanced. Therefore, as a result, information on companies is easy to obtain. This transparency builds the trust of investors from around the globe. Thus, the U.S. stock market draws in more investors. That makes it much simpler for a U.S. organization to open up to the world.

The general U.S. stock market presentation is followed by its three head accounts: the Dow Jones Industrial Average, the S&P 500, and the NASDAQ. Various parts of the markets are also followed. For instance, the MSCI Index tracks stocks' presentation in developing market countries, for example, China, India, and Brazil.

Major World Stock Markets

Each significant nation has a stock trade. Here are the best 10, positioned by total market capitalization. They are accounted with the most quoted indices that are nearest to estimating their performances:

- New York Stock Trade – NYSE.

- NASDAQ - The trade likewise has an account with a similar name.

- Tokyo Stock Trade - Nikkei 225.

- London Stock Trade - FTSE 100.

- Shanghai Stock Trade - Shanghai Stock Trade.

- Hong Kong Stock Trade - Hang Seng.

- Toronto Stock Trade - SPTSX.

- Bombay Stock Trade - SENSEX.

- National Stock Trade of India - NSE Nifty.

- BM&F Bo Vespa (Brazil) - The file is additionally called BOVESPA.

Other Financial Markets

The stock market is only one type of financial market. Before you invest, ensure you know about them all:

Items are generally traded in future options, which makes them increasingly confounded. They incorporate grains, oil, and the abnormally named pork bellies.

Foreign trade is the place individuals purchase and sell currencies. It's high risk because the qualities can change drastically for no evident explanation and change rapidly.

Derivatives are exceptionally complicated bonds that get their incentive from the hidden resources, for example, subprime mortgages. Singular investors should remain away. Although they can give huge returns and can also reduce your entire life savings in a day.

Supply and Demand

If an organization reports shockingly low profit, demand for its stock may fade, and as the value drops, the harmony among buyers and sellers is changed. Buyers will begin mentioning discount on the present cost, and many prodded sellers will oblige them to dispose of the stocks. Once there are more sellers than buyers, this generates more supply than demand, so the value starts to fall.

The Role of Prices

Eventually, a stock's cost may drop to a level where buyers find it attractive, or some other factor will change the dynamic. As buyers move into the market, demand becomes quicker than supply, and the expense correspondingly goes up. Sometimes supply and demand discover a balance, a value that purchasers acknowledge, and that seller obliges. Costs will bounce up and down when market supply and demand are generally equivalent, yet they will do it in a narrow price range. It's workable for stock to remain in this range for a considerable length of time or even a very long time before another outside factor disturbs the supply and demand balance, and causes either a perceptible increase or decrease in cost.

If interest for a stock surpasses the supply, its cost will rise, yet it will just increment to a point where buyers speculate that demand is disappearing. By then, holders of the stock will probably start selling. Some may have ridden the cost up and accept an inversion is coming, so they sell their shares and take their benefits while they are still ahead.

When stock costs start to fall (which can occur for a few reasons), and more owners begin selling their shares, there will be more supply than there is demand. To tempt buyers, sellers must drop costs to oblige the saturated market. A similar unique deal with the opposite side, however, is a switch. As the value falls, it will arrive at a level that buyers find attractive. As buyers get shares, the stock's cost will rise because sellers must be lured to let go of their shares.

Understanding Stock Market Fluctuations

It is surely known that the stock market is unstable and hard to anticipate. What is less well understood is why. What are the raw sources of economic factors that drive these sporadic changes? By a long shot, most of the discourse in the press, additionally most economic hypotheses, declares that the market is driven by shocks (erratic variances) to macroeconomic basics that have significant consequences for economic growth. The most significant irregular powers behind the more drawn out term gains in the U.S. stock exchange have not been drivers of financial development. However, it has rather been an aggregation of irregular shocks to a great extent uncorrelated with economic development that has brought about redistribution among laborers and investors.

There is a little puzzle that the genuine estimation of the stock market floats upward over significant stretches to a great extent unsurprising path as efficiency (driven by innovative advancement) improves. Likewise, this same deterministic pattern has pushed yield per capita, and the average way of life upward in the course of the last several centuries. It is rather the random shocks, the bloom, and busts around this trend, about which we have little information, yet on which a continuous stream of media theory centers. Such random shocks can steadily displace the market from its long-term pattern for periods up to quite a few years.

CHAPTER 33:

The Benefit of Having a Good Mental Attitude as a Trader

I f you have decided to get into trading, then it only means one thing. Your mind lives to analyze, and you are fascinated by monetary trends. This alone gives every beginner an edge over those who do not. You do not need to worry if you are a beginner. At least you are doing what most are not.

The mind of every trader needs not only to be fast but also laser-focused. This is because, in the instance of day trading, the whole dance happens in one song. Meaning, all the money you invest in has the chance to multiply or decrease all in one day.

Resilience is an excellent mental attitude that all traders must abide by. Some days you make incredible profits, and the stocks are all in your favor. Other days, not so much, and you end up feeling worse when you exit than when entering. The art of resilience, to say to yourself that you will try again tomorrow, is essential.

Discipline with your account is also another vital attitude a trader should have. This is helpful while buying stocks as they experience a losing streak, and then one might be tempted to use more than they had planned. Learn to discipline the mind in stopping to avoid heavy losses.

Every trader must be high on caution. Eagerness tends to be the greatest mistake that ruins not only traders but also big companies. This is because in the race to make more money, one tends to overlook a few things that might cause him more harm than good in the stock market. Pausing and observing is important as it helps avoid risky money behavior.

Helps You Achieve Your Goals

Your thoughts are essential in shaping your life and ensuring that you accomplish the goals that you have set. As humans, we like making specific goals for our lives, and you might have set that at a certain time, and you want to earn a certain amount of money. As a day trader, you might be having some goals on the amount of money you wish to correct at the end of the day. These goals are good as they keep you motivated.

Ensure that You Stay Focused

A positive mental attitude can have a huge impact on your ability to focus. Set your mind to achieving something, then constantly remind yourself to give your best to achieve what you have planned to get. This can be done by having some daily affirmations. You will be surprised by the impact that these affirmations will have on your life. Every day that you wake up say something good about yourself. Remind yourself that you can tune your mind into focusing on the plans you have for the day.

Increases Your Potential of Earning an Income

It is amazing how our thoughts influence our level of productivity. When we have a positive attitude, our productivity levels are likely to increase. The vice versa is also applicable. When our thoughts are negative, we are likely to experience a decrease in our level of production. As a trader, you need a positive mental attitude as you conduct your trades.

It Minimizes Stress Levels

At times life can move quickly, and you are not adequately prepared for it. You may feel overwhelmed as it could result in stress. When it gets to some extreme levels, the stress can result in something major like trauma. We have had people engage in day trading to encounter a loss at the end of a trade. You will find that some invested in more than they could afford. Some traders borrow loans so that they can trade.

Helps You Know How to Handle Failure

As a trader, not every day will be a celebration day. Some days you will win, and on other days you will lose. You cannot get in a trade with a full guarantee that things will go as you planned. You will often come across some losses, and there is no need to feel overwhelmed by the losses. With the help of a positive mental attitude, you can avoid some of these frustrations. All you have to do is tune your mind to having the right positive attitude. It makes you ready in case anything happens.

Provides Room for Growth

One of the beautiful things about life is that it allows us to grow. One can experience growth in all aspects of their life. For you to grow, you require a positive mental attitude. It propels you towards success in life and allows you to make the right choices and decisions. As a beginner in day trading, you will have to learn a lot of things. Some of these things you will have to teach yourself. Your performance will be influenced by how much you know, and how willing you are to learn.

Helps You in Taking Care of Your Emotions

Emotions are part of who we are. Someone might tell you something that upsets you, and your emotion is ruined. At that point, you can become sad or angered. If you achieve something good, you automatically become happy and proud of yourself. On a good day, you may have made several trades and acquired a huge profit. This is something that you will feel happy and proud of. It can automatically bring you in a cheerful mood, and you will feel so good about your success.

Allows You to Be Hopeful

As a beginner, you will come across numerous challenges while trading options. It is entirely up to you to ensure that these challenges do not interfere with your growth and general output. You need to reenergize constantly so that the challenges become bearable. One of the benefits of having a positive mental attitude is that it allows one to be hopeful. You believe that things will get better with each passing day. This will boost your confidence, and enable you to get better at what you do. This attitude will be helpful while trading options.

Helps You in Making Sound Decisions

While day trading, there are a lot of decisions that you will make. Some of these decisions will determine if you expose yourself to more risks or make a profit or a loss. A single decision can make your investment worth your while or make you lose all you have worked hard for. While trading, there are several factors that you will have to consider. These factors determine if you will make a profit or make a loss. When it comes to selecting the appropriate option strategy, one needs to make a lot of choices.

You Learn from Your Failures

No one gets in anything with the expectations of failing. You find that you have an exam, and even though you have not adequately prepared for it, you still expect to pass. As entrepreneurs establish various businesses, their end goal is to become successful at what they do and get profits at the end of the day. We have people engaging in options trading to generate an income. No one enters a trade with the expectation that they will fail.

CHAPTER 34:

What Every Investor Should Do

While all the information in this guide should prepare you to enter the world of options trading with some degree of confidence, nothing can prepare you for live trading. Every situation will be different and may require any one of the strategies or some combination of them. However, no one can prepare any options trader for every conceivable transaction, event, or opportunity. Success in this field will come with the continued application of the methods, strategies, and knowledge you have learned.

This includes what we consider to be the most important do's and don'ts of options trading. We hope not only that you put these strategies to work, but also that you start formulating your compilation of road-tested options trading secrets.

Understand Market Basics

In the modern world, investment has been made accessible to the average person. Most employers who offer retirement savings plans often sponsor an education day, so employees can gain some familiarity with the types of retirement plans and available options. Also, with the proliferation of cable news networks, specialized programming, the internet, and social media, there is no shortage of information widely available to virtually anyone, anywhere.

Especially in the information age, knowledge is power. Before you jump right into trading on the options market, take some time to familiarize yourself with market dynamics basics. Options traders use a unique language to their niche in the investment world, and many outsiders may be completely perplexed and unable to understand much of what they say. The ability to tolerate a certain amount of financial risk is an inseparable component of successful investing. Thus, by understanding the terminology of the options market and the fundamental dynamics of the stock market in general, investors can exponentially increase their chances of assembling a profitable career in options trading.

Play by the Rules

As an options trader, you will compete with other traders and investors. Much of your success in investing, including making valuable connections in the investment world, will result from your ability to play by the rules. The stock market is a living thing, and traders' activity has a significant impact on its health and volatility. We are all tempted to be maverick investors who leave a legacy of innovation but understanding the fundamentals will work in your favor.

Specifically, option prices increase or decrease as a result of changes in share prices and volatility.

When share prices increase, call options to make money and put options to lose money; when share prices decrease, put options make money and call options to lose money. Options also move to volatility; when share prices are stable, greater volatility can increase option pricing. So, when volatility rises, buying options make money; when volatility decreases, selling options makes money.

Understanding these four basic rules can help you become a better trader.

Adapt Your Strategy to Market Conditions

Once you're up and running in the world of professional options trading, you will gain confidence as you see your efforts pay off in returns to your options account. As you move from a Level 1 trading account to a Level 2 trading account, you will likely develop a preference for a certain type of options trades, maybe covered calls or married puts. Familiarity with the language and mechanics of the options trading profession is something that will work in your favor. However, it is important to remember that you will gain access to a wider array of trading tools and strategies as you move up the ladder.

As you gain knowledge and experience, remember that no matter how comfortable you have become with a select number of options trading strategies, there will always be additional aspects of nuance that can enhance your skill as a trader and increase your efforts' profitability. The key to ensuring success is not just choosing the best strategy for the underlying asset's performance. You must also consider the overall market conditions, and whether those conditions may affect that asset's future performance. Although one strategy may have worked in the past under similar conditions, considering changes in current conditions will help you adjust your strategy to ensure you continue to build on your past success.

Always Have an Exit Plan

Picking a stock, formulating an options strategy to generate income from the stock's performance, and then contacting your broker to initiate an opening transaction is a good beginning. But this plan is not a complete strategy. The most important part of any options strategy is not how to get in; it's how to get out.

The payoff of an options strategy may result from buying the underlying stock at below market value, from accepting a cash settlement deposit for a put option on the stock with declining value, or even from profiting from an increase in the cost of the options premium by selling the contract before it expires. However, you believe the asset you have identified may provide you with an opportunity to construct a profitable options trading strategy, conjecture, and hope should not be part of that strategy. Before you complete an opening transaction, make sure you know your specific goal for entering the contract. After you complete the opening transaction, you will be faced with one of three possible outcomes:

- The market and the target stocks moved in the direction you predicted.

- The market or the target stocks move in a direction you did not predict, resulting in unexpected losses.

- The market or the target stocks move in a direction you did not predict, resulting in unexpected gains.

Conclusion

The options trading crash course is all about options trading. I hope this guide will teach you everything you need to know about options trading, from basics, why people trade options, and how you trade options. It will teach you everything you need to know on this important topic so that you can start making money right now with options trading without having any knowledge at all. You will find out precisely what kinds of investments there are available, and exactly how much your broker will charge for each one so that you can choose the one that is best for your situation.

It is a great way to make money through leverage. With options, you can make money by selling an asset at a specific price and buying it back after rising in price. It's an exciting and profitable way to gain financial freedom. The options market is the largest and most liquid market globally, which means that it is also very popular. Options trading is an attractive option for anyone looking to make money from their investments. It's a way of investing in stocks or other securities without actually having to buy them.

Options' trading allows you to make money and increase your wealth. There are many different types of options, but most people are familiar with the call option. It is one of the best ways to make money in the stock market. Options are contracts that give you the right, but not the obligation, to buy or sell an asset at a specified price within a specific time frame. Options trading is one of the most popular ways for traders to earn money. However, it's one of the riskiest ways to start making money.

Options trading is a great way to make money while watching the markets. Although options trading can be a complicated process, there are plenty of resources to help you get started.

This can be a great way to make money, but it's essential to do your research and know what you're doing. It is one of the most fun and lucrative forms of investing, but it's also one of the most challenging. The goal of options trading is to buy stock or other assets at a price you think will go up in the future.

It is very lucrative, but it's also risky because you can lose a lot of money if you don't know what you're doing. Options are a derivative contract that gives the holder the right, but not the obligation, to buy or sell an underlying asset at a set price. Options contracts can be purchased and traded on exchanges. Options trading has become a popular investment strategy for many. Both beginners and experienced traders can benefit from the basics of options trading. The essential part of options trading is understanding the different options available and how to use them.

The Options Trading Crash Course is a great place to start. The course walks you through the basics of options trading and teaches all the concepts you need to know.

www.ingramcontent.com/pod-product-compliance
Lightning Source LLC
Chambersburg PA
CBHW081802200326
41597CB00023B/4122